LOVE MAKES THE RIDE WORTHWHILE

Jane Kemp Baker

PublishAmerica
Baltimore

© 2006 by Jane Kemp Baker.
All rights reserved. No part of this book may be reproduced, stored in a retrieval system or transmitted in any form or by any means without the prior written permission of the publishers, except by a reviewer who may quote brief passages in a review to be printed in a newspaper, magazine or journal.

First printing

At the specific preference of the author, PublishAmerica allowed this work to remain exactly as the author intended, verbatim, without editorial input.

ISBN: 1-4241-4292-X
PUBLISHED BY PUBLISHAMERICA, LLLP
www.publishamerica.com
Baltimore

Printed in the United States of America

LOVE MAKES THE RIDE WORTHWHILE

Jane Kemp Baker

Dedication

To all who have traveled with me

For long or short distances over the years—

Family and friends,

Strangers and passersby

Of all colors, creeds, and cultures—

And have helped to make my journey

Through life on this planet

So full, so blessed,

And so very worthwhile,

I humbly and gratefully dedicate this book.

Special Thanks

To my dear parents, Horace and Marion Kemp,
*   who left their children a legacy of integrity,*
*   hard work, love of God and country,*
*   respect for authority*
*   and just plain common sense,*
*   all of which prepared us for the changes*
*   we would encounter and the decisions*
*   we would make later in life.*

To Klinedale, my beloved husband of 55 years,
*   whose exuberant love for life*
*   and unshakable faith in God*
*   have made our ride together,*
*   not only an exiting adventure,*
*   but a meaningful spiritual journey as well.*

To our four children, each a precious gift and source of joy,
*   who have unknowingly provided material*
*   for many of the stories and poems herein:*
*   Teresa, Phillip and Marianne,*
*   who are living happy and productive lives,*
*   and have given us eleven fantastic grandchildren;*
*   and Gregory, whose short life on this planet*
*   taught us what love is all about.*

To Eleanor Pratt, my dear friend and fellow teacher,
*   who was never too busy to read whatever I wrote*
*   with a professional and critical eye,*
*   and who said I needed "a wider audience."*

Most of all, I am thankful to Almighty God.
*   Creator of life,*
*   and source of all love and inspiration.*

CONTENTS

PREFACE — 13

I - FAMILY LOVE - — 17

Introduction — 19

Expressed in Prose
A Special Gift — 21
A Country Road — 24
My Day in the Cellar — 27
Memories of a Bridge — 29
A Little Prayer and How it Grew — 31
Report Cards — 34
Marianne's Gift — 38
The Paper Route — 40
Turning Point — 44
The Blue Card — 50
Finding the Key to Greg — 55
Making Cookies With Mother Baker — 58
A Cup of Cold Water — 63

Expressed in Poetry
The Day After — 67
Welcome, Jackie! — 68
To Betty on her Birthday — 69
Graduation Day Meditation — 70
Anniversary Gift — 72
To Greg in Heaven — 73
Shower Gift — 74
Trees — 75
Dear Eleanor — 76
Bon Voyage — 77
Birthday Blessing — 78
Dear Bobby — 80

II - ROMANTIC LOVE - 81

Introduction 83

Expressed in Prose
How We Met 84

Expressed in Poetry
Returning Veteran 87
In Retrospect 88
The Weaver 89
Woolgatherer 90
Mirage 91
Prudence 92
Reclamation 93
April 94
To Robert Burns 95
Memento 96
My Heart 97
Coquette 98
Sonnet on the New Year 99
Idealist 100
To My True Love 101
To My Love on his 74th Birthday 102
To My Valentine on Valentine's Day 103

III - DIVINE LOVE – 105

Introduction 107

Expressed in Prose
A Country Church 109
Fairwell Sister, It Was Happy When You Were Here 113
My Lost Love 119

Expressed in Poetry
God's Call   121
Heartfelt Prayer at a Religion Teachers' Workshop   122
You Say You Want Peace   125
Moving Day   126
Murphy's Ten Cent Store on a Summer Day   128
First Meeting of the Monday Night Group   130
Advent   132
The First Christmas   134
New Year Prayer   136
A Pilgrim's Prayer   138
Holy Year Prayer   140
The Mysterious Holy Spirit   142
Bicentennial Prayer   144
Thanksgiving for God's Blessings   146
Prayer for Spiritual Renewal   148
Renewal   149
Message From Jesus in the Eucharist   150
Jubilee Year   152
Message at Summit Lake   153
The Hands of Jesus   157

IV - LOVE OF LIFE -   161

Introduction   163

Expressed in Prose
Depression Years on the Farm   166
Boot Camp   172
Rosemary   176
Honolulu   178

Expressed in Poetry
The Burning Schoolhouse   179
Autumn   180

On Meeting Mrs. G.	181
Sonnet	182
Spring	183
Summer Night	184
The First Snow	185
All Through the Night	186
Plenty Papaya	188
The Lei Lady	189
Mormon Temple in Hawaii	190
The Geode Speaks	191
On Taking Psychology 101	192
Poets are Terribly Sensitive People	194
To My Successor in Office	196
College Daze	197
Sonnet to a Friend	199
Windy Days	200
Rainy Days	201
Early Snowfall	202

PREFACE

Love is not what makes the world go around.
It's what makes the ride worthwhile.
—Franklin P. Jones

Years ago a friend gave me a colorful banner bearing these words. I appreciate the wisdom of them. The forces that make the world spin around on its axis are beyond our comprehension, but most of us would agree that it is loving relationships that bring us the greatest happiness and enhance the quality of our lives as we travel through space on this planet. Indeed it is love that makes the ride worthwhile.

The word *love* is used so casually today that it is losing its real meaning. For instance, ten-year-old Michele *loves* her new puppy, her mother *loves* Richard Gere, her father *loves* golfing, her brother *loves* blueberry pie, and her grandmother *loves* crossword puzzles. They are a happy family and they all *love* each other!

On the other hand, there are caring families, especially those of earlier times, who never used the word *love* at all. Take Tevye and his wife Golde, for instance in the play *Fiddler on the Roof.* Tevye asks Golde in song, "Do you love me?" She is insulted by the question and replies angrily, "Do I love you? For twenty-five years I've washed your clothes, cooked your meals, cleaned your house..." and after recounting other things she does for him, she tells him slowly, as if she had never thought of it before, "I suppose I do..."

How different from the psychology of today! We are advised to tell our children often that we love them, or they are likely to suffer emotional damage from feelings of rejection, neglect or inadequacy.

As I look back, I cannot remember my father ever saying he loved me, though I never doubted that he did. He was a man of few words, but his actions were unmistakable. One stern look from him was enough when my siblings and I were misbehaving. He never lectured or nagged us, but he expected us to obey him, and most of the time we did. His love came through to his family in the things he did for us. He made a teeter-totter for my brother and me, and he made a wonderful swing from an old rubber tire. I have vivid memories of him pulling me over the snow in a sled when I was four or five years old. We went out to our woods to find a Christmas tree. When we had decided on one, he cut it down, piled it on the sled, and away we went. I *loved* (there's that word again!) being all scrunched up, with the cedar branches tickling my face, and holding on tight as the sled glided over the snow.

This book is about love, both expressed and unexpressed—love of family and friends, love of God, love of country and love of life itself. It covers a variety of topics, and includes, among other things, childhood memories, depression years on the farm, glimpses of military life as a Navy Wave, special events in the lives of our children, prayers and meditations, and Grandma Baker's recipe for Pennsylvania Dutch cookies.

A few years ago, I decided to collect all the poetry I had written and saved. As I looked for my poems, I came across a number of short prose pieces, and gradually my collection evolved into a book of both prose and poetry. This collection is not in itself the story of my life, nor even the highlights of my life, for at some of the most interesting times, I was too busy to write.

It does, however, depict the lifestyle and values of my generation, and reflects the living and loving I have experienced through family and friends, through my faith, and through the circumstances of my life. Some of it has been published or written for special occasions. The name of the publication or the occasion is given at the end of the piece.

I have been blessed with more than my share of love, and I would hope that these bits and pieces of life as I have known it would stir up warm memories of your own childhood and your own dreams and longings, as well as a deeper appreciation of your family, your faith, your country, and the generations that have gone before you.

I - FAMILY LOVE

"He ain't heavy, Father, he's my brother."
—Father Flanagan's Boys Town, Omaha, Nebraska

Introduction

Family love is different from any other kind of love. Our families are imposed upon us, whether we like it or not. We can choose our mates and our friends, but we cannot choose our parents and siblings, or for that matter, aunts, uncles, cousins and grandparents. We inherit them all at birth. The characteristics we share with family members—our ethnic backgrounds, our strengths and weaknesses, our gifts and talents—are all qualities we cannot change or ignore. They bind us together as family. They are constant reminders that we belong to one another in a special way.

The stories and poems in this section relate to family, or in some cases, "extended" family—close friends or people who have been members of our household at some time. They cover three generations—stories of my own childhood, stories and poems about our children, and one story about their Grandmother Baker.

The stories relating to our children were often written down immediately after that particular incident occurred; for example, *Marianne's Gift* and *Report Cards*. I wrote the conversations in detail, thinking the children would enjoy reading them in later years. Actually, I enjoy reading them myself, as they bring back memories that are dear to me, though the children may not remember the incidents at all. What amazes me is that these stories reveal personality traits in the children that are still prominent in the adults today.

Two of the stories about our children are devoted entirely to Greg. They speak for themselves. All I need to say here is that Greg opened our eyes to the needs of physically disabled and mentally challenged children, and made us keenly aware of handicapped and troubled people, wherever we meet them. Our compassion and understanding for those who need a helping hand is a gift from Greg, which he passed on to his parents and siblings. We have all been blessed by this gift and we are grateful to God for the opportunities he has given us to use it. Greg would be pleased, and I believe he is smiling down on us from heaven.

A Special Gift

It was the day before my sixth birthday, a typical July day, hot, dry and dusty. My brother Charles (whom we always called Bud) was four years old. He was my shadow and tagged along behind me every place I went. When Mother sent me to get the mail from the mailbox on the corner or to take a letter to be mailed, I would try to sneak out of the house so he wouldn't see me leave. But before I could reach the mailbox, I would hear him calling, and turn around to see that sturdy little figure standing in the middle of the road and yelling with all his might, "*SIS-TER! Wait for me!*"

On this particular day, Dad took Bud and me to the home of Ed and Maggie Payne, our closest neighbors, about half a mile away. They were an older couple with two unmarried daughters living at home. Ed's father, a Civil War veteran, was also living with them. We felt very much at home there, as they took care of us any time Mother and Dad had to go any place without us. Mrs. Payne was a grandmotherly figure, always ready to welcome us with open arms and give us cookies, books, or toys to keep us busy. In fact, my sister Mary, when she was two or three, began to call her Grandma. When Bud said to her, "She's not your Grandma," she replied, "I know her name Mit Payne, but I ist call her Grandma."

How Mrs. Payne kept us occupied that day I don't remember, but when it began to get dark, I asked her why Dad did not come to get us. She assured me he was probably busy and would come as soon as he could. It was night when he came, and Bud and I were getting sleepy. He didn't offer any explanation for being late, and we didn't ask any questions. We just climbed into the truck, glad to be going home.

When we reached our house, I saw that it was dark inside, except for a light in Mother and Dad's bedroom. I was the first to go in and, as soon as I opened the door, a neighbor lady whom I knew took my hand and pulled me into the bedroom, saying, "Come and see your birthday present." Several other ladies were standing around the room, all watching and smiling. She led me to the bed, where Mother was lying with a small bundle beside her. At first I thought it was a doll and reached out to touch it. Mother said, "It's real. It's your baby sister."

I touched her pink little cheeks, and Mother unwrapped her so I could see her tiny fingers and toes. It was love a first sight! She was beautiful! She was perfect! In all my short life I had never been so surprised and so delighted as I was that night! The women were asking, "Now what do you think of that?" and "How's that for a birthday gift?" but all I could do was smile. I really believed what they were telling me—that this little baby was my birthday present—and I was so overwhelmed that I could not speak.

We named her Mary Frances. I felt protective and responsible for her from the beginning. I helped Mother care for her, played with her when Mother was busy, did tricks to make her laugh, and began to teach her words when she was only a few months old. She was cute and smart and learned quickly. A neighbor started calling her "Windy" because she chattered so to everyone who came, and spoke distinctly at an early age.

As time went on, I realized that Mother and Dad probably had *not* actually gone out and looked for a baby for my birthday, but I still clung to the notion that Mary belonged to me in some special way, since she had arrived the day before my birthday.

When Mary was about three years old, another boy was born into our family. He was named Robert and we called him Bobby. Bud was glad to have a brother, since I already had a sister, and he was tired of playing house. I remember thinking, "Two boys and two girls. That's a perfect family." I do not remember any details of his birth, or wondering where he came from. I was almost nine, so I must have been satisfied with whatever I was told.

Bud, however, was more curious. When he was eight or nine, he began to ask me questions that I could not answer. It was his idea that we go together to ask Mother for answers, and I would be the spokesperson. So we accosted her, and I told her we had two questions for her: *Who made God?* and *Where do babies come from?* She gave us a quizzical look and replied, "You're too young to understand such things. We'll talk about it when you're older." We never mentioned it again and Mother never did either. We had to find the answers for ourselves.

Every age brings changes in the way we teach our children. For example, just one generation later, when I was very pregnant, I heard our five-year-old daughter talking on the phone to a neighbor who was apparently asking her about kindergarten. Our Terri was explaining, in a very grown-up way, "I might not start to kindergarten the first day. It depends on when Mommy has the baby. If she's in the hospital, then she won't be able to take me. I won't start till she gets home, so she can take me."

We mothers always want the best for our children. When it comes to teaching them the so-called "facts of life," sometimes we follow the latest theory of the child psychologists and sometimes we follow our intuition. I wonder how much it really matters, so long as we do it with love and understanding.

As for Mary, under my tender care and guidance, (she might question that!) she grew into a beautiful young lady, and married her high school sweetheart. They are enjoying retirement now, as my husband and I are. We have always kept in touch, though at times we have lived far apart. Now in the sunset of our years, we treasure our visits together. Mostly we talk about our children and grandchildren— their interests, their talents, their hopes and dreams, their work and their accomplishments. We are glad they have opportunities we did not have, and we are proud of them all.

Sometimes we reminiscence about growing up on the farm, how things used to be then, and how I thought she was my birthday present. She is my only sister, and we have shared our lives through joyful times and sad times. I still think of her as my special gift, not from my parents, but from the Father above, giver of every good and perfect gift.

A Country Road

From the state highway, you can see the white farmhouse on the opposite hill. To reach it, you take the gravel road, go down the hill, across the bridge, up another hill and turn left.

All through my school years, I walked this road to and from the school bus. During that time, there were from two to eight children who caught the bus at this corner, sloshing through the puddles on rainy days and crowding into the "shack" our fathers built for us to wait in; hurrying along in cold winter weather with heads down, hands in pockets, and scarves blowing; or tramping through the snow in heavy boots, laughing, shoving, chattering, arguing.

Tim Smith's farm was to your left. His cornfield was always neat with few weeds, but he couldn't lick the honeysuckle that choked his fence. It still climbs over and through it, permeating the air with its sweet fragrance.

The Bowers' cow pasture was to your right and behind that, the thick dark woods. That land is now being cultivated and soybeans are growing there. How strange that looks!

At the foot of the hill, to your right, there is a persimmon tree. Each fall, on our way to the bus, my siblings and I used to stop there and brush away the autumn leaves to find the plump ripe persimmons that dropped from the tree. I have never since tasted persimmons that matched the quality of those I picked up under that tree. (It was also there that I learned what it was like to bite into a green one!)

Beyond the persimmon tree is the iron bridge. I remember when it was built to replace the narrow wooden one. The bridge was a halfway mark, a meeting place, a parting place, and a point at which to stop and dawdle. When my best friend would come over to play, and I begged to walk part-way home with her, my mother would say, "Only as far as the bridge," and we would stand there, leaning over the iron rail, kicking stones into the shallow stream below, talking idle girl talk.

Across the bridge and to your left, in Tim Smith's pasture, stands an old oak tree, its strong branches set in splendid symmetry against the sky. In winter it looked like a Christmas card, its bare limbs outlined with snow. In summer, the great tree gave a large pool of welcome shade. We girls used to play house around its roots, scraping out the grass and dried leaves to make rooms, with the protruding roots as partitions. We fashioned furniture from stones, leaves, sticks and stones. Tiny imaginary people inhabited these dwellings.

As a child walking home from school, I used to feel a curious excitement soon after I passed the old oak tree, for it was there that the roof of our house came into view over the crest of the hill. At that point, I would break into a run. Dashing up the hill and around the corner, I would cut across our lawn, clatter up the wooden steps to the porch and push open the door breathlessly. More than likely I would be greeted with the delicious aroma of yeast bread baking or molasses cookies fresh from the oven. My mother was a firm believer in after-school snacks. Before chores or homework, my siblings and I would be given a glass of milk and a cookie or maybe a thick slice of homemade bread with real butter.

Another family lives in this house now. It has been remodeled and painted, and the three maple trees in the front yard have grown so tall and full you can hardly see the house. The summer my father planted them, my brother and I pumped six buckets of water and poured it on them every evening to keep them alive. He told us that, if we jumped over them every day, we would be able to jump over them when they were tall. We tried it for a while, but they outgrew us!

Another generation of children now play under these trees, walk this road, and slide down these hills on their sleds. I wonder if they too pick the honeysuckle, eat the persimmons, and drop pebbles over the iron rail of the bridge. I hope they may grow to cherish memories of a serene and uncluttered childhood as I do now, remembering a small girl who trudged along a country road, down a hill, across a bridge, and up a hill to home.

—1963

My Day in the Cellar

My father loved sorghum molasses. He grew his own cane, cut it in the fall and hauled it to the mill where it was boiled down to a dark pungent syrup that lasted our family all year. My mother flavored baked beans with it and baked spicy gingerbread with it. We made popcorn balls with it, and poured it over our pancakes with lots of butter.

One fall the new molasses was brought home in a twenty-gallon wooden keg with a spigot on the side. It was set on a low table in the cellar where it would be handy when we ran out upstairs.

The first time that happened was on a Saturday morning and we were having pancakes for breakfast. I was sent to the cellar to fill up the pitcher. I set the pitcher under the spigot and turned, but nothing came out. Molasses gets thicker when it is cold. Given a few minutes, it would have found its way through the small opening. But in the unthinking haste that was typical of me at that time (I was 16), I tipped the barrel to start the flow.

Suddenly the heavy barrel fell against me, and I was not strong enough to push it back in place. The lid slipped off, and the thick syrup flowed out like lava down a mountainside. When I could find my voice, I screamed, "Mother!" She came hurrying down the stairs, gave one horrified look, and called for Dad. Then she went back upstairs and Dad came down. He took in the situation quickly and his dark eyes flashed in anger at such foolish waste. He took three steps to reach me, and used the palm of his hand to give me three smart whacks on my plump bottom.

"Don't come upstairs till you get that all cleaned up!" was all he said. Then he clumped up the stairs in his heavy boots and was gone.

When I heard Dad leave the house, I called again for Mother and she brought me the necessary tools to clean up the mess. I was able to set the keg upright and save some of the molasses, but most of it had spread slowly over the cellar floor, and I had taken off my shoes and was wading in it, wondering where to begin.

The job took all day. First, I scooped the spoiled molasses into a bucket and poured bucketful after bucketful into a big lard can. This would later be mixed with silage and fed to the cattle. Then I scrubbed the cement floor with hot soapy water which Mother brought down to me. I had no help with the cleaning and didn't expect any.

The hardest thing about that day I spent in the cellar was the realization that, in one thoughtless moment, I had ruined our year's supply of molasses. The humiliation of the spanking also hurt. I cried bitter tears into those sticky buckets, but in the end I resolved to make up for my carelessness by being more helpful at home. I think I grew up a little that day. It was my last spanking.

It was characteristic of my father that he never referred to the incident again. He was not one to hold grudges or to cry over spilt milk, or in this case, spilt molasses. Once my brother mentioned it before guests to embarrass me, but my father's only comment, with a wry smile, was, "Mighty expensive feed for the cattle!"

Memories of a Bridge

We used to dream the most wonderful dreams, Penny and I, hanging over the rusty iron rail of the bridge on summer afternoons, kicking rocks into the water with our bare feet.

The bridge was our meeting place and our parting place. It was built over a muddy little creek full of tadpoles and crawdads. Honeysuckle vines climbed the sagging fence on one side of the country road and there was a persimmon tree on the other. The narrow dirt road wound uphill on either side of the bridge. Penny's house was on top of one hill, and mine on the other.

Penny was a scrawny little girl with big eyes and flying blonde hair and she was my best friend. Oh, the long talks we used to have on drowsy summer days, standing on the bridge squelching the hot dust between our toes! The very atmosphere inspired confidences. There was hardly a sound but the soft trickle of water and the hum of insects in the tall grass. When we saw a car coming, we scrambled under the bridge because we liked to hear it rumble over our heads. Sometimes we waded in the creek or wandered up to where the water was knee-deep, took off our clothes and splashed in the water to get cooled off, careful not to wet our hair, so our mothers wouldn't know.

Sometimes we picked the little blue flowers that grew along the banks of the stream, and sometimes we looked for four-leaf clovers. Penny found them often, but I seldom did, and she would give me hers in token of our friendship. But most of all, we liked to talk about "when we grow up and go away." It never entered our foolish little heads that we might possibly grow up and stay right there on the farm. Our faith in each other was marvelous. I never doubted that Penny would some day become a real honest-to-goodness nurse, and she thought my poems were "just as good as the ones in the magazines."

As we grew older, our conversations were more likely to dwell on the opposite sex. It was there on the bridge I confided to Penny that I was in love with my history teacher, and she showed me her first love letter, written in pencil on blue-lined paper.

Penny was a year ahead of me in school, and the first to "grow up and go away." When she graduated from high school, she was offered a job in the County Home, commonly known as "the poor farm." She would help care for elderly people who were homeless, poor, or sick. She would live at the Home, the work would be hard, and the pay very little. But Penny saw it as a preparation and stepping stone to her nursing career, and she was very excited about leaving.

The day she was to go, she came over to tell me goodbye. I walked with her as far as the bridge, where we lingered, wondering when we would see each other again. The little stream was swollen with the spring rains, and yellow water gushed under the bridge carrying sticks and dead leaves. I promised to write often and she vowed to answer every letter.

I walked home slowly because there was an aching emptiness inside of me. My best friend was going away, but that was not all. For the first time, I realized that I could not always share my life with Penny. *This is what it is like to grow up,* I thought. *Only children share everything, and we are no longer children.*

—*Hill Thoughts*, 1948
Hanover College, Hanover, IN

A Little Prayer and How It Grew

In the early days of our marriage, my husband and I, both recent converts to the Catholic faith, looked forward to the challenge of rearing a Christian family. Among the things we planned was an old-fashioned ritual—family prayer.

I envisioned it like this: Father, Mother and children gathered around the fireplace just before bedtime, firelight flickering on devout little faces, joining in a prayer led by Father. It was a lovely fantasy, but not at all realistic. Our babies came close together and the first two had colic. We spent our evenings rocking, patting and walking with them to get them to sleep. As they grew older, we kept trying, but they were restless or wandered off. We ended up by praying with each child individually at bedtime. Family prayer was forgotten.

Then, quite innocently and with no planning at all, we slipped into the perfect way for us to pray together. A family prayer had been developing all along and we had never even noticed it.

It all began with grace before meals. With our marriage, we had begun to pray the Catholic version. But it was not long before we added another line we had heard somewhere because it expressed so perfectly what we wanted to say: *Make us ever mindful of the needs of others.* Later, we were surprised to learn that there is a Catholic *after-meal* prayer. My husband thought we should adopt this practice, but we could never remember to do it, so he simply added the after-meal prayer to our before-meal prayer, remarking matter-of-factly, "What difference does it make *when* we say it?"

And so our children learned to say this prayer before meals: *Bless us,*

O Lord, and these thy gifts which we are about to receive through thy bounty, and make us ever mindful of the needs of others. May the souls of the faithful departed, through the mercy of God, rest in peace. Amen.

We soon began to add to it, however. We all had needs, concerns, and thanks to express, and we added lines like this: *Bless Grandma and make her well...Help Terri to do well in her piano recital tomorrow... Thank you, Lord, for bringing us home safely.*

Sometimes the prayers were surprising. I was pleased to hear one evening: *Bless Mother and all she did for us today*; and I noticed our little girl's startled look on hearing this one: *Bless Marianne and help her stop sucking her thumb.*

When my husband's work took him out of town overnight, we prayed for his safe return, and this began the practice of praying for any family member who is not present. Once when Greg was about two or three, I called to him, "Come to dinner, Greg, or we'll have to pray for you." When I found him hiding under the coffee table, he smiled and said, "Go ahead." That is what he was waiting for. Since he was never absent, we had never prayed especially for him!

Our children pray for the needs of their friends. Phillip still prays for a Nigerian student who once visited us. We know God answers our prayers. We have prayed that God will make us aware of the needs of others and he has done that. We have been privileged to know and work with the handicapped and the mentally ill in meeting their special needs, and it has proved to be very worthwhile.

One evening as my husband was beginning to say grace, I was pricked by an odd nostalgia. It may have been the sheen of the candlelight on the bowed heads, or the sudden stillness as my husband began, "Bless us, O Lord..." when my long-ago fantasy of family prayer came to mind, and the truth struck me with amazing clarity: *This is family prayer!*

And so it was! And is! Over the years, our meal-time prayers have reflected our family interests, our current needs and our spiritual growth. They vary from day to day, but are always fresh and spontaneous. Without intending it, we have discovered our own method of family prayer. It keeps us close to God and to each other in a simple loving way. Flexible and casual, but sincere, our little prayer that grew into a big one has meaning for us all.

—The Family Digest, 1968,
Huntington, IN

Report Cards

The evening before Phillip's sixth birthday I was baking cupcakes for his party the next day, and my husband was supervising baths. I had just taken a pan of cupcakes out of the oven and put them on the counter to cool when Terri, 8, and Greg, 7, came in, fresh from the tub and ready for bed.

"Can we have one, Mommy?"

"Okay. Just one, then off to bed."

Daddy heard that. "You just undo what I'm trying to do," he said.

"They've just brushed their teeth. How can we cut dentist bills if you let them eat before they go to bed?"

"You heard what Daddy said," I told them. "I'll put one in your lunch tomorrow."

"Please, Mommy. Just one."

I gave in to their pleas. "Okay, if you brush your teeth again."

Phillip and Marianne, 3, came into the kitchen just in time to hear that. All four of them grabbed a cupcake. Greg took a bite out of his, then quickly grabbed another one and took a bite. I took away both cupcakes, and walked him to his bed with the promise, "You'll get them in your lunch tomorrow." I tucked him in, kissed him goodnight, and left him sniffling into his pillow.

Back to the kitchen. The other three were sitting quietly at the table eating their cupcakes. I started baking cookies. My husband had recently asked, "Why don't you make some of those good molasses cookies, just for us?" It seemed to him I was always baking for church or school.

Daddy was calling to the kids, "Come on now. You're finished. You're going to bed. It's 7:30."

"But bedtime's not till 8:00," Terri reminded him.

"If I say it's 7:30, it's 7:30," he replied, but his bark was worse than his bite. He sat down at the piano, and started playing *This Old Man Came Rolling Home*. The kids loved it and they all joined in singing the words. Then he heard Greg crying and went in to him. I sent the others to the bathroom to brush their teeth, and took out a pan of cookies. In a few minutes Terri was back. "Can you put my hair up now, Mommy?"

"Okay. Bring me the curlers, and I'll do it while the cookies bake."

Just then there was a crash of glass, and I whirled around to see Marianne standing on a chair, the spice cabinet over her head swinging on one nail, and jars and bottles on the floor, some of them broken.

"Move, Marianne! Get down off the chair! Get down!" I shouted.

"But...but...but," she stammered, "I didn't mean to, Mommy, I didn't mean to!"

"It's okay, honey. It was just an accident. But don't stand up on the chair any more. Now sit down and stay out of the glass!"

Daddy is standing in the doorway surveying the debris on the kitchen floor and shaking his head in disbelief.

"Don't step in it!" I told him. "Stay in there and keep the kids out of the kitchen. I'll clean it up in a few minutes. Just keep out of it!"

Daddy disappears. Suddenly, Phillip is in the doorway. "What happened?

"Just a little accident. Don't come in. There's glass on the floor. Why aren't you in bed?"

"Nobody put me."

"Did you brush your teeth?"

"No."

"What have you been doing? Go brush your teeth!" I take him bodily to the bathroom, only to open the door and find Daddy emerging from the shower. He jumps on Phillip. "Why aren't you in bed?"

I explain, "Because I told him to brush his teeth."

"Brush his teeth? He's already brushed his teeth. I saw him do it."

"The first time, or after the cupcake?"

"I don't know. I can't keep track of what you're doing."

"Okay, Phillip," I tell him. "Go on and brush. You don't need all that toothpaste. And then go to bed."

Back to the kitchen. Look at the cookies. Put a curler in Terri's hair. Take out the cookies. Put in another pan. Put in two curlers.

"Mom-eeee!" It's Phillip.

I go in. "What now?"

He is in bed at last, sitting up in his top bunk. "How come Marianne is still up?"

"She'll go pretty soon. She was scared because she accidentally knocked the spice rack and it fell down. She needs to calm down a little bit. Then she'll go."

"Oh." Satisfied with this explanation, Phillip lies down and pulls up the covers.

Back to the kitchen. Three more curlers and a goodnight kiss to Terri. She goes happily to bed. I take out the last pan of cookies, then sweep up the broken glass and spilled spices on the kitchen floor.

Marianne comes in, sucking her thumb and trailing her blanket. "I'm hungry," she says. She is getting over the flu and her eyes look unusually big and dark.

"Come on, let's fix a surprise for Daddy." I put some cookies and a glass of milk on a plate and we take it in to him.

"Oh, thank you!" he says, beaming. "My favorite cookies!" He takes Marianne on his lap and they eat them together.

I clean off the counters and begin to frost the cupcakes, putting extra frosting on the two that Greg had taken bites from. I hear him coughing. His cough is getting worse. I must call the doctor tomorrow.

"Aren't you finished yet?" My husband has put Marianne to bed, and they are all sleeping. Heavenly silence!

"Almost. I found the nail for the spice rack. Could you put it back? There weren't many jars broken. Marianne stood up on a chair, and must have hit it somehow to knock it loose."

Mumbling something about the kids and their antics, he put the spice rack back in place and went into the living room to read the paper. My thoughts turned to the report cards that Greg and Terri had brought home that day. Terri had received all G's (meaning Good in the parochial school they attend), but there was a note that she was not doing the work she was capable of doing. Greg had received G's in Religion, Art, Reading and Numbers but L (Low) in writing. We would have to help them more with their homework.

I wanted to look at the report cards again, and found them on top of the piano. But what were the two green sheets beside them? I picked up one on which MOTHER was printed at the top, with grades under it.

VG in Baking
VG in taking care of us
VG in being good

VG means Very Good—the highest grade. I picked up the sheet marked DADDY and read the grades under it.

VG in playing the piano
VG in reading to us
VG in telling stories

I showed the report cards to my husband and we stood there reading them together, feeling humbled and proud at the same time. This was Terri's work. How could she have felt inspired to even think of such a thing on this crazy evening? Strange as it seemed, one thing was clear: our 8-year-old daughter, of her own accord, had thoughtfully rated us as parents on qualities she considered important, and she had given us the highest possible marks! It was one of those surprising and wonder-filled moments when parenthood, with all its challenges, brings its own rewards. We could only hug each other and thank God for this amazing day!

Marianne's Gift

Under our Christmas lies a small package wrapped in green and silver paper and tied with a red ribbon. The attached card bears a fat Santa waving heartily, and the words, "To Daddy from Marianne."

Insignificant as it appears among larger and more colorful boxes, this modest gift nevertheless represents such love and sacrifice that it almost seems to glow as I single it out each time I pass the tree.

"You'll *never, never* guess it!" Marianne tells her father after she has let him shake it one more time, and they have both listened with cocked ears. It makes a soft rattle, and he guesses, "Cuff links? A tie clip? A gum ball?" After each guess, she goes into peals of laughter. "That's enough for today," she says. She takes the package and carefully places it under the tree.

I am one of the favored few that know what the package contains. I await the day it is to be presented with almost the same ecstatic anticipation as the young giver.

A few days ago Marianne announced to me in her decided way, "I know what I'm giving Daddy for Christmas!" and then added mysteriously, "Have you noticed anything different about me lately?"

I searched the pert face for clues—the enormous brown eyes under the shiny black bangs, the smattering of freckles across the short straight nose, the smiling rosy mouth. The mouth! Suddenly I knew her secret! "Your thumb! You've given up sucking your thumb!

"Do you think Daddy will like it?" she asked.

"Oh, honey, he'll love it! It will be the best Christmas present he ever had! Have you really stopped?"

"I really have," she answered with such dignity and pride that I knew *this* time there would be no going back to baby ways. "And please don't tell him, Mommy. I want to surprise him. Do you think he'll notice before Christmas?"

"I'm sure he won't. *I* didn't, you know, until you made me think about it."

Marianne sat down at the kitchen table and, with her left hand, she carefully drew around her right thumb on a piece of paper. She wrote under it: *I gave up you-know-what.* She folded the paper into a small square, and placed it inside a ring box with a pop-up lid. Then she put the ring box inside a larger box and wrapped it with care, giggling and sighing by turns, as she thought of how delighted her father would be, and then of the long wait till Christmas.

There's a new radiance in Marianne's smile, and a confident swing to her step. She has learned that she is master of her own will. Then too, she is filled to bursting with the joy of giving, and of knowing the recipient will value the unusual qualities of her gift more than any material thing.

Certain signs of character development have not been overlooked by her father. "Our little Marianne is growing up," he remarked this morning, "Have you noticed how considerate she is lately? I hope she doesn't go and spend all her money on that gift for me she's so excited about."

"Don't worry, she didn't," was all I said, but in my secret heart, I added, "Money can't buy that gift, my dear. It's one of those rare treasures that can only be given away."

The Paper Route

The rain was coming down at a fast clip when I opened the front door to pick up the morning paper. It was only 6:15 a.m. but our *Indianapolis Star* was tucked neatly inside the storm door, thanks to our efficient and trustworthy paperboy.

A paperboy, as everyone knows, must go on his appointed rounds 364 days a year (no paper on Christmas) through snow, rain, howling dogs and below-zero temperatures to deliver the newspaper to your door. What some people *don't* know is that, behind most of those polite little paperboys is a paperboy's Mom, without whom you would come up paperless on many a winter's morning.

I speak from experience. Our son Phillip was not quite 12 when he announced that he had been offered a "bicycle route." He could hardly wait to begin. All he needed, he told his father and me, was our permission and a down payment on the bond. The district manager came out, and my husband and I signed the papers and turned over the money. We all agreed it would be a wonderful thing for Phil.

"We're always glad to find the boy's family interested in his route," the man said. He wasn't just making conversation. The significance of *that* statement was to sink in later.

When Phil's alarm clock went off that first morning, I wondered if we had made a terrible mistake. It was unbelievably dark at 4:30 a.m. and I envisioned Phil on his bike, trying to find the addresses on his list in that blackness. I thought of drunken drivers and the deep swift water under the bridge he had to cross. I was tempted to get up and drive him, but I knew that would defeat the whole purpose. Weren't paper routes famous for teaching responsibility and developing character? So I

LOVE MAKES THE RIDE WORTHWHILE

listened for him to leave, and didn't sleep a wink until I heard the front door slam and knew he was home again.

Plenty of opportunities to drive Phil came later. In spite of the toughest bikes and the tightest all-weather gear, there are times when paperboys' Moms have to come to the rescue. There is snow so deep that bikes bog down, cold so biting it freezes fingers and toes, driving wind and rain that tear up the papers. The Sunday papers are too big to be carried in one trip, so paperboys always welcome a family member who is willing to drive them around on Sundays.

The first time I drove Phil, it was pouring rain and foggy. I drove slowly along the unfamiliar streets, trying to follow Phil's directions: *Turn right at the next corner and stop at the second house on the left...Turn into the driveway on the other side of the brick house...Let me out at the corner, and drive on down to the fourth house on the right.*

Phil hopped in and out of the back seat, dripping and cheerful, offering interesting bits of information between stops. For instance, precisely *where* the paperboy places the paper is very important to the customer.

"Mr. Miller wants his paper inside the big jar on the step," Phil told me, "but if it's raining, I'm to put it inside the storm door." Mrs. Wilcox wanted her paper put in her milk box, and Mrs. Jensen wanted hers at her side door. As for Mr. Fullbright, Phil explained, "I'm to go through the garage and leave the paper at the back door. But when the dogs are in the garage, I can leave it at the front door."

At one house, Phil went up on the porch and, after a few minutes, returned with this explanation, "Mr. Crandell wants his paper on the table by the door with the stone on top, but there for a minute, I couldn't find the stone."

I learned that Phil had a healthy respect for dogs. "Let me out here, and meet me at the corner," he instructed me at one house, and disappeared into the shrubbery. When I picked him up at the corner, he explained, "They have a big dog, and I didn't want to attract too much attention."

Phil would take four or five papers, stick them under his yellow slicker and splash off into the darkness, while I would creep along the wet streets, peering between the flashing windshield wipers, trying to find the place where he would come out again.

As I waited for him, I wondered what his customers were like. When he said, "Stop at the house that's indented in," I strained to see the little house back off the street. "That's where Mrs. Umber lives," Phil said. "I put her paper under the mat. She's old and lives by herself, and she always gives me a tip when I collect." At this, my heart warmed toward dear old Mrs. Umber.

Rarely did we find anyone up. Mrs. Ford was an exception. "She's a school teacher, and she's always waiting for me," Phil said. Sure enough, a woman in a robe opened the door and reached out a hand for the paper.

Little by little, the pile of papers dwindled, and Phil sighed with satisfaction. "Six more left. We'll come out even." As I learned, the number of customers is never static. People move in and out, take vacations, and stop and start their papers. A shortage means a boy has to buy papers at the newsstand to make it up, and is later reimbursed. When he has "extras," he pays for them out of his own pocket if he has failed to inform the newspaper office of a "stop." Coming out even is good.

After the last paper was delivered, Phil said, "It's early for school. Let's go to the Big Donut." This invitation turned out to be one of the fringe benefits that came from driving Phil around to deliver his papers. And the doughnuts were always his treat.

As we found stools at the counter that morning, rumpled and damp, I felt a bond with the three other customers—two truck drivers and a waitress. There is something intrinsically satisfying about being up and working before the rest of the world is awake. The coffee was especially good, the doughnuts fresh from the oven, and Phil talkative and hungry. We shared the good feeling of having completed a worthwhile task in spite of obstacles.

Phil has gone away to school now, and another boy is "passing papers" on his old route. But I remember fondly those pre-dawn drives, and I will always have a warm spot in my heart for the paperboys who carry on the business of newspaper circulation with all its hazards, not only because the experience is character-building, but also because having a dependable paperboy is one of life's little treasures.

—1972

Turning Point

The over-sized office calendar above Greg's desk is strikingly incongruous in the friendly clutter of his bedroom. In numerals twelve inches tall, it shouts the date my mind is reluctant to register. It tells me the year is 1968, the month is April, and the day is Tuesday. Emblazoned in black on the square page is a bold-faced 23.

Who will tear off the pages day by day now that Greg is gone? Or, like Little Boy Blue's toys, will they gather dust and await his return, halting time on this momentous day when his father and I drove him to a state hospital and left him there?

Greg is 15 now and, since the age of two, when he suffered a head injury, he has had epileptic seizures. He has been on as many as five medications at a time, but his seizures have never been completely controlled.

In Bible times, epilepsy was thought to be caused by a demon, and Jesus of Nazareth had the power to cast it out. His disciples, however, were unable to heal the possessed boy who "foamed at the mouth" and "often fell into the fire and into the water." (Mark 9:14-29). Medical science has given the demon a name, *epilepsy*, from the Greek word meaning *to seize upon.* When it seizes its victim by the throat and throws him down, writhing and unconscious, the person is said to be having a *seizure.*

Greg has enjoyed interludes of comparative freedom from seizures, and these times have been filled with the good things of life—a brother, two sisters, and parents who love him, school, sports, trips, pets, much laughter and many friends—all sandwiched in between the dark periods when his demon Epilepsy has had the upper hand.

Twice he has been hospitalized for seizures so severe no medicine would control them. Twice he was hospitalized for "emotional disturbance" and once for gum surgery because of abnormal gum growth, a side effect of dilantin. Many times he has been struck down at school and at play, while riding his bike or swimming, because his insidious demon gives no warning.

Greg is not physically disabled and does not think of himself as handicapped. He has compassion for blind and crippled persons, and is gentle with small children. He is tall and slim, and has honey-colored hair and brown eyes which light up when he smiles. A friend remarked of him, "When he smiles, he smiles all over."

Greg gets a kick out of the smallest things—finding a penny on the sidewalk, a game of checkers with Grandpa, a romp with our dog Tippy. He delights in surprising someone, especially his father, and does a perfect imitation of Gomer Pyle's "Suh-prahs, suh-prahs, suh-prahs!" He likes swimming, camping and hiking, and tans to a lovely golden-bronze color. Once when he was seven or eight, and he and his brother were taking a bath together, I asked, "Greg, why is it you get such a beautiful tan when Phillip only burns?"

"We-e-el," he drawled, smiling that mysterious smile, "It's 'cause God made me special."

And special he is! I've always thought he might have been the scholar of the family because of his love for books. He keeps a pile of them by the side of his bed to read when he has trouble sleeping, which is almost every night. When we go to the library, he can never decide which book he wants to take out, there are so many he likes—animal books, science books and adventure stories, plus all the wonderful children's classics. Only God knows what he may have become had not his enemy Epilepsy struck him down again and again, finally attacking his mind as well as his body. Severe *grand mal* seizures eventually caused brain damage, and he has been in Special Education classes since then.

When mental development is arrested in the early years, the innocence of childhood is prolonged. There is a trusting, childlike simplicity that is characteristic of Greg. It is this spiritual quality about him that both humbles and inspires us.

One spring day when Greg and I were in a public park, he had a seizure and fell to the ground. An old man with a white beard peered down at him and spoke in a shrill cracked voice, "This kind will surely go to heaven."

Yes, they surely will, and in a way, I think they never quite leave heaven, for they are always children, still innocent and trusting, as if the Father has never let go of them completely.

And so, tonight, I remember all these things and ponder them in my heart as Mary, the mother of Jesus, did. It is what we mothers must do as we seek to understand our children.

There were no tears today as we left Greg in his new surroundings. He took his clothes, two joke books, his Rummy cards, and his Magic 8-Ball. Casual and smiling, he stepped into a world which will exclude us. Others will supervise his waking and sleeping hours. Someone else will cook his meals, give him his medicine and see that he takes a bath and brushes his teeth. Will he be homesick? Will he be sad? Will he rebel? How long will it be, I wonder, before a day goes by that I do not think, "It's time for Greg's medicine," or wake with a start in the middle of the night, thinking I hear him having a seizure?

Greg's break with home was inevitable. Adolescence brought physical and emotional changes. New tensions and pressures developed. Greg's old enemy struck with greater force, and school was no longer feasible. After several months of indecision, frustration, and consultation with specialists, we have placed Greg in a state institution which promises to give him what we cannot give—further education and job training—so that he may be able to work in a sheltered workshop, and live a more normal life. We will be able to visit him often and bring him home on holidays.

We will all miss him, but my loss will be the greatest. He and I spent long hours together these last two months, reading, playing games, and watching television. How still the house will be without the blaring voices of Popeye, Superman and Mighty Mouse!

His room is exactly as he left it, his record player still open on his chest, ready to play Wizard of Oz, Side 2. His records are piled up haphazardly on the discarded ice chest, which holds his school papers. His model airplanes, cars and boats, all glued together by him, carefully, crookedly and with great patience, are displayed on the open shelves.

His shelves also hold other prized items: the Indian plaque he molded from wet *papier mache*, then dried it in the sun and painted it with oil paint when he was a cub scout; his cub scout manual, battered and very dear, having spent rainy nights under a tent with him; the electric clock he bought with his own money, and on which the alarm has long ago ceased to work; his metal lock-box with a secret combination known only to him and his brother Phillip; a funny clownish doll that sits with its hands folded over its knees; his peanut butter jar full of marbles, serving as a bookend; and a jagged row of big and little books, including *Peter Pan,* the *Lassie* books, *Robinson Crusoe, Grandfather Frog, Reddy Fox, Bible Stories,* and *Fairy Tales.*

On his desk are his pot-holder frame and yarn with four brand-new red pot-holders which he turned out these last few weeks at home; the pencil holder he made from an orange juice can, painted blue, with *PENCILS* printed in wobbly black letters on one side; a small plastic statue of the Virgin Mary and two holy cards; a broken pocket watch; a coin purse, a lock and key, and some little plastic animals from cereal boxes.

Other treasures are hidden in the top drawer of his desk, and still more, no doubt, under his bed. Tomorrow I will clean his room, wash the bedding, and put away some of these things…

It is late. The kids are in bed, and my dear husband also. Emotionally drained from the events of this day, his only need is for rest, while I must have my time alone, my hour of purging and self-renewal, in order to face this turning point in our lives and move forward again.

Our house will be oddly silent without Greg and the humorous banter that goes on between him and his father, the joking and the good-natured arguing that always seems to accompany Greg. Our other three children have gone about their chores, their homework and their baths quietly this evening. They will all miss Greg, especially Phillip, just a little younger than Greg. The boys have shared toys, clothes, treats, and friends for as long as they can remember. It was Phil who taught Greg to play fairly and scorn cheaters; who saw to it that no one took advantage of Greg, and just as carefully watched to see that no special favors were granted him.

Teresa is 17, our first child, cheerful and responsible, our baby-sitter, who mothers and disciplines the others, and knows how to supervise them lovingly but firmly. She plans to be a teacher and she will be a good one. She said tonight, "It's different already without Greg."

Marianne, our youngest, is 12, dark-eyed and intense. To her, Greg is a puzzle. She is disturbed by his odd behavior, worries about him an prays for him. She said to me one day, "Sister Ann says God sends suffering to those he loves, so I think he must love Greg an awful lot."

What will Greg's absence mean to these three? Now they are sad, but as time goes on, they will experience greater freedom than is possible with Greg at home. In the end, it may be better for them.

Greg's calendar with the bold-faced 23 meets my eye, and I realize that this day that began a new life for him is over. It is already another day. Yesterday is gone…I rip off the 23, crumple it in my hand and contemplate the big black 24 underneath…Today is a new day, a different day. I must quit musing and get on with it…Suddenly I know what I am going to do! Greg's room can wait. I can clean it another day…Tomorrow I am going to get out the sewing machine and start that new dress for Marianne…And I'll tell Terri she can invite some friends over for snacks and record-playing after school. They can use the family room. Greg will not be in there watching T.V…And I'll talk to Phil about his assignment for the school anthology that has been bothering him. I've put him off too long…I have so much catching up to do! I must begin!

I shiver in my thin robe, but not from the cold. A heady exhilaration has taken hold of me and little prickles of excitement are running around inside me. I feel slightly intoxicated.

I snap off the desk lamp, tiptoe out of Greg's room and shakily close the door. I stop at the girls' door and listen for their quiet breathing. At Phil's door I pause and hear him mumble incoherently in his sleep. I hurry to our bedroom, throw off my robe and slip in beside my husband...I know what will make him happy. Pancakes for breakfast! Pancakes with maple syrup, served with love...

The clock on our bedside table points to 1:15 a.m. I slide closer to the broad warm back beside me and smile in the dark with pure uncontrollable idiotic delight. *The crisis is past and all is well!*

The Blue Card

Phil looked taller when he came home from the seminary workshop and he wore a serious expression, almost as if he were afraid to laugh.

"Look at the halos around their heads," his father said in a teasing way to Phil and his friend Kim. Both boys had attended the two-week workshop, and Kim's parents had picked them up when it was over and brought Phil home. The boys looked at each other and smiled, but didn't answer.

After Kim and his family left, my husband put his arm around Phil's shoulders and said, "Now come in and tell us all about the workshop, Phil."

The other children were playing in the back yard. Phil glanced at them, then led the way to the living room. He sat down in the big chair by the fireplace and told everything in a detailed organized way, first things first.

"We had Mass every morning at seven, and we went to communion every day. We had evening prayer every night, and didn't talk from then till breakfast the next morning. You know, (he paused as if remembering), it was a good feeling going to Mass every day."

"Fine!" my husband exclaimed, well pleased. "We knew you would like it, Phil. Now tell us about your classes. Were they hard?"

"Math was interesting. I liked that. Latin was hard!"

"But you never had Latin before," I said, "That makes a difference."

"Well, I knew a little Latin from serving Mass," he explained. "Then we had English. Man, are they strict in grading! I misspelled one word—dormitory—and he took off five points! I would have had 100 in English if it hadn't been for that! We had a test in everything at the end.

I'll show you my papers." He ran upstairs to get them, and my husband and I looked at each other and smiled.

"It's been good for him, hasn't it?" I said, "He's different, more grown up." And he nodded in agreement.

Phil came back with a brown envelope and took out an 8 x 10 photograph. "Here's a picture of our group," he explained. "I had just got back from the kitchen when they took it. I was washing dishes." He handed me the picture, and I found him, with a thatch of brown hair over his forehead, along with around 60 other boys, and a few priests and Brothers, standing on the seminary steps. The boys looked bright and pleasant, all smiling.

"This is a good picture of you, Phil," I told him. Do you know these priests?" He pointed them out to us, naming them all, the classes they taught, and also naming some of the boys.

"Father Hillman said our group was the best-behaved bunch of boys he ever had. There wasn't *one* who caused any trouble!" Phil spoke with pride, obviously taking this as a great compliment. Then he rummaged through the brown envelope and took out the English test marked 95. We looked it over and commented on it.

"This is a good paper, Phil," my husband remarked, "And what did you make on the other subjects?"

"In Math, 92. That's a B+. Just one more point and it would have been an A." Phil was disappointed in this grade, as Math was always his best subject.

"B+ is a good grade," I told him. What about Latin?"

"C. Here's my paper. I just couldn't get on to that Latin!"

"That's all right, Phil. I think you did just fine." his father told him. "Now, what did you do besides study? Did you have a good time up there?"

Phil brightened up. "They've got an indoor swimming pool, and we could go swimming in our free time. I went every day. We had classes in the morning, then in the afternoon we had work to do. Our team's work was to keep the pool clean. Boy, was that cool! They've just got *everything* there—all kinds of sports!

"So I hear!" I exclaimed. "Kim told me you won the track

tournament. That's wonderful! I bet Daddy doesn't know about that yet!"

"Track?" his father asked. "What did you win, Phil?"

Phil smiled. "Well, they had this Field Day, see? They divided us into groups. I was on Team 1 for the 440. I came in first. Then the winners of the teams ran the mile race. I came in first on that." He pulled out the picture again. "This guy came in second. And Father Bell, here he is, he said "Well, I see we have a track star for next year."

"For next year?" I asked, holding my breath.

"They want me to come back, to go to school there next year. Father Hillman said he would come and get me and drag me there himself if I didn't come back." He smiled, and for a moment, looked like his old self again.

"You mean," his father asked, "they want you to study for the priesthood?"

"You mean," I parroted, "They want you to be a priest?"

Phil blinked a couple of times and answered, "Yes."

He didn't enlarge on that, so I asked weakly, "How do *you* feel about that, Phillip?"

He hesitated a moment, blinked again, and his gaze was on the carpet in front of him as he replied, "I'd like to go back."

My husband was the first to speak. "We'd be proud of you, Phillip, if you decided to be a priest, but we'd want you to think it over very carefully first to be really sure you have a vocation."

"I know," he answered, "I've been thinking about it."

"You don't want to make a decision until you know more about it," I said, "more about the Order, more about the school, about what you'd do as a priest…" I fumbled. There was so much more that *I* wanted to know!

"They told us that if we changed our minds, or couldn't make it all the way through, we'd still have a fine education. This school has a very high rating…"

I didn't hear about the school's rating because my mind was racing…*He is barely 14! Why do they take a boy away from home so young? He has just finished 8th grade. There's so much he has to learn.*

Why so young?

Phil was blinking again and, with his dark-rimmed glasses and his big eyes, he had an owlish look. *Is he nervous?* I thought, *or is he going to cry? Our son is telling us he wants to be a priest. He wants us to understand. Why are we making it so hard for him?*

I found myself speaking again, "We want you to do whatever you think is best for you, Phillip, whatever you will be happy doing, so long as it is good and worthwhile work. We can give you advice, but only you and God know what is right for you."

Phil nodded. It was as if he had expected a lecture and was prepared to listen until it was over.

My husband was on a different tack. "I know how you feel, Phillip," he said. *Funny how we both keep calling him Phillip.* "You have been living in a religious community with Mass and communion every day, and that inspires you to do more for God. I have been on retreats and always come back feeling I want to do more to serve God. But when I get back again, with my work and my family to think about, I realize I am serving God right where I am. A priest lives a different kind of life, and must really feel called to give his whole life to serving God. That means giving up marriage and family. That's why you need to wait to be sure God is calling you to this kind of life, that you do have a vocation. You understand this, don't you?"

"Yes," Phil answered, and waited for more.

"I think we should all pray about this," I offered, "Let's just wait, and pray that God will lead you to make the right decision, Phillip."

"Yes, I'll do that," Phil promised. "They gave us this blue card to fill out. If you send it in, they'll send you an application blank. Most of the boys filled theirs out there, but I brought mine home." He handed me the blue card with his name and address filled in. Below it were these words in large print: I WANT TO BE A PRIEST. PLEASE SEND ME AN APPLICATION.

"I wanted to talk to you first, before I signed it," he said.

How like him, I thought, *our thoughtful conscientious son who has always been a joy and never a problem. He wanted to talk to us first, but he really wants to go.*

I handed the card to my husband, and Phil began to explain to him about the tuition…"You can pay it by the year or by the month…" He showed us pamphlets of the school, pointing out the various buildings, and spoke with enthusiasm and humor. With their two heads bent over the pictures, my mind wandered again…

Did Phil have the makings of a priest? I remembered Phil at seven, making his First Confession, and hoping he would not commit a sin until Sunday morning when he would receive First Communion…Phil a Cub Scout, marching in parades…Phil a Boy Scout, chosen by his troop the best all-round Scout, and zapped out for the Order of the Arrow…Phil serving Mass, carrying the Book, ringing the bell…Phil on his paper route, getting up at 4:30 a.m. to deliver papers…Phil cheerful, always busy, full of jokes…now sitting here, serious, quiet, just waiting for us to speak…to tell him that what he wants to do is all right…

"It will be your decision, Phillip," my husband was saying. "We know you'll be in good hands, and we know you'll be a fine priest if you decide to be one. Will you agree to think seriously about this and pray about it for two weeks? In the meantime, we'll find out more about the school and we'll talk about it, then if you still want to go there next fall, we'll send in the blue card. Is that fair enough?"

"Fair enough," Phil replied in a business-like way. He tucked the blue card carefully inside the brown envelope, along with his other papers, and fastened the clasp. He gave a little sigh, and then smiled a tiny smile that was more to himself than to us, and ran upstairs to his room.

Finding the Key to Greg

Our son Greg returned home to the Father when he was only twenty-three, but he could have said, as Jesus did, "It is finished...I have completed the work you gave me to do."

The work God gave Greg to do could never be separated from who he was as a person. From the age of two, when he suffered a head injury, Greg was epileptic. As he grew older, severe seizures caused brain damage, and he attended special education classes in both public and private schools, and in a state hospital.

From the time Greg could remember, there were doctors, nurses, therapists and neurologists in his life. Hospitals were friendly, familiar places for him. His seizures were never completely controlled with medication, so he sometimes had accidents which required stitches. He could be riding his bike, swimming, or playing in the backyard, and suddenly wake up in a hospital. For Greg, it was all part of the adventure of living.

Early in his life, my husband and I began to search for "the key to Greg," as we called it—the key that would unlock the mysteries of epilepsy and lead to a cure. Naively, I thought it would be only a matter of finding the right medication, or a really good neurologist, or a special kind of surgery, and that little spot in his brain that was causing all the trouble would be healed or removed, and Greg would be well again.

We tried all the things the specialists recommended. When Greg was eight, we were advised to put him in a state hospital for three months, so the doctors there could make a "thorough diagnosis." After the three months, we were called in for an interview and told that Greg had a degenerative brain disease and would not have long to live. We were advised to leave him in the hospital, but we took him home that same day and resolved to care for him ourselves as long as possible.

A few weeks later we received word from the hospital that their diagnosis was "incorrect." In checking Greg's medical history, they had decided he did not have the brain disease with which they had first diagnosed him. That is when we realized that the specialists, with all their medical knowledge, did not hold the key to Greg at all. God alone held the key, and Greg was in his hands!

There was a serenity of spirit in Greg that defied the turmoil in his body. He had a childlike simplicity; yet, his eyes seemed to hold some mysterious secret. It was as if the Father had never let go of him completely, and he was quite sure of his identity. He knew to whom he belonged.

When Greg was in first grade, his teacher, Sister Judith, wrote on his report card, "Greg has an understanding of God far beyond his years." These words were, for my husband and me, a clear confirmation of Jesus' prayer, "What you have hidden from the wise and the clever, you have revealed to the merest children." (Matthew 11:25)

Later, when Greg attended a Catholic day school operated by the Benedictine Sisters, he was taught that heaven is our real home. He took those words to heart and, when asked where he lived, he would give his address and then add solemnly, "But heaven is my real home."

The Bible was very dear to Greg. For years, a children's Bible was the only Bible he knew. He discovered the "real Bible" when a friend gave him a copy of *The Way* version. He determined to read it all, from beginning to end. First, he made a list of all the books. Then as he finished each book, he drew a line through it. We often heard him late at night, reading softly. He never learned to read without sounding the words.

In the end, epilepsy conquered Greg's body, for he died of a brain concussion, the result of a fall caused by a seizure. But nothing could conquer his spirit! I sometimes wonder what he would have become, had he been free to choose. He loved to read and had great determination. But God called him to be one of his "little ones," whose work was simply to show forth the glory of God to those around him.

After his death, I found Greg's list of the books of the Bible in the drawer of his bedside table. The last book marked off was Daniel.

Curious to know what words he had last read, I turned to the book of Daniel and found his bookmark on the last page of Daniel. In *The Way* version, the last verse is this: "But go on now to the end of your life and your rest, for you will rise again and have your full share of those last days." What prophetic words!

As our children were growing up, my husband and I often wondered whether the other three resented the time we spent with Greg, helping him with homework and speech therapy, giving him medication, taking him to his medical appointments, and sometimes missing their school events because of his seizures. After his death, we asked them if they had felt neglected. They all assured us they had not, but realized Greg had special needs, and wanted to help him and protect him, as they had seen us do.

When Greg was about five, and his brother Phillip a year younger, our family attended my husband's office picnic at a state park. The boys and I were taking a walk along a gravel path when Greg had a seizure and fell, cutting his head on a sharp stone, causing it to bleed. Phillip immediately turned to me and said, "Mommy, you go get Daddy, and I'll stay here and keep the flies off Greg." Even at that young age, he knew what needed to be done!

We can't begin to count the lives Greg has touched. Because of his special educational needs, my husband and I were instrumental in starting a private school for mentally challenged children, and I taught in that school for two years. My husband worked hard to make special education mandatory in Indiana and to pass legislation to benefit disabled citizens of all ages.

Because of Greg, his sister Terri and two of his cousins became special education teachers. Because of him, our whole family has been made acutely aware of people with disabilities and their special needs. We have been led into ministries we would never have chosen and into places we did not plan to go. God has used us to do his work, and he used Greg to show us the way. Alleluia!

—*The Word Among Us,* August 2003,
Ijamsville, Maryland

Making Cookies with Mother Baker

She was always "Mother Baker" to me from the day I married her son, but it seems that half the people she knows call her "Gramma Baker" and the other half call her "Aunt Nellie." She is 95 years old and so tiny and wrinkled you would think a wisp of wind would blow her away. But her Pennsylvania Dutch blood keeps her going.

"Oh, I don't have the strength to make cookies any more," she said with a sigh, as we discussed the Christmas menu. So I offered to help her, for how could we celebrate Christmas without her cut-out sugar cookies? "You mix the dough," I told her, "and I'll roll out and cut."

Mother Baker doesn't hear well, but we communicate. She frowned and shook her head, but I insisted, and finally she said, with a shake of her finger for emphasis, "We'll make cookies on Thursday."

Cookie Day came and I was ready and eager to begin, but Mother Baker waved me away when I tried to help, and I got the feeling I was only in the way. She wouldn't let me do a thing except put the cookies in the oven and take them out when they were done. Even then, she wasn't entirely pleased with my performance, for she looked with disapproval at one sheet of cookies I had left in the oven just a tad too long.

As I watched her graceful movements, I realized that this cookie-making was a ritual, much like a tribal dance, learned when cooking was an art, passed on from mothers to daughters, and performed as a labor of love for their families. Every move was meaningful and made with the sureness and perfection that comes from experience. I had a sense of viewing a drama that had been enacted thousands of times before.

First, the kitchen table was cleared of all but the plastic table cloth.

Then Mother Baker brought forth a worn and warped breadboard which she wiped with a damp cloth and placed on the table. I wondered why she didn't use her counter top. Was it too high for her? But I decided it was more likely that she had made cookies and kneaded bread on the kitchen table long before she had a counter in her kitchen, and continued to use the table from habit, not convenience.

Next, she took out a big yellow bowl and sifted flour into it. "How much flour?" I asked, notebook in hand, trying for the umpteenth time to get the recipe for these famous cookies. She shook her head. "I never measure the flour," she said.

When the bowl was about two-thirds full, she began to hollow out the middle and pat the flour around the sides. Then she put a stick of margarine and half a cup of vegetable shortening into the hollow space. This I knew was a concession to modern times. The original shortening was butter.

Mother Baker then plunged her right hand into the bowl and began to squeeze the shortening, working a little of the flour into it with each squeeze. She shook her head as she worked, saying, "It's not soft enough. I should have set it out last night," then added, "I haven't made cookies in a long time. They may not be any good."

After a while, she added two cups of white sugar to the shortening and continued to blend it with her hands, still complaining about the consistency of the shortening. "Why don't you use your electric mixer?" I suggested. "That would do it." A shake of the head.

When she was satisfied with the mixture, she broke two eggs into a bowl and began to beat them with a fork. Again I suggested the electric mixer. She shook her head vigorously. "I never use the electric beater for cookies," she said, "only for cakes."

The eggs went into the softened mass in the middle of the yellow bowl and were blended by hand into the mixture. Next, she measured a cup of buttermilk, and stirred two teaspoons of baking soda into it. She sprinkled two teaspoons of baking powder over the ingredients in the yellow bowl. "I usually use just one teaspoon of soda and one of baking powder," she explained, "but I've had this so long it's lost its strength."

A little at a time, Mother Baker added the buttermilk to the mixture in the yellow bowl, blending the mass with her right hand after each addition, and moving the bowl in a slow circle with her left. At the same time, she brought more and more of the flour from the sides of the bowl into the middle, working it into the dough. She added a little salt and a teaspoon of vanilla, and continued to squeeze and knead the dough until it was a soft but firm mass. Then she lifted it out of the bowl, and lightly floured the breadboard with some of the left-over flour in the bowl. She broke off a chunk of dough from the large mass, patted and kneaded it tenderly, then rolled it out to about a quarter of an inch thick.

Next came the cutting. I wanted to help with this, so she could sit down and rest a while, but Mother Baker wouldn't give up the cookie cutter. With her old-fashioned tin cutters, she carefully cut the dough into Christmas trees, Santa Clauses, reindeers, bells, and angels. Each one was a work of art, and she lovingly lifted it onto the cookie sheet with a spatula so as not to break it or distort the shape. After each rolling, she wadded up the scraps of dough, rolled it, and cut another cookie or two from it, using up every smidgen before taking a fresh chunk of dough. I wondered why she didn't save the scraps and roll them out together at the end, but I didn't ask. I was too busy with the baking. Mother Baker spread a neatly ironed linen cloth on the table, and I placed the fresh cookies on it to cool. Then I stacked them on platters to be frosted.

When the last of the dough had been cut into cookies and I had put them in the oven, the work of cleaning up began. This was also a part of the ritual. There was still unused flour around the sides of the yellow bowl, and this Mother Baker sifted back into her flour canister. No wonder she never measured the flour! Whatever was left over, she saved! The rolling pin was carefully scraped with a knife, wiped and wrapped in a soft cloth, and tucked away in a cabinet. The breadboard was also scraped, wiped, and put away. Neither of them would ever see soap or water.

We cleared the table and Mother Baker allowed me to wash the dishes and also to do the frosting, in which she took little interest. "Too sweet," she said. She was exhausted, but pleased. For one more

Christmas, she had made the Christmas cookies which had been part of the family tradition for as long as anyone could remember.

—1982

Note: This may have been the last time Mother Baker made Christmas cookies because she died two years later. I experimented until I came up with cookies which my husband claims taste just like hers. I make them every Christmas, and have passed the recipe on to my children. I never make them without remembering Mother Baker, and I make them carefully and lovingly as she did, or I know they wouldn't be any good!

Grandma Baker's Christmas Cookies

1 cup shortening (half margarine and half vegetable shortening)
2 cups white sugar
1 cup buttermilk (or sour milk)
2 eggs
1 teaspoon baking powder
1 teaspoon baking soda
1 teaspoon vanilla
1 teaspoon salt
5 to 6 cups flour

- Cream shortening and sugar. Add eggs and vanilla. Beat well.
- Add baking soda to buttermilk and stir well.
- Sift 5 cups of flour and add baking powder and salt.
- Add the buttermilk mixture alternately with the dry ingredients to the shortening and sugar mixture.
- The dough should be soft but not sticky. Add more flour if needed.
- Chill dough overnight. (makes it easier to work with)
- Roll out on lightly floured board, a little at a time, and cut into shapes.
- Bake at 350 degrees for 10 to 12 minutes, or until done.

Frosting

1 box of powdered sugar
1 egg
1 stick of margarine or butter
1 teaspoon of vanilla or other flavoring
Coloring if desired.

- Beat well until it is a smooth consistency. Frost cookies and sprinkle or decorate as you wish.

A Cup of Cold Water

After our last child was married, and my husband and I were living alone in the house, we began to discuss how we might use a large bedroom with twin beds, now vacant, to serve the Lord. Should we provide a home for a foster child? Rent the room to a college student? Take in the local bag lady? Nothing we considered moved us to act.

One Sunday morning as we were starting off to church, I said casually, "Maybe we'll get a message today at Mass." I remember these words because of what happened next.

The first reading was from the Old Testament—the story of the Shunammite woman who welcomed the prophet Elisha into her home and invited him to stop there and dine whenever he passed by. She said to her husband, "I know he is a holy man of God. Since he visits us often, let us arrange a little room on the roof and furnish it with a bed, table, chair and lamp, so that when he comes to us, he can stay there." This was done, and her hospitality was returned in a miraculous way. (See II Kings 4:817)

My husband was sitting with the choir and I was sitting on the opposite side of the church. Across the assembly, our eyes met. The words of the Shunammite woman spoke to our hearts. We were both thinking the same thing: *Of course! We already have the room, and it is already furnished with these very things. All we have to do is wait for the Lord to send someone. "When he comes to us, he can stay there." How simple!*

The Gospel reading went a step further in defining our future ministry. In this passage, Jesus is instructing his disciples as follows: "He who welcomes you, welcomes me; and he who welcomes me, welcomes him who sent me. He who welcomes a prophet because he bears the name of prophet receives a prophet's reward. He who welcomes a holy man because he is known to be holy receives a holy man's reward. And I promise you that whoever gives a cup of cold water to one of these lowly ones because he is a disciple will not want for his reward." (See Matthew 10:40-42)

Jesus is saying that, when we welcome a disciple of his, whether it is a prophet, a holy man, or the simplest of believers, we welcome Jesus himself. His words gave us the answer we were looking for. They were also a confirmation of what we were already doing, but in a different area.

Three years before, our son Greg had died from a fall caused by an epileptic seizure. His childlike love of God was an inspiration to our family and all who knew him. He made us aware of handicapped and troubled people of all kinds. We had been working with and through organizations for the disabled and mentally challenged, but now we heard Jesus' words as an invitation to work personally with an individual, to open our house to a "disciple" of his. That meant a Christian or a person with a Christian background, which would eliminate other possibilities we had considered. He was leading us one step at a time. We looked no further, but waited expectantly for the person he would send.

About two and a half months later, a friend from our prayer group stopped by with his son Billy, and asked if we would consider taking Billy to live with us for a while. Billy was 19 and unemployed. His parents were divorcing and he was an angry and disturbed young man. He moved in that very day and quickly became part of our family. He lived with us for a year and a half, then enlisted in the Air Force and served at San Antonio Air Force Base, Texas for six years. He is now a Sergeant on the city police force there. He has married and has three beautiful children. He and his wife have shared their home on three occasions with young people who have needed a safe haven from the storms of life. (Billy says he learned this from us!) He has also made his peace with both parents.

After Billy left, other troubled people came to our door from various and diverse sources. We did not advertise or invite anyone to come, and we never turned anyone away. They were all "disciples" in the sense that they were of the Christian faith. Each had a different story, but all had one thing in common. Like Billy, they needed a place of refuge—a safe non-threatening environment where they could find order in their lives, sort out priorities, and find the courage to deal with the challenges that faced them.

Those with whom we shared our home during a six-year period (Billy jokingly refers to this as the Cup of Cold Water Ministry) include the following: a young woman with anorexia; a middle-aged woman and her handicapped daughter; a business man whose marriage was in trouble; a priest who had requested to leave the priesthood, and was granted a year's leave to reconsider; and a young woman who was mentally ill and came to our church rectory seeking help early one Christmas morning

One summer two young women shared the room. One was a University student from England and she returned home after three months. The other, who was in the Army Reserve and studying to be a nurse, stayed on and became pregnant. She threatened to have an abortion, but could never bring herself to go through with it. When her beautiful baby boy was born, she named him Matthew because, she told me, her eyes shining with tears, Matthew means *gift of God*. Moments like this made everything worthwhile.

She and Matthew lived with us for three months, until she could make other arrangements. She completed her training and became a Registered Nurse, married, and has two more boys. She is now head nurse in a prison facility. Matthew is in college and, in her own words, is "a wonderful young man."

Our ministry came to an end abruptly. In fact, we had to ask our last guest to leave sooner than he had planned. Our daughter, her husband and two children were returning to the U.S. from Germany, where he was stationed in the Air Force. They would be staying with us for a while, and we would need the extra bedroom.

After that, the Lord sent us no more disciples. The room was used for visiting grandchildren, and we moved on to other activities.

We were blessed in many ways during those six years. We thank

God for the opportunity to offer a cup of cold water to our brothers and sisters in Christ who were thirsting for peace, order and love in their lives. We were able to provide a place of refreshment, refueling and healing until they could find the energy and the will to go forward and become what God meant them to be. To watch this happen has been our greatest reward!

>—*The Word Among Us, Family Insert*, February 2005, Ijamsville, MD

The Day After

How still is a house after death has visited it!
My mother speaks softly when she speaks at all,
And my father's eyes are bloodshot.
The pain in them is so great
I cannot bear to look at him.

The bedroom looks the same again
Except for some dried mud on the floor
Where the casket stood,
(A very little casket, white and silver)
For the people had come
Through the rain with muddy shoes
To view the little body lying there.

The furniture is back in place
Except for a few chairs
Standing stiffly in the living room,
Brought from other parts of the house
For the extra people to sit on.

Outside, the sun is shining.
The wreath has been taken down from the door.
You would not know a child had lived here
Except for a little red wagon,
Half-hidden by a sprawling rosebush,
That no one had remembered
To bring in out of the rain.

—*Recalling the death of my little brother Bobby, who died of rheumatic fever at the age of eight.*

Welcome, Jackie!

Newborn babe with sleepy eyes,
You're an angel in disguise,
Lately come from heaven above,
Bringing healing, bringing love.
Every gurgle, every coo,
Every single thing you do,
Every move is counted dear.
What a blessing you are here!

Precious infant, sweet and small,
You will learn to love us all.
You'll be nurtured carefully,
Given love, yet never be
(None will dispute what I say)
Loved as you are loved this day!

—Recalling the birth of my little brother Jackie, who was born two years after Bobby died.

To Betty on Her Birthday

There are poems of moonlight and poems of love,
But this one's to *you*, Betty Schmidt, on the move!
I've tried for three days, goodness knows,
To catch your psyche in repose.
Though you have virtues sweet and noble,
I can't see you any way but mobile.

You can't be written. You can't be sketched.
You're like a bird with wings outstretched,
Reaching for heights that can't be reached
By any creature, man or beast.

You are always so full of new ideas,
You inspire us who take our life "as is."
Though your hands are busy with diapers and things,
You've a mind that bright and a heart that sings!

You'll never be fully resigned to your lot,
No matter how much you have or have not,
But your cheerful persistence in spite of it all,
And your faith in the God who created it all,
Prompt me to thank you for what you have done
To make my life a happier one!

—1955—
To my dear friend Betty Schmidt

Graduation Day Meditation

A little less
Than eighteen years ago,
You weighed a mere six pounds or so.
I kissed your tiny bean sprout toe
And took off all your clothes to see
If you were well and strong.

One tiny flaw I found—
A wee pink spot on the side of your hand
Like a jelly smear,
Or a kiss that stuck,
And wouldn't go away.
It grew with you, and it's still there,
Shaped just as I found it
On your natal day.

Love grows like a baby's toes.
It never runs out.
There's always more.
The first is never loved the less
Because there are four.

You are my firstborn,
Dear to my heart,
As each is dearest
In some special way.
You opened the wondrous door to motherhood
And I have never been the same
Since that day.

LOVE MAKES THE RIDE WORTHWHILE

Now, with your classmates,
You march and pose,
And sit on the platform
In stately rows.

You've been so sheltered.
Your life is ahead.
What can I say to you, child of God,
Whom I've bathed and rocked
And diapered and fed?
What words that haven't been said before?
What can I tell you of peace and war?
What can I tell you of brotherhood,
Of life and courage, and love and renown?
It has to be lived to be understood……

"Oh, there you are! Congratulations!
How nice you look in your cap and gown!"

Anniversary Gift

The first year is paper, they say,
And this is paper,
We've gotten that far.
Already, you see,
We've eliminated the color TV,
The weekend away,
The golden goblets,
The built-in bar.

From now on, it's easy.
We look for things paper,
Nothing to eat,
And nothing to wear,
Just stationery, envelopes,
File cards and calendars,
Magazines and picnic plates.
What wonderful gifts
For Bobby and Mare!

But this gift is different,
So please understand
That, paper or not,
These things are forgot.
The paper you're getting
Is right in your hand!

That sixty or seventy dollars
You owe us…I could look it up…
Our gift to you is:
We cancel that debt,
Just go on from there.
God bless you and keep you
And fill up your cup.
We love you, Bobby and Mare!

To Greg in Heaven

Dear Greg,
Today is your birthday,
Your first birthday in heaven!
How can we say, "God bless you on your birthday!"
When you have already received
The greatest blessing of all?
No worldly gift would do.
All the gifts of eternal life are yours!

What can we give you?
What can we wish for you?
What joy is not already yours
In that bright world of the spirit
Where there is no darkness at all?

We can only wish that, because you are there,
Heaven will be more beautiful.
The choirs of angels sing more gloriously,
And the heavenly alleluias ring out so loud and clear
They burst the barriers between God and mankind,
And God's message of love pours forth
To all the world!

This is our wish for you, Greg,
On your birthday,
From all of us here
Who have not seen what you have seen
Or heard what you have heard.
It comes with much love
And the sure knowledge
That this will be
Your happiest birthday ever!

—*December 13, 1976*

Shower Gift

Cleanliness is next to godliness, they say,
And so to be sure you start out together
In just the right way,
With love and care, these gifts we've selected,
And when you use them as directed,
No sign of dirt can be detected.
These gifts aren't the kind you hang up to be seen,
But they *are* guaranteed to keep your place clean.

How sad it would be for a newlywed
To discover roaches under the bed!
And there's nothing quicker to fade a romance
Than to find in your pantry those pesky ants!

If your cabinet is empty, these things will help fill it.
There's a product here to take gunk off your skillet,
And for mold in your bathroom, here's something to kill it.
Here's something for windows, for floors, and for rugs,
For laundry and dishes, for bathrooms and bugs.
You can wash, you can scrub, you can wax, you can rub.
You can cope with the dirt with the things in this tub.

These household helpers keep things clean and bright.
We know your apartment will be a delight,
And you'll never hear mice nibbling at night.
Your drains will be open, your mirrors will be sparkly,
So you see your image clearly, not darkly.
May your windows be shining to let in the sun,
And your counters all clear when the dishes are done,
For the Father will bless your work from above
If it's done for each other and done in his love.
May your home be so lovely your friends will all know
That you're both *clean* and *godly,* dear Terri and Joe!

Trees

Trees! What memories they evoke!
What joy they held in childhood days!
Oh, to climb the highest branch
And over the countryside to gaze!

The old oak tree with its tire swing
That thrilled us with its windy ride!
Trees we've planted, trees we have loved,
Trees we've nurtured, trees that have died!

Your life, dear friends, is like a tree.
You've weathered storms, and drouth and rain,
And yet you've grown and blossomed out
And borne good fruit in spite of pain.

Now is the time to thank the Lord
For fifty golden love-filled years.
We pray that He will grant you peace,
And send you joy instead of tears.

God bless you both in all you do.
God bless your family and your home.
May you stay always close to Him
For many happy years to come!

—January 29, 1999—
To Leon and Carol Gibson,
with the gift of a rain tree on their fiftieth wedding anniversary

Dear Eleanor

It's not *your* birthday, this I know.
It's just because I love you so,
I'm thinking of you every day
And sending happy thoughts your way.

I pray to God that all good things
Will come to you on angels' wings.
I pray that God will smile on you
And let you know he cares for you
In his own deep mysterious way
Through every moment, every day!

I'll always treasure, thankfully,
The special gift you've been to me—
My friend, my guide, my sister dear.
In joy or sorrow, you were there.
We're sisters still, though miles apart.
My love I send with all my heart.

—July 2, 2001—
To my dear friend Eleanor on my birthday

Bon Voyage

God grant you safe passage, John,
As you move from
This world's darkness and pain
Into His marvelous light!

Floating on a cloud of prayers,
Surrounded by those who love you,
May God's strong arms hold you,
His peace enfold you,
And His Spirit move within you.

Secure and unafraid,
May you slip quietly
Into eternity,
Like an infant
Who falls peacefully asleep
At its mother's breast.

—July 2002—
To our good friend John LaTora after he called
to tell us that his doctor had given him three months to live.

Birthday Blessing

May God be with you and bless you
With friends and love and laughter
Through the years,
With satisfying work to do,
An open mind, the gift of joy
And a few tears.

May your children rise up
To call you blessed,
Your home be a haven
Of refuge and peace
And, like Abraham's tent in the desert,
A place where wonders never cease.

May the Lord guard your coming and going,
And keep you from going too fast.
May he grant you the faith
To place in his hand
Your future and your past.

LOVE MAKES THE RIDE WORTHWHILE

God has called you to be a disciple,
A husband and father, too.
May he give you the courage
To answer his call,
Whatever he asks you to do.

Never lose your sense of wonder.
May you treasure each new day.
Fifty years you've blessed *us*, Phillip,
So we're blessing *you* today!
Know our love and prayers are with you
All the way, all the way!

—February 1, 2004—
To our son Phillip on his fiftieth birthday

Dear Bobby

Can't believe you're really fifty
Since you're still so neat and nifty!
You've worked and played and shed some tears.
You've learned a lot in fifty years!

The Air Force quickly grabbed you up
When you were only twenty.
They transferred you from base to base;
In twenty years you saw a plenty!

You've served your country far and near,
Protecting freedoms we hold dear.
You've had a full and busy life—
Three great kids and a loving wife!

Now manager at Home Depot,
You still have many miles to go.
Today we wish for you the best—
Good health, good friends, and happiness!

We love you for the way you've lived,
We're proud of all you've done,
For when our daughter married you,
We got another son!

Our birthday prayer for you is that,
No matter what you do,
The peace that God alone can give
May always be with you!

—August 12, 2005—
To our son-in-law Robert Ball on his fiftieth birthday

II - ROMANTIC LOVE

*" 'Tis better to have loved and lost
Than never to have loved at all."*
—Alfred Lord Tennyson, *In Memoriam, A.H.H.*

Introduction

The deep feelings of romantic love can run the gamut of emotions—all the way from Rosalind's facetious remark to Orlando in Shakespeare's play *As You Like It,* "Men have died from time to time and worms have eaten them, but not for love," to Elizabeth Barrett Browning's famous sonnet, beginning, "How do I love thee? Let me count the ways."

Love makes poets of us all. Poetry flows easily from the hearts of lovers, as they seek to express their deepest feelings toward their beloved. Even when betrayal, rage, jealousy, or the bitter pangs of a lost love bring anger and hurt, poetry expresses it better.

It is not surprising that this section on romantic love is mostly poetry. Some are cynical with the cynicism of youth, and some are full of fantasy—love portrayed as a female entity, capricious, fickle, and sometimes cruel. Some are to my husband, the love of my life.

One poem in this section was written to a famous Scottish poet. When I was 15, I discovered some old books Mother had inherited from her father, all classics. A collection of Robert Burns' poetry was my favorite, and I memorized the Scottish dialect (given in the back of the book) so I could pronounce the words and understand it as Burns wrote it. I fell in love with Burns and his beautiful poetry (as did many other young ladies of his time!) and I have included in this section my poem *To Robert Burns*, written that summer.

How We Met

Children always like to hear the story of how their parents met. This story is one our children have heard many times. I am including it here because our grandson Christopher thought this book would not be complete without it.

My husband and I both grew up in Indiana, both served in the Navy in World War II, and both went to college on the G.I. Bill. However, our paths did not cross until the summer before my senior year, when I decided to take two six-weeks courses at a branch of Indiana University in Jeffersonville, IN. The day I registered, I was given a list of people in the city who rented rooms to college students. I selected an address within walking distance of the college and went to look at it. Mrs. Phillips, the landlady, was very pleasant and showed me a big front room on the first floor. I moved in immediately.

Later in the day, she came to me and announced, "There was a young man here today, and he needs a room right away. I thought if you wouldn't mind moving upstairs, I could give him this room." I didn't mind at all, as the upstairs room was cheaper. Two ladies, with whom I would share a bathroom, were renting the other two rooms on the second floor. I quickly moved my baggage to my new quarters.

The next morning, Mrs. Phillips came up to my room. "The young man is here," she said. "He has a lot of books, and I wonder if you would mind giving him the bookcase in your room." I was happy to oblige and offered to carry it downstairs for her.

My husband always tells people that the first time he saw me, I was coming downstairs backward, and bumping a bookcase slowly down, a step at a time. Then he adds, "Jane gave me her room, then she gave me her bookcase, and she has been giving to me ever since."

There he was, standing at the bottom of the stairs. He seemed to be in a hurry and was saying something to Mrs. Phillips about an important phone call. She turned to introduce us, "Jane Kemp...Klinedale Baker." I thought the name was unusual, and he must have a nickname, so I asked, rather facetiously, "And what do people call you?" It was obvious he did not think this was funny. I still remember how he looked straight at me, lifted his chin slightly, and responded firmly, "Klinedale." Then he hurried off to make his phone call.

We hardly saw each other after that, as he worked during the day, and my classes were from 6:00 to 10:00 every evening. Sometimes we would pass each other coming or going and exchange greetings, but that was all. However, dear Mrs. Phillips was keeping us well informed! She often invited me down to have coffee with her in the morning, after everyone else had gone to work. She related to me that Klinedale was a Navy veteran and was working at the Indiana State Board of Health, his first job after graduating from Indiana University. In the evening, she related to him what she had learned about me. So we knew each other's background before we ever had a real conversation.

One day about 5:30 p.m. as I was getting ready to walk to my classes, it began to rain. Klinedale happened to be in his room at that time, and I heard Mrs. Phillips call to him, "Klinedale, why don't you take Jane to school? It's raining."

I didn't want him to feel obliged to drive me, so I took an umbrella and slipped quietly downstairs and out the front door. I was walking along briskly in the light rain when he drove up to the curb and called out, "Do you want a ride?" I got in, and thanked him for picking me up. He said it was no problem, and asked when I would be getting out. I told him I would be out at ten o'clock, and he said he would he would be there to pick me up, as "it might still be raining." He was waiting for me at ten and, after that, he began to meet me after classes almost ever evening.

That is how we got to know each other, riding around town after my classes, sometimes stopping for ice cream or something to eat, and talking, talking, talking! We shared our Navy experiences, talked about our families and friends, my college life, his job, our interests and hobbies, and our plans for the future. We found we had much in common and enjoyed our time together.

We soon discovered that Mrs. Phillips' household was a real community. She invited anyone who was around on Saturdays to have coffee and rolls with her, and we would sit around the table and talk, relating to each other like a family. One Sunday she cooked a delicious dinner for all of us. When anyone in the house had a birthday, she made sure we all met to celebrate with cake and ice cream. She loved ice cream, and when Klinedale and I were both there weekends, we would take her for ice cream, or to visit her son, or some other place she wanted to go.

When I returned to Hanover College in the fall, Klinedale and I continued to see each other. In December, we became engaged, and in June we were married. No one could have been happier about our marriage than Mrs. Phillips. She always took the credit for bringing us together, and said it would never have happened if it hadn't been for her.

And who are we to say it wasn't true? Was Mrs. Phillips part of a Divine plan for us to meet? Or was it purely coincidental that we arrived in Jeffersonville on the same day, just happened to live in her house for the same period of time, and that our relationship flourished under her loving watchful eyes?

We have been happily married for 55 years, and Mrs. Phillips has long ago returned home to the Father, but we still remember her kindness and wisdom, and her unique role of matchmaker.

One last note: My husband's friends and associates call him *K.J.* but I still call him *Klinedale*.

Returning Veteran

Battles could not hurt you.
You came back strong,
Wrapped in a suit
Of self-sufficiency.
Your laughter is bold,
Like a proud new song.
Go find yourself another love.
You don't need me.

Duty may be binding,
But love flows free,
And why it is I cannot tell;
Yet this I know to be:
Tenderly I'd love you,
And everlasting long,
Had you come back limping
Of a wounded knee.

—*Hill Thoughts*, 1948,
Hanover College, Hanover, IN

In Retrospect

I thought I'd wear my best for Love
And put a flower in my hair,
But she slipped in the back way
And caught me unaware.

Since I have come to know her ways,
I've seen her scorn of sham,
And I am, oh, so thankful
That she found me as I am.

—*Hill Thoughts*, 1950,
Hanover College, Hanover, IN

The Weaver

Bewitched by heaven a million years ago,
Love sits enchanted in a golden room,
Under a spell to weave forever
On a crazy loom.

Her shuttle carries yarns from every land—
Bright and drab, and coarse and silken yarns,
Tangled, dirty, fine and ugly yarns,
Smooth and soft, and gay and glittering yarns.
Swift and sure it moves beneath her hand,
Weaving ancient crazy patterns
On a ancient loom.

Blood-red and bitter-black, plucking in and out,
Twisting mad and frenzied figures in its wake,
Winding threads in angry puzzles,
Black and white and purple puzzles,
Every thread a silly heart
Beating but to break.

Woolgatherer

Once, because I dreamed too long,
My heart soared high and caught a star,
But when it sought reality,
The journey was too far.

Mirage

I glimpsed Love through a glass of wine
    On a silver, starlit night.
I thought she paused and winked at me
    Ere she resumed her flight.

Prudence

Though your eyes
Were ever tender,
And your kiss
Like any lover's,
And your manner
Jubilant,

Still, the words you spoke
Were guarded,
And the words you wrote
Well-chosen,
So that, some day,
When the time came,
You could speak
Without a quaver,
Or a blot
Upon your conscience,
Clear and proper,
Custom-bred,
"After all, I never said
I loved you.
I never said…
I never said…"

Reclamation

Last spring
When skies were blue,
And waters splashed upon the beach,
I gave my heart to you.
Carelessly, unknowingly,
You held it in your hand.

Today,
I thought of you.
I walked again upon the beach,
And found the pieces,
One by one,
You strung along the sand.

April

It is nothing but the spring.
It is the bright warm sun
And tender grass.
It is the budding tree
Where bluebirds pass.
It is but the robin's song,
The path along
Our last year's rendezvous
That makes my sentimental heart
Long suddenly for you.

Next winter when
The trees are bare again
And winds are fierce
Against my windowpane.
I shall be secure and warm,
Inside my house with books and pen.
I shall not remember you then.

To Robert Burns

Thy works so charm me, Bobby Burns,
Thy poems so delight my heart
That I would fain a poet be,
As loved and gifted as thou art!

Other bards have yet to write
With such a gentleness and grace,
With love and humor to reveal
The frailties of the human race.

With trials to try an angel's patience,
All the faults of mortal men,
Thou ever kept thy humorous sense,
Thy gift of gab, thy trusty pen.

So sensitive to other's hurts,
So jubilant at small success,
So penitent for some misdeed,
So soon to beg forgiveness!

Whatever after-world thou hailed,
Thou'lt have thy bit of fun in it—
Write heavenly anthems for the saints,
Or regale Satan with thy wit!

Memento

Last night, among old letters,
And bits of verse
And stories half-begun,
I found a scrawled note
Written in pencil
On blue-lined paper.

It was not long
And had been ripped
From a notebook.
"Darling…"
Dashing letters they were, but faded,
The paper yellowed, dull, old.
Silly to have kept it there,
A long-forgotten note
Written in pencil
On blue-lined paper.

My Heart

My heart is made of iron, you say.
Oh, no, 'tis not of such
Substantial stuff.
A chemist might know.
Brittle it is,
And easily broken
And then,
So easily welded again,
The cracks hardly show.
A peculiar metal,
If metal it is,
Complex and fine,
And though
Formulas are out of my line,
A chemist might know.

Coquette

She flicked the graying ashes
Of a flippant love,
And winked at the moon
Over her left shoulder.
She caught the darts of Cupid,
Tossed them back,
Heaped her flameless passions
…And grew older.

Sonnet on the New Year

Today I pause to think and reminisce.
A year has passed again, and through the dawn,
The future's hard to guess. We stand upon
The shaky threshold of a year that is
Untried, unsure, unsafe, a changing day.
I wonder, looking back on yesteryear,
If you and I will be the same, my dear.
I cannot guess. I've only this to say:

If I should ever cease to love you, dear,
And lose the clear-cut memory of your face;
Should time erase the short-lived ecstasies
Or dim the sweet goodbyes of this last year,
Still none in all the world will take your place,
Nor memories more beautiful than these.

Idealist

Because her dream went far astray,
    She will not dream again.
She shields her heart and cautions me
    That I may know no pain.

Though Time should wantonly destroy
    Sweet fancies Love has made,
I think that I shall not regret
    Nor ever be afraid.

And if the distant years are not
    So fair as they now seem,
I'll hold no grudge against the Fates.
    I shall have had the dream.

To My True Love

My dear, do you not think it strange
The way our lives turned out to be?
Of all the guys and girls we met,
That I chose you and you chose me?

I've wondered why we tarried so
For wedded bless, but now I know.
The secret is that we were led
Where we had never planned to go.

All through the years of World War Two
As Navy tars, we learned and grew.
We worked among our country's best,
Attired like us in Navy blue.

So many others came our way,
Those years we spent on shore and sea,
But still we waited, passed them by.
They were not right for you or me.

Through college on the G.I. Bill,
The Lord was working with us still,
And then he brought us face to face,
Spoke to our hearts with love and grace,
"Now is the time! This is the place!"

Our God has led us, day by day,
In his own time and his own way.
How blessed are we! 'Twas meant to be
That I'd find you and you'd find me!

To My Love on His 74th Birthday

You asked for a poem as your birthday drew near,
So I'll try to come up with some verses, my dear.
My poetry-writing days are long past.
The words and the rhythms aren't coming so fast.
My memory's fading, my brain is too slow,
But here are some things that I want you to know.

Our whole life together has never been dull.
It's a merry-go-round with hardly a lull.
So enjoy your day, take a slower pace,
And thank the good Lord for his goodness and grace.
He's blessed you so much these 74 years
With music and travel and laughter and tears.

Look back and you'll see that you've had a great life—
A warm loving family and a *wonderful* wife!
I love you and wish you the best of all things.
I'll be by your side whatever life brings.
So give thanks for this day, and for yesterday too,
And give thanks for this poem. It's the best I could do!

—1997

To My Valentine on Valentine's Day

(Incorporating three of our favorite songs)

Forty-nine Valentine Days have gone by
Since that day in June when rain hid the sky
      And wedding bells were ringing!
Forty-nine times we've spoken in signs,
Expressing our love through valentines
And heart-shaped cookies, and pale pink wines,
Vowing anew a love that binds.
      How can I keep from singing?

Forty-nine years in all kinds of weather,
We've laughed together and cried together,
And all the years we have lived together
      We've placed our trust in the Father above.
In times of stress, when a child needed care,
Or a payment was due, or the cupboard was bare,
His words were true. He was always there.
      "I love you with an everlasting love."

As the pages turn and the years move on,
As our vision fades, and our memory's gone,
We await the Light of another Dawn,
      Joyfully, hopefully, heart to heart.
And so, *this* Valentine's Day, my dear,
As the Third Millennium draws near,
I thank the Lord we have each other
To love and bless and cherish forever.
      My God, how great thou art!
      How great thou art!

—1999

III - DIVINE LOVE

"God is love, and those who abide in love abide in God and God in them."
—First Letter of John 4:17
New Revised Standard Version of the Bible

Introduction

Religion is complicated, but God's love is simple. Many writers and speakers have attempted to express the love of God for his people, but what could be simpler and more eloquent than these words of John?

I have found God's love shining through his people in small faith communities like the one described in *A Country Church* in this section. I have also found God's love in huge stadiums where fifty thousand people of over forty different Christian denominations were worshipping and praising God together.

I have found God's love among the so-called "unchurched" and among cultures very different from my own. I like this Cherokee Indian prayer because it is short, simple, and covers the essentials of a happy life: *Grant, O Great Spirit, that I may live as good as I can, learn as much as I can, and love as deeply as I can.*

This section reflects some of the changes that were taking place in the Christian churches in the 1960's and 1970's. The story *Fairwell Sister, It Was Happy When You Were Here* depicts the loving relationship between elementary school children and their principal in the parochial school where I taught.

On the other hand, the "flower children" were proclaiming, "Make Love, not War," with banners and signs. They stood on street corners, playing guitars and singing songs of love and peace. But secretly they smoked marijuana and rebelled against society by withdrawing from it, and living in an unreal world of their own making. Their lifestyle appealed to teenagers who were not too crazy about school in the first place. The poem *You Say You Want Peace* speaks to this situation.

Vatican II brought a new approach to religion in the Catholic schools, and religion teachers had to adjust to new ways of teaching.

The emphasis was on God's love for his people and how to respond to that love by using the mind and conscience he gave each of us, rather than memorizing answers and depending on Father or Sister to make decisions for us. *Heartfelt Prayer at a Religion Teachers' Workshop* addresses this challenge.

By the late 1960's, the charismatic movement had begun to spread, first in the Protestant churches, and later among Catholics. This fresh "breath of the Spirit" swept like a mighty wind through all branches of Christianity, transcending the doctrinal barriers that divided the denominations, bringing us back to the basics of our faith, and creating a unity of spirit that no one had thought possible.

In 1971, my husband and I became actively involved in this movement, also called the *Charismatic Renewal*, as it was definitely a renewal of faith for the traditional Christian churches, as well as being ecumenical and charismatic (using the spiritual gifts or *charisms.*)

Many of the poems in this section were inspired by this movement and the people in it. The prayers and meditations reflect the highs and lows of my spiritual journey, which has been greatly blessed by the beautiful people who traveled with me.

A Country Church

My first recollection of "church" was the small faith community my family attended during my growing-up years on the farm. It was called New Hope Community Church and had a congregation of around ten families who actively supported it. That meant maybe fifty in attendance on Sunday if it was a good day. The white frame structure had only one big room, with two outhouses in the back, one marked MEN and one marked WOMEN.

The congregation could not afford a regular pastor, so they managed to have a preacher for most Sundays by using students from two different seminaries in Louisville, Kentucky. The seminarians were required to have a certain number of hours in Practice Preaching before they could be ordained. Little churches like ours helped them meet this requirement. Every seminarian that came to New Hope to give the Sunday sermon understood that his remuneration would be only what the collection basket produced that Sunday, plus dinner after the service at the home of a family in the congregation.

I remember one dear lady who was always prepared to take a seminarian home with her after church for a scrumptious chicken dinner, in case no one else volunteered. Mother invited them from time to time, and one summer Dad hired one of them to pick green beans. This was during the Great Depression of the 1930's, and most of them were working their way through the seminary. No such thing as student loans at that time!

The ladies of New Hope met once a month for a day of quilting. Their quilts were raffled off and the proceeds given to the church. That is where I learned to quilt, and also learned what was going on in the community. For instance, some one might report that a woman with a family is sick, and needs to have food brought in, so please take whatever you can. Another woman has just had a baby, and could use some baby clothes if you have any to spare. One family has more peaches (or apples or tomatoes) than they can use, so anyone in the church is invited to come and pick as many as they want. This is the way they helped each other. No one had much, but they shared what they had with those in need.

The men cared for the grounds and the buildings. In the winter, someone had to go early and start a fire in the drum stove. When Dad was superintendent of the Sunday School, that was his job, and we all went early so he could get the building warmed up in time for Sunday School at 9:30 or 10:00 a.m. He was also responsible for providing Sunday School teachers, and when I was 16, he had me teaching a class of children from toddlers up to about 10. I loved it, and was always looking for pictures in magazines to use for visual aids.

The potluck dinners on the lawn stand out in my memory. Every summer when fruits and vegetables were plentiful, a church picnic was held, the food spread out on long tables on the lawn—fried chicken, potato salad, green beans, sliced tomatoes, corn on the cob, cucumbers, homemade pickles, cole slaw, and yummy desserts of all kinds–fruit pies, custard pies, cocoanut pies, four-layer chocolate cakes, fruit salad and, of course, watermelon, that beautiful refreshing fruit of summer. I remember those watermelons being sweet, very red on the inside and the seeds big and black. Something has been lost in the flavor and color of watermelons since we have learned to grow them without seeds!

These picnics included fun for everyone. There were games for the children, horseshoe pitching for the men, and clean-up and socializing for the women.

Then there were the "hymn sings." When word got around that a church was having a hymn sing, there was usually a full house. People simply gathered for an evening to sing hymns and meet friends. While the adults sang, the kids sat in the back rows, whispering and giggling. Sometimes, we even slipped out the back door and went outside to play games.

Some of the larger churches presented a Children's Day program every spring. New Hope did not have enough children to do this, but for several years, a neighboring schoolteacher gathered up children in our neighborhood and took them to her church to participate in the program there. She directed the whole thing, and we had many practices. I remember being in a group of about a dozen girls who marched around the stage, making motions with our hands while she played a march on the piano. It may have been *Onward Christian Soldiers* or *Glory Glory Halleluia*. She was very strict and made us all keep in step and do the motions in unison. There were songs, dances, and recitations of poems by the little kids, and short plays and pantomimes by the older ones. The production always brought good reviews from the local papers and much enjoyment to the proud parents of the children who performed.

Once a year, New Hope held a week-long "revival." Everyone turned out for these, including members of neighboring churches. The services were always exciting, with a visiting clergyman doing the preaching, much fervent and joyful singing, and an altar call every night.

When I was eleven, and my brother Bud was nine, a minister by the name of Dr. Cobb was a big attraction at one of these revivals. He had visited the Holy Land and showed clothing, pottery, jewelry, hyssop, carpentry tools, and other items he had brought from there. He explained how the items were used and what life was like in the time of Jesus. He called people out of the congregation to come up and model the clothing, and named people in the Bible who would have worn this type clothing. He evangelized by showing slides and pointing out places where Jesus had lived and taught. Bud and I were fascinated by his beautiful slides and the Bible stories he told. He made the message of God's love come alive for us. At the altar call one evening, we went forward and promised to follow Jesus as our Lord and Savior.

On Dr. Cobb's last Sunday with us, all who had responded to the altar calls were baptized by him in the Ohio River. We waded out, one by one, till the water was waist-deep, then Dr. Cobb dunked us backward until we were fully immersed, as he said the words, "I baptize you in the name of the Father, and of the Son, and of the Holy Ghost."

The congregation stood on the shore and sang *Shall We Gather at the River?* We waded back to shore to receive hugs and congratulations, dripping wet but full-fledged members of the church. Our Christian journey had begun.

Fairwell Sister...It Was Happy When You Were Here

Dear Sister, I've herd your leaving this school. Mrs. Bucket told me you were changing your name to Sister Marie. I think that is a pretty name. I will miss you.
Your friend, Rita

And so it was that Rita said goodbye to her "favorite principal" who was being transferred to another school. Many of the children wrote farewell messages to Sister Julie in their own words (not to mention their own spelling and grammar). Sister was so impressed with these literary gems that she consented to share them. Refreshingly honest and clear-sighted, they give us a child's-eye view of Sister and reveal their deep feelings for her.

Some commended her highly for her good works:

Dear Sister, you have been a wonderful principal. I know you tryed hard to keep us good Chrishians. And I hope you more fun than you ever done.
Your friend, Darlene

...You were a good principal. I liked you more than school. This year I have never been absent. Please come again.
Your friend, Chris

Note the oratorical ring to this one. This little girl will make a great club woman some day:

Dear Sister, you were a nice and respectful and thoughtful person. So for your great responsibility, the whole school says goodbye. But not only for the first time, but for the last time.
Your dearest friend, Christie

The sadness of parting comes through in these wistful notes:

...I will miss you when you leave St. Monica Shool. It was happy when you were here. God bless you.
Brian

...I am sorry to see you go. I know whatever you do will be good. Thanks for everything.
Love, Jean

Dear Sister, I wish you won't leave. I think your so good. And you bleve in God.
Your friend, Andy

Goodbye for the rest of my life, wrote one little girl dramatically, and then added, *Come back and visit us sometime.*

From a third grader...*I wish you were not leaving. But I hope you like your new job. Are you going to the race?* It was unsigned. Perhaps he was in a hurry to get to the race.

This one has a nice conversational tone:

Dear Sister, I hope you enjoy the school your going to. Did you have six nice years at St. Monica? Do you know who your replacement is? Whoever she is, I hope we enjoy her as much as you.
Scott

This one must have given Sister a jolt:

Dear Sister, I'm hoping to see you before you live are school. My whole family doesn't want you to live.
Your friend, Earle

But this one makes up for it:

...We are all sad to see you go. But I wish you could come about once a month to play the organ.
Sincerely yours, Luanette

Children are flexible and soon accept what they cannot change:

Dear Sister, we are sad to see you go. But the Archbishop said you must...

...You did a nice job as principal, but your six years are up and we get a new principal...

...Everyone in the third grade is sorry to see you go. But I cannot do anything about it.

Luanna

Dear Sister, I am sorry to see you leave, but that the way the cookie crumbles...

Some of the children expressed doubt about the future:

...It is too bad you leave St. Monica. I not so shur of the new principal. But she looks nise and I hope she nise as you are...

Dear Sister, I wish you didn't have to leave. You been nice to us. I hope you will have a nice place to live. And I hope you have way to get there...

The writer must have left something out of this one:

Dear Sister, I hope you have next year. And I think you the best principal I ever seen in my life.
Your friend, Terry

But this one is even more startling:

...You are a very good principal. I don't want you to live, Sister. Know one wants you to live. I hope you have a nice trip. Goodby.
Linda

The writer of this one would make a fine politician:

...I'm sorry you can't be principal any more. We're all going to miss you guiding us and helping us know right from wrong. I'm sure our new principal will do very well since she has such a good example to follow.
Your pal, Sally

Many of the children expressed thanks:

...Thank you for helping us to be a loving child...

...Thanks a lot for being a good principal. You'll probley be just as good where your going.
Your friend, Jane

...You are the best. I thank you for let us wearing coolots. I hope you have a good year at St. Gabriel.
Kathleen

...You make fair and good rules...

...Thank you for giving us four years of your life...

...Dear Sister, we are sorry that you have to leave. I think you are nice to the kids in the school. I like the suit what you are wareing.
A student, Pamela

...Thank you for doing things for us and helping us learn. And thank you for your kindness and love.
Your friend, Linda

...Thank you for the nice playground. I hope you have a nice vacashun...

...You were nice to us in all ways...

...Fair Well Sister. I think you were the best princeable this school had and I hate to see you go.
Love, Greg

...Thank you for the work you have done...I have really liked you for a principal even if I did come late.
Your friend, Shari

...Thank you for being a principal for six years. Even now I haven't been here that long, but you have been working...

One child was not above giving a little friendly advice, among other things:

...Good luck and goodbye! I hope you have a nice time traveling. I'll try to remember you if I can. I hope I can. Will you teach or will you not teach? I think you should not teach for a while so you can have a break. Teaching isn't very hard except when you have to shout and scold children.
But when you get mad at them you should still like them.
Your friendly nabor, Barney.

Some of the letters were illustrated with original artwork in crayon. One little girl who drew flowers around the border of her letter explained it like this:

Dear Sister, I think that flowers will be better to make you chear up, as it will also be sad to leave. You have been a nice teacher to everyone. We will miss you and you will miss us.
Goodbye Sister, Nikita

A few expressed their sentiments in poetry. For instance:

Of all the Sisters there may be,
I choose the one who worked on me.
Roses are red, violets are blue.
God loves you and I do too.
—Johnny

No one summed up the feelings of the whole school better than a little boy who put it into two lines:

Dear Sister, you are very holy. You have done a good job. I thank you. God bless you.
David, third grade

All we can add is *Amen.* We wish you well, Sister. It was happy when you were here.

—Today's Family Digest, May 1970,
Huntington, IN

My Lost Love

A green macramé wall hanging which adorns my kitchen wall is a gentle reminder of God's love. The macramé of heavy cotton cord is knotted around the letters L-O-V-E and hangs perpendicularly with a ring at the top and a tassel at the bottom. It was a Christmas gift from a dear friend and when I opened it, I knew immediately where I would hang it, but at the moment, I simply laid it under the Christmas tree.

When the holidays were over and the decorations taken down, I was ready to hang my gift, but I couldn't find it! After searching the likeliest places, I asked my husband if he had seen it. Absorbed in his newspaper, he mumbled, "Oh, I probably put it away with the Christmas ornaments. I'll look for it later." But he continued reading and forgot all about it.

The next day I went down to the basement and pulled out the boxes of Christmas ornaments. As I opened box after box without success, I became increasingly frustrated and angry. I resented the time I was wasting on this futile search, and blamed my husband for treating my loss so casually and for having carelessly misplaced a gift that he knew was special to me.

Suddenly, the irony of the situation struck me. Here I was, searching desperately and angrily for L-0-V-E when my heart was far from loving! "Lord," I said aloud, "There's so use looking any more. I know you're not going to let me find L-O-V-E until I am able to love. Help me get my priorities in order and I'll leave the rest to you."

I put away the boxes, went upstairs and opened my Bible to First Corinthians 13: *Love is patient, love is kind...is not prone to anger, does not brood over injury..."* As I read, the warmth of God's love enveloped me. Praise and thanksgiving welled up in me. I thanked God for my husband, my home, and my children. In the light of all my blessings, this one thing seemed very insignificant. I resolved to say nothing more about it and surrender it entirely into the Lord's hands.

Weeks passed. Then one Saturday morning when we were having a leisurely breakfast, I felt moved to share with my husband my angry feelings at that time and how the Lord had led me to count my blessings.

He admitted he had not given the matter another thought, but he was sure he could locate the gift. He proceeded to look around the house in all the places I had first looked, but to no avail.

Then I had a thought, "Do you think it would be with the artificial Christmas tree?"

"No," he said, "I don't think I would have put it there, but we can look."

We went downstairs together, opened the artificial tree box, and there it was, right on top! He held it up victoriously and we hugged each other, with the restored L-O-V-E caught in our embrace. "I think the Lord wanted us to find it together," he said.

As I look at my lost and found L-O-V-E, hanging placidly where it belongs, I am reminded of two lessons the Lord taught me in my search: (1) We cannot find love when we are angry and (2) We cannot find love alone.

—*Guideposts*, February 1984,
Carmel, New York

God's Call

When I was young, I said a prayer,
Simple and childlike and true,
*"I offer you my talents, Lord.
What would you have me do?"*
I thought the Lord would answer me
With signals loud and clear.
I listened but no answer came.
No voices did I hear.

The years went by. As a teacher
I labored lovingly.
Content with my role, I reasoned,
"This is God's plan for me!"
Then marriage came, and children too.
I murmured fervently,
*"This is the work that I do best.
A mother God wants me to be!"*
When later I felt called to serve
The poor and mentally ill,
The need was great. I thought, *"At last!
Now I am doing God's will!"*

Today my son had a question,
Frowning most earnestly,
"Mother, how can I know for sure
What God is asking of me?"
I said to him (for I knew that God
Had answered my long-ago prayer),
"It's God's own work he calls you to,
And his work is everywhere!
Don't wait for a God-given sign
Or a flash from a radiant star.
The roles are many, the call but one:
Do God's work wherever you are!"

Heartfelt Prayer at a Religion Teachers' Workshop

Lord, we are gathered together like the disciples in the Upper Room.
We are here to prepare for the apostolic work you have called us to do.
We are surrounded by reference books, study guides, lesson plans and visual aids.
We have called in a psychologist, a priest, a youth director and a coordinator of religious education.
We have before us posters, film strips, video tapes and games.
We have fortified ourselves with coffee and cookies,
And we are ready to be filled with the wisdom and knowledge we need to carry out our important mission.

You can see, Lord, that we are an intelligent and well-organized group.
In fact, we represent a variety of degrees from a number of institutions of higher learning.
Not only that, but we keep ourselves abreast of the times.
We are familiar with the lifestyles of the youth we teach—their music, their dress, their values—
So that we can meet them on their own level,
And converse with them in their own vocabulary.
We know all about Reaching Out, Touching, Loving, Caring and Sharing.
We have talked with them about sex, drugs, war, pollution, hunger, injustice and love.
Mostly, we talk about love.

Pull us out, Lord.
We are buried in a sea of semantics.
We are voices crying out in a wilderness
Of words, words, words,
A wilderness of more books that we can ever read,
More philosophies than we can ever assimilate,
And as many methods of teaching as there are teachers.

In this maze of controversy, we are not sure what we should be teaching or what we are trying to accomplish.
We are not making excuses, Lord. We are sincere.

We have shared some beautiful moments together, and a great deal of wine.
We have laughed and wept and agonized together, and we have come a long way in a year,
But here we are again, in doubt.
We have decided that a little doubt is a good thing.

So here we sit, Lord.
We have heard all the speakers and seen the filmstrips, listened to the tapes, and played the games.
At last we begin our discussion.
We focus on goals.
We talk about structure, content, process and efficiency.
We are very earnest, rather wordy, and not at all clear,
But we keep trying.
In the end, we cannot agree on a single objective.

Lord, you said, "Where two or three are gathered in my name, there am I in the midst."
Lord, we need you in our midst.
Let us not be ashamed to ask for your help.
"Ask and you shall receive. Knock, and it shall be opened," you said.
Give us the courage, Lord, to ask, right out loud, in front of everybody.
Let us not be afraid to knock, so that the door can be opened.
Let us meet, not simply for the pleasure of being together, but for being together with *you* in our midst.

Help us to look at ourselves honestly,
And not be puffed up with pride
At our own accomplishments,
Realizing that whatever is accomplished through us is the work of the Holy Spirit.

But neither let us waste time grieving over our mistakes,
But get on with the work at hand.
Let us be strengthened by the Scriptures.
May we not stand in awe of reading the Bible
No matter which translation,
For the message shines through the words,
And you know we need to be constantly reminded of the message,
Lest it grow dim in our minds and fade away altogether.

Lord, send the Holy Spirit to us *now, tonight,*
As you sent him to the disciples in the Upper Room,
So that we may be filled,
Not with a dozen new theological concepts,
Or formulas for teaching, or rhetorical skills,
But with an intense desire to "go…and preach the Good News" in
    whatever way he inspires to do it.

Enlighten us day by day and minute by minute,
And give us the courage to speak for you, Lord.
May your Spirit shine in us and through us,
So that the world may say,
"They are Christians, for see how they love one another."

—Religion Teacher's Journal, May 1972,
Twenty-Third Publications,
West Mystic, Connecticut

You Say You Want Peace

If you say you want peace
and you will not let your brother live in peace,
I say you are a hypocrite.

Peace does not begin with nations.
It begins here
in this classroom
with you and me.

Yes, *you*, brother,
with the rapt, attentive gaze,
gently molding a spitball
against the roof of your mouth.

Yes, and *you*, brother,
unobtrusively moving a stack of books,
inch by inch,
with your foot,
so they will soon fall
with a loud crash.

I mean *you*, brother,
slumping in your chair,
and leafing aimlessly through your book
because you have lost the place,
shuffling and snickering,
and talking, always talking,
because you have never learned
to listen to anyone but yourself.

Talk no more about peace to me, brother,
until you can find it in your heart
to stop disturbing mine.

—1970

Moving Day

My footsteps echo on the bare floors
Of these familiar rooms.
The curtains are down, the rugs rolled up,
The pictures removed from the walls.
Tall packing boxes, sealed and labeled,
Give silent testimony to the fact
That we are moving.

How vulnerable now is this house I have loved!
Like an unclothed person, each flaw is revealed.
How glaring and ugly the dirty window,
The patched wall, the crack in the ceiling!
Every defect is visible. Nothing is hidden.

How much like houses are we,
The faults in our structures
Known only to God!
How covered with patches and scars
Is the house of my soul,
Could it be bared to view!
How worn the floors!
How cracked the walls!
How odd-shaped the rooms!

LOVE MAKES THE RIDE WORTHWHILE

But the Spirit who dwells in my house
Is a careful and loving homemaker.
He has taken this poor house of mine
With all its weaknesses and eccentricities,
And turned these infirmities into beauty!
He has filled the dark corners with light,
And the bare empty places
He has covered with the drapery of his love.
He has made it a place of peace and tranquility
Because he has touched it, transformed it,
Loved it and lived in it!

Murphy's Ten Cent Store on a Summer Day

Thank you, Lord, for black raspberry ice cream, purple and cold,
Piled high on a cone and ready to drip.
Thank you for the scorching sun that burns the sidewalk
And also for the person whose creative mind invented air conditioning.

Thank you for swinging doors and department stores
And neat little salesgirls who smile and say,
"Have a nice day!"

Thank you, Lord, for the white-haired couple walking hand in hand,
And stopping to look at this and that as they wander through the store.
Who is leading whom, I wonder?
Bless them in their golden years and keep them close to you.

Thank you for the 16 flavors of ice cream,
The five shelves of beauty aids,
And the endless supply of cosmetics.
Whoever thought of a nail polish called mushroom?

LOVE MAKES THE RIDE WORTHWHILE

I sense your presence in your people, Lord,
In the lady who sits on the bench with me,
Holding packages, tired and hot,
Waiting for her son to pick her up,
And in the lithe suntanned boy
Sweeping the sidewalk with a wide broom.
How could we make so much litter in one day?

I know you're present, Lord,
In all these people, young and old, fat and thin,
Black and white, brown and yellow,
Coming through the swinging doors.
Help us to remember
That we are sisters and brothers under the skin
You're the Father of us all, and we are yours,
All yours!

First Meeting of the Monday Night Group

Dear Lord, this meeting of your "committed people"
Is a disaster!

How could we have sunk so low
After that inspiring weekend?
Only two days ago
We humbled ourselves before you
On our knees,
And begged forgiveness
For all the things
That keep us from you.
We asked you to take away
All our self-centeredness
So that your will could be done
Through us.

Was it a dream we had together?
Did it really happen?
Here we are, together again,
Interrupting, all talking at once,
No one listening,
Can't wait to get our own word in.

…Guess what happened to me.
I'm a changed person!…
…I can't come on Mondays.
I gave up my Slimnastics class
To come tonight…
I have a Scripture to share.

It's here in Timothy...
The Lord really spoke to me...

Let's start with a prayer.

...Monday is okay for me,
But not Tuesday or Thursday...
...That's what I mean!
We have to be an example
To the rest of the community,
Show them what it is to be Christian.
...We have to be honest with each other,
Ready to listen and accept criticism...

Can we pray now?

Oh, I'm sorry I'm late!
I had a liturgy meeting.
We're making banners for Easter.

Let's pray now.

I have a Scripture I'd like to read.
It's from Colossians...
...Where's the order in this meeting?
I thought the Holy Spirit
Is supposed to bring order!

We're going to pray now.
Let's just kneel and hold hands
Around this coffee table.
Lord, we commit our lives to you...

Advent

I am looking for him.
They tell me this is the season he comes.
They are making wreaths and candles
And a crib for him,
And planning celebrations in his honor.
They are all preparing for him,
And I am preparing too
Because I want to find him for myself.

"Seek and you shall find," he said.
So I am seeking, and I will not stop
Until I find him,
For if all those others find him
And I do not find him for myself,
What good is that to me?
The wonder is not so much that he *came*,
But that he still *comes*,
And that he will continue to come
To all who call on his name,
Even me!

LOVE MAKES THE RIDE WORTHWHILE

"Knock and it shall be opened to you," he said,
And I repeat his promise
As I stand before that closed door.
"Knock and it shall be opened…"
But what if I knock and nobody answers?
What if he does not hear
My weak and trembling knock?

Oh, please, Jesus, open the door to me!
I know you are there,
And my heart is ready for you!
Come as you promised
And give me a new life!
Come, Lord Jesus, come!

The First Christmas

'Twas the night before Christmas in Bethlehem town
And Joseph was anxious. No room could be found
For Mary, his wife, so gentle and mild,
Who soon would give birth to her firstborn child.

The village was filled—every house, every bed.
"No room in the inn," the innkeeper said.
And very sadly he turned them away.
Yet they lingered, wond'ring where they might stay,
Till the innkeeper mentioned a cave in the hill.
"Let's go there," said Mary, "It must be God's will."

The moon had come out and the stars were aglow.
They brightened the path for the donkey to go.
It led to a cave where cattle were kept,
And, gratefully, Mary and Joseph slept.
And there in that cave, on a bed of soft hay,
Baby Jesus was born that first Christmas day.

God the Father rejoiced, and from heaven above,
Sent an angel to earth announcing His love.
And while shepherds guarded their sheep that night,
They saw in the sky a dazzling light!

"Do not be afraid," the angel exclaimed,
"There is good news for all, and it must be proclaimed!
I bring you glad tidings of joy on this morn.
In the city of David, your Savior is born!
Let this be a sign: in a manger he'll be.
An infant in swaddling clothes you will see."

LOVE MAKES THE RIDE WORTHWHILE

The shepherds were struck with wonder and awe
At the sounds they heard and the sights they saw!
They left their sheep and hurried ahead,
And found the babe as the angel had said.
They knelt on the floor of that cave so bare
And lifted their hands and worshipped him there.
With Mary and Joseph, they looked on his face,
And the glory of God filled that humble place!

'Twas dawn when the shepherds returned to their sheep,
Touched by the mystery their hearts could not keep.
Yet many greater than these would come
To worship the fruit of Mary's womb,
For all who came to him would be healed
And by him would the Kingdom of God be revealed.

We all know the story, two thousand years old.
We love it the more, each time it's retold.
Yet the greatest gift we can wish for you
Is to know the joy that the shepherds knew
In that little cave one wondrous morn
In Bethlehem where Jesus was born!

—1983—
Written for a children's Christmas party
given by Community of Light, Rockville, MD

New Year Prayer

Thank you, Lord, for new beginnings
And for the gift of hope
Which makes me eager to face the challenge
Of a new day,
A new week,
A new year.

Thank you for the joy
Of opening a new book,
Making a new friend,
Beginning a new project,
Moving into a new house,
Holding a new baby.

Life is a series of new beginnings.
When the plans I make do not work out,
Or I have made a mess of things,
I thank you for giving me the strength
To begin again.

I thank you especially for *this* new year,
So fresh, so untouched,
So full of hope.

LOVE MAKES THE RIDE WORTHWHILE

Yet, if I do not accomplish all that I intend,
If I do not slay any dragons,
Or make my mark in the world,
Or grow spiritually to any noticeable degree,
If I flub my opportunities,
And close the doors you open,
And make wrong decisions,
I know you will love me still,
Wipe clean the slate,
And give me another chance
In the *next* new year!

A Pilgrim's Prayer

Lord, as I kneel to pray,
Widen my mind to include more of your people:
The gentle Arab shepherds with their flowing robes,
The deep-voiced Muslim chanting from the minaret at dawn,
The young Israeli soldiers hitching a ride home,
The smiling Sisters who do your work
In Rome, in Nazareth, in Jerusalem,
And the dear Franciscan Fathers who care for the Holy Places.
Oh Lord, let your blessing fall on all who seek peace,
Of whatever nation, of whatever creed!

Provide food for the wandering Bedouins, Lord,
Roaming the rocky mountainside with their sheep.
Lead them to the grassy spots
And bring them to the clear water.

Thank you, Lord, for the experience of thirst
That I may know the blessing of water.
Thank you for the privilege
Of climbing the mountains you climbed,
That I may pray with understanding,
"You will not allow my feet to slip."
Thank you for the great abundance of bread in your land,
At every meal a reminder of your words,
"I am the Bread of Life."

LOVE MAKES THE RIDE WORTHWHILE

Thank you for being present to me in this land you loved.
Thank you for speaking to me through simple things
Like water and bread and rocks and sun,
And for proclaiming so majestically
From every mountain top and every valley
That Jesus Christ is Lord!

Let the reality of this truth dominate my life
So that I can never be judgmental and shallow again.
Give me the courage to proclaim
That you are the God of all nations and all people,
And that you are gently calling us to love one another.
Teach us to love with your love
That this may be so.
Amen.

—1975—
Written after a pilgrimage to the Holy Land

Holy Year Prayer

Father, look down upon us and hear our earnest prayer.
Forgive our pettiness and our lack of love.
Forgive our selfishness and our failure
To be aware of the needs of others.
Forgive us for being cozy and comfortable
In our own little world, and shutting our eyes
To suffering and hunger and poverty.
Stir us up, Lord, and keep us from being
Proud and smug and complacent
In our abundance of material things.

Help us, Father, to make a fresh start this Holy Year,
To make it a time of forgiveness and reconciliation
With our brothers and sisters in Christ.
Help us to forget our differences, and remember only
That you are at work in all of us,
And that nothing but your love will bring us together.
Let us see your light shining through your children
Of other faiths, other races, and other cultures.
Let us keep our eyes on that light
Until our differences drop away.

LOVE MAKES THE RIDE WORTHWHILE

Thank you, Father, for your many gifts to all of us.
Help us to use them for *your* glory, not our own.
Teach us to follow your way and listen to your voice.
Help us to become more holy this Holy Year.
Allow us see ourselves more clearly.
Let us come closer to you and bear fruit for you.

Thank you, Father, for your mercy, your forgiveness,
And your everlasting, unconditional love.
Help us to repent. Help us to forgive.
Help us to love with your love.
In Jesus' name we pray. Amen.

—1974—
Written in celebration of the Jubilee Year

The Mysterious Holy Spirit

The Holy Spirit who dwells in me
Is a great mystery!
I carry him wherever I go—
The third person of the Holy Trinity,
Living in me!
This is the wondrous, awesome,
Inexplicable mystery!

Sometimes I ignore him.
For days at a time,
I forget him completely.
Then suddenly, surprisingly,
He is overwhelmingly present,
Surrounding me with his love.
Filling me with his joy and peace
To the point of tears.

There are times
When I make
A concentrated effort
To call him forth.
I set an appointed time.
I designate a meeting place.
I make all the arrangements,
But he is strangely uncommunicative.

LOVE MAKES THE RIDE WORTHWHILE

I do not understand him at all,
This Spirit who dwells in me.
But one thing I know—he loves me
And he will never leave me!
This Jesus has promised.

So I will place my future in his hands.
I will learn to wait,
To abide, to grow,
To respond in humility and joy
To his love and his gifts.

I know that his presence within me
Is the greatest gift of all.
And for now,
That is enough.

—September 12, 1976—
Written on silent retreat with Father Keith Hosey,
Dayspring, Maryland

Bicentennial Prayer

Father of all nations and all people,
We are grateful for the blessings you have poured out
Upon this land we love,
For the diversity and beauty of our landscapes,
For the abundance of natural resources,
And for the rich productive soil
Conducive to growing grains, fruits and vegetables.

Father, we thank you for the people who have come
From all parts of the world to form our nation,
And for the various cultures and traditions
That make up this patchwork quilt of America.

We thank you for the courage of the early settlers,
And the faith which enabled them to endure the hardships
Of this wild new country.

We thank you for the two hundred years
We have survived and grown as a nation.
You have blessed us with wealth and prestige and power,
And we have often taken them for granted.
We have been wasteful and destructive and self-seeking.
Help us to repent and return to you with renewed faith.

LOVE MAKES THE RIDE WORTHWHILE

Father, forgive us for the sins we have committed as a nation,
And the sins we have committed against one another
Within our nation.
Give us the grace to forgive and forget.
Lift us out of the darkness of pride and greed,
And bring us into the light of your truth.

Inspire us with the high ideals and the simple faith
Of our founding fathers,
Realizing that all we have comes from you,
For yours is the kingdom and the power and the glory,
Now and forever. Amen.

—July 4, 1976 —
Written for a celebration of Independence Day
held by the Community of Light prayer group, Rockville, MD

Thanksgiving for God's Blessing

(A meditation on Psalm 65, relating it to our time and place, but retaining the spirit of the psalmist)

To you, Father, we give praise and thanksgiving
Because it is to you we come with all our needs.
You alone can answer our prayers and forgive our sins.

How blessed we are that you have called us to be yours!
You have filled us with all good things.
You have sent your Spirit to dwell in us.
Through your son Jesus, you save us from our sins.
You are the hope of the world!

We acknowledge you as our Creator,
Maker of heaven and earth.
You formed the mountains.
You control the raging waters of the seas
As easily as you quiet the tumult in our hearts.

Your glorious works are marvelous to behold!
The beauty of the sunrise and the sunset
Makes our hearts leap for joy!

LOVE MAKES THE RIDE WORTHWHILE

Just as you water the earth with showers,
Softening the soil for seeds to take root and grow,
So you continually refresh your people
At the spring of Living Water,
So we may bring to fulfillment
The new life within us.

Just as you prepare the earth to yield crops
By sending the sun and the rain in due season,
So also you prepare your people to bear fruit
By using the joys and sorrows in our lives
To bring us closer to you.

You have given us a year
Overflowing with good things—
A rich harvest of loving relationships,
Inner peace, newfound joy,
And healing of bodies and spirits.
We, your people in the Community of Light,
Sing for joy, and lift up our hearts
In praise and thanksgiving!

—1978

Prayer for Spiritual Renewal

Father,
you have called us to be your people.
Then why do we so often behave
like sheep without a shepherd?
You gave your son to die in our place
that we might have life.
Then why do we try so hard to make it alone
as if we did not know that Jesus is our brother?
You sent your Holy Spirit to be with us always
and to lead us to the truth.
Then why are we burdened and restless
as if your Spirit did not dwell in us?

Lord,
we need your healing touch!
Stir up our faith and give us the courage
to live what we truly believe!
Enkindle in us the fire of your love,
the love that motivated the apostles!
Pour out your Spirit upon us, Lord,
that we may become the faith community
You have called us to be:
a people who read your word and listen to your voice,
a people who experience your joy and your healing,
a people who do your work and witness to your truth.
This we pray in Jesus' name. Amen.

—1984—
Written for the three-year RENEW program,
and recited after every Mass during the RENEW seasons at
Shrine of St. Jude Catholic Church, Rockville, MD

Renewal

See what the Spirit is doing among us!
Behold our new leaves—
A visible sign of our prayers,
A symbol of hope and new life
In Jesus, our Lord!

Together we grow, together proclaim
Our oneness in him who calls us to love
And be loved!

—1984—
Written to set before the Prayer Tree, symbol of the RENEW program,
Shrine of St. Jude, Rockville, MD

Message from Jesus in the Eucharist

My people,
Why do you encase me in a fancy frame,
Pay homage to me on your knees,
Lift me high on a golden plate,
And yet you do not see me on the street?

When you pass me by, and hurry to the chapel
To bow down before me,
I am not there for you,
For if you do not recognize me on the street,
You will not recognize me on the altar.

Your rituals put distance between us.
Come closer, and do not be afraid
To touch me in the Eucharist,
To reach out your hand for me.
My touch is healing.

LOVE MAKES THE RIDE WORTHWHILE

My people,
I am always with you.
Look deep within yourselves,
And in those around you.
I live in the least of these.
When you welcome them,
You welcome me.
When you reject them,
You reject me.

Wherever you go, I am with you.
You are the temple of my spirit.
You are my dwelling place.

—March 19, 1987

Jubilee Year

(An up-to-date version of Isaiah 61:1-3)

The Holy Spirit is with us now, in our time and place.
The Lord himself has anointed us to do a special work.
He has chosen us to bring the Good News of Jesus Christ
To all who despair,
To heal those who have been hurt,
To proclaim to fellow Christians
That they can be free in the Holy Spirit,
To release them from their bonds of guilt, fear, and anxiety,
To announce a year of special grace from God,
A Jubilee year,
A time when God is drawing his people together
By a great outpouring of spiritual gifts,
A time when God is absolving us from our sins,
A time to comfort all who are sad,
To give those who mourn the peace of Christ
Instead of guilt for sin,
To bring them the joy of the Lord instead of sorrow,
A banner of love instead of apathy,
So they may grow strong in the Lord
And stand like oak trees planted by the Lord
To show forth his glory!

—*2000, Jubilee year*

Message at Summit Lake

I heard the Lord calling,
"Come away with me.
I have a message for you."
I answered, "Yes Lord, I am coming,"
And I opened my heart and my mind,
And laid before him my will.

At Summit Lake, on silent retreat,
I walked in the woods
And saw the tall pines bending in the wind.
"The Spirit of God is like the wind," I thought,
"He blows where he wills.
He cannot be contained.
He cannot be limited
To one theology,
Or one spirituality.
He is utterly free.
Is this your message, Lord?"
But all I heard was the rustling of the leaves
And a woodpecker knocking at his tree.

Later I stood by the rippling lake,
And I was reminded of the Living Water
Which wells up inside me, fresh and bubbling.
"Is this why you have called me, Lord," I asked,
"That my own spring, which is only a trickle
Might be renewed?"
But the only answer was the splish-splash
Of the water against the shore.

Dinner came, and there were platters
Of fresh-baked bread.
The words of the Mass came to mind,
Through your goodness, we have this bread to eat,
Which earth has given and human hands have made.
I prayed, "Lord, you are truly the Bread of Life.
You feed my Spirit as this bread feeds my body.
Give me always your bread to eat."

At sundown, I walked along the shore,
As the shadows fell across the lake,
Watching the dusk gather in the low places,
Listening to the awesome silence of the wilderness,
Humbled by the majesty of God's creation.
How glorious are the works of your hands, O Lord!

Then I saw a small figure
On the other side of the lake,
Climbing into a rowboat and shoving off.
Instantly, I was drawn to him.
The splendor of the sunset was forgotten.
I wondered if he could swim
And if his mother knew he was alone
Out there on the lake.

LOVE MAKES THE RIDE WORTHWHILE

My fears were groundless.
He rowed with confidence,
A true captain of his ship.
Engrossed and elated,
My eyes followed him.
His triumph became my triumph,
His joy, my joy.
In some mysterious way,
My spirit was linked with his spirit.
We were one.

In that moment, a mighty truth
Was singing in my heart:

*The Lord's greatest handiwork
Is not the highest mountain,
Not the deepest ocean,
Not the stars or the trees or the sunset,
But his people!
We are his geatest glory!
He has poured into us a part of himself.
No other created thing is so glorified!
The Spirit of God in me
Is forever calling out
To the spirit of God in you,
And that answering,
That responding, that communicating
Is the glory of the Lord among us!*

And the message of the Lord
Came to me that day at Summit Lake:

Seek my face in my people.
Love me in my people,
For I am present in each of them.
I have made you to be complete
Only when you are in union
With one another.
Look deep into every heart,
For I am there.
I am present in your suffering.
I am present in your joy.
I am present even
When you think nobody cares.
Look for me in the faces
Of your brothers and sisters.
When you discover me in others,
I rejoice,
For it is then
That we are one.

The Hands of Jesus

What were they like—
The hands of the carpenter from Nazareth
The hands that touched and healed,
The hands that blessed little children,
And calmed the winds and the waves?

They must have been callused and rough,
Those strong young Jewish hands
That did the work of a builder and a fisherman;
Yet they were gentle and comforting
To the blind and the crippled.

They reached out to touch a leper,
Whom nobody dared to touch,
And the leper was made whole!
They mixed a mudpack for a blind man's eyes,
And he began to see!

They washed the feet of twelve men
Not worthy to tie his sandals.
They ministered to the sick and the dying,
And they were lifted in praise to the Father.

The hands of the Son of God
Received a drink of water
From the hands of a prostitute,
And broke bread in the houses of sinners.

The hands that overturned the tables
Of the money changers, and held the whip
That drove them out of the temple
Are the same hands
That reached out in compassion
To the poor and the suffering.

With his human hands,
Jesus blessed bread and broke it,
Blessed wine and shared it—
The sign of a new covenant
Between God and mankind.

With his hands, he carried a cross
To the site of his death
And, in the end,
His hands were pierced with nails
That those yet unborn
Might have eternal life.

His hands were like yours and mine—
No different!
There is nothing that Jesus did
With his human hands
That you and I
Cannot do with ours!

They responded to the warmth
Of a friend's hand,
And they felt the numbness of cold.
They got dirty.
They experienced bruises,
And splinters and blisters.
They throbbed with pain from the nails.

LOVE MAKES THE RIDE WORTHWHILE

Dear Jesus, let me hold
Your hurting, blood-soaked hand
By holding the hand
Of a brother or sister in pain.
Let me respond in love
To a hand outstretched in need,
And know it is your hand I touch.

Just as your human hands
Were channels of Divine power,
So let my hands be channels
Of your Spirit within me
That rejoices in the Father
And all his gifts—
The blessings and the burdens,
The laughter and the tears,
The surprises and the disappointments,
The labor and the rest.

Let my hands be open wide, like yours,
To receive with thanksgiving,
And to give with joy,
So that, at the end, I may say with you,
"Father, into your hands
I commend my spirit."

IV - LOVE OF LIFE

*"I asked God for all things that I might enjoy life.
I was given life, that I might enjoy all things."*
—Attributed to an unknown soldier of World War II

Introduction

When I consider a truly full and joyful life, I think of a friend who died recently. He was born in Puerto Rico and his family moved to New York when he was a young child. He had that joyful spirit and love of music and dancing that is so typical of the Spanish community in our parish. Several eulogies were given at his funeral service, and every one of them spoke of his love—his love for his wife, his children, his God, his church, and his love for music and poetry.

One of his greatest joys was to perform with a small music group that visited nursing homes to entertain the residents. With this group, he sang, played the harmonica and the *maracas,* and sometimes danced Spanish dances with his wife.

He loved to sing his grandchildren to sleep. He wrote poetry, including a book of love poems to his wife. He composed a song in praise to God, which was sung at his funeral. His joyful spirit brought happiness and laughter into the lives of those who knew him.

People like our friend are the ones who make the journey through life on this planet a new adventure every day—a mystery to be lived, not a problem to be solved. Their love of life uplifts those around them.

Love is a gift to be nurtured and cherished, for where there is love, we thrive, we grow, and we enjoy life. Where there is no love, we become discouraged and depressed, and life is merely a jumble of unrelated events. Love connects the dots, making it whole and complete, and giving it purpose and meaning.

As I look back over my own journey, I feel blessed, for I have had a loving family and helpful companions along the way. I have lived through times of poverty and times of prosperity and know that I can live with either of them. During my lifetime, I have seen drastic changes in our society and serious challenges to our nation. Our country has engaged in five wars, and we are still deep into the fifth one—the War on Terror.

When I was growing up, life was simpler, slower paced, less complicated and less competitive. As children, we worked hard, but we had time to be creative, and time to spend with our families. We helped each other. We trusted people. We felt safe and secure in our homes and never locked our doors.

My generation has been dubbed "the greatest generation" by Tom Brokaw in his book by that name. He is referring to those of us who are now in our eighties, and grew up during the Great Depression of the 1930's, when our country's economy was at the lowest ebb in its history. Thousands of families lacked the very necessities of life, and survived by means of soup lines and government aid.

We reached adulthood just in time to serve in World War II. To those who returned, Uncle Sam offered the G.I. Bill—funds to start a business, or a free college education. I was among the thousands of veterans who registered for college in the fall of 1946, and I am extremely grateful for that opportunity, for it changed the course of my life.

Brokaw interviewed many men and women for his book—those who were in the armed services, and those who served on the home front in factories, ammunition plants, and on the farm. He points out that these men and women were united, not only by the common purpose of winning the war, but also by common values—duty, honor, economy, courage, service, love of family and country, and above all, personal responsibility.

Of the veterans who returned from World War II, he wrote, "They won the war. They saved the world. They came home to joyous and short-lived celebrations, and immediately began the task of rebuilding their lives and the world they wanted. A grateful nation made it possible for more of them to attend college than any society had ever educated, anywhere. They gave the world new science, literature, art, industry, and economic strength, unparalleled in the long curve of history."

I am proud to be numbered among those labeled "the greatest generation," for though my service in the Navy did not lead me into dangerous war zones, I shared the same values, the same work ethic, the same respect for authority, and a strong sense of responsibility, as well as hopes and dreams for a better life.

Depression Years on the Farm and *Boot Camp*, in this section, reflect the values that united our nation and gave Americans the will, the strength and the discipline to endure those years of hardship and war.

Depression Years on the Farm

I grew up on a farm in Indiana in the 1930's, the oldest of five children, during the "depression years," as my mother always referred to that time. The Great Depression, as it came to be called, began in 1929 with the Wall Street stock market crash and lasted until the U.S. entered World War II. When ammunition and aircraft factories began to operate at full speed, and other businesses turned to producing food, clothing and supplies for our troops overseas, this brought prosperity to the whole nation. Every able-bodied adult was called to go to work to help the war effort. Even farm wives left their kitchens and gardens, and went to work on assembly lines to help pay off the debts they had accumulated during the depression.

Electricity did not reach our rural area until the late 1930's and early 1940's. Until that time, we had no running water in the house. We did have a cistern, which collected rainwater. The water was pumped up from the cistern below by priming a small hand pump. We used it for washing clothes and other things, but the water we used for drinking and cooking came from the pump in the back yard. Pumping water and carrying it to the house to keep the water bucket filled for drinking and cooking was the responsibility of my brother Bud and me.

Our school homework was done on the kitchen table by the light of an oil lamp. We had a big wood-burning range with a reservoir for water on the side. It was used to heat the kitchen, as well as for cooking. In the summer, when it was too hot to use the range, we cooked on a three-burner kerosene stove.

Our telephone hung on the kitchen wall. We had to crank it to get the operator, who would then ring the party we wanted. If we were on the same line, however, we could ring them ourselves. People on the same line often listened to their neighbors' conversations. This is how they found out that someone was sick, or had died, or had a new baby. But Mother would never let us do that. "If the line is busy," she told us, "hang up. Don't listen to someone else's conversation."

Farm life was never easy. By the time electricity reached us, we were in the throes of the depression. However, Dad wired the house for electricity and put in electric lights. An electric refrigerator came next and, gradually, other conveniences were added. A Maytag washing machine with a wringer on the side replaced the big old washtub and washboard. My great-grandmother Hatt (Mother's grandmother) was leery of these new-fangled machines. She asked, "But how does it know when the clothes are clean?"

Finally, a sink with hot and cold running water was put in, and a shower and toilet installed in a small room we called the "washroom." The outhouse was torn down. The water bucket and the dipper, which hung on the kitchen wall close to the water bucket, were put away. I still have the dipper, which is now an antique.

By today's standards, we would have been considered poor, but my siblings and I did not think of ourselves as poor, because our neighbors were on the same level of poverty. We learned to "make do" with what we had. Nothing usable or wearable was thrown away. Sugar and flour came in white cotton bags, which were used for dishtowels, pillowcases, curtains, dresser scarves, and other household items. When my mother made dresses for my sister and me, she always saved the odd-shaped scraps for quilts. These were called "crazy quilts."

We raised chickens, milk cows, and beef cattle. Dad butchered every year. We had a vegetable garden, and also apple, pear, and plum trees. We canned green beans, tomatoes and peaches every summer. Blackberries grew wild in our woods, and we picked buckets of them, getting chiggers every time we picked. We canned what we couldn't use at the time, so we were able to have blackberry cobbler in the middle of winter, always a treat.

Mother saved cream and took it to the creamery in town every week. She received around $3.00 for it, and with that money, she bought staples—sugar, flour, cornmeal, baking powder, soda and lard. We churned our own butter in a hand churn. That was always a job for us children. It took half an hour or longer to make butter.

Early in life, my siblings and I had regular chores to do. In the winter, after school, my brother Bud and I carried in wood for the kitchen range and the drum stove in the living room. We also pumped water for the cattle. In the summer, we picked green beans and tomatoes, which Dad grew for a canning factory. Usually, the whole family was involved in harvesting them. Dad paid us a penny a pound for "snipping" the green beans (breaking or cutting off the tips) because the factory paid more if they were snipped. We were delighted to earn a little money. We never heard of an allowance.

In the spring, tobacco planting was a big job. Tobacco plants were pulled from the tobacco beds (where they had been started from seed) and planted in the field. All children old enough to do so would be called upon to carry a bucket of freshly pulled tobacco plants and drop them, one by one, about eighteen inches apart, in furrows. Adults came behind them with a hoe to set the plants in the ground. As the tobacco grew, the children in the family were expected to help hoe it, "worm" it, "sucker" it and help hang it in the barn to dry after it had been cut.

But our life was not all work. My sister Mary and I were involved with 4-H projects every summer. Standing for head, heart, hand, and health, the 4-H Club was a great incentive for young people to become good homemakers and farmers. We could select projects such as sewing, baking, canning, home decorating, raising a calf or a pig, or raising vegetables. We held meetings where adult leaders instructed us and monitored our progress. Our work was displayed at the Country Fair and, if it won blue ribbons there, it was taken to the State Fair. Mary always took sewing, and moved from making pillowslips to making her own clothes. She became an excellent seamstress.

A big event each summer was the Fourth of July celebration There was a marching band and a parade, with men wearing World War I Army and Navy uniforms, and one old veteran of the Civil War, who sat in an open truck or wagon and waved to everyone. People always clapped when he passed by. After the parade, a short service took place at the cemetery honoring the veterans buried there, and we said the

Pledge of Allegiance to the Flag and sang *The Star-Spangled Banner.* Even as a child, I was proud to be an American.

In the winter, when the creek froze over, we made ice cream. Dad would go down to the creek and chop out some big chunks of ice, put them in a gunny sack and crush them with a hammer. He then packed the crushed ice all around the container holding the creamy mixture that Mother poured into it. We kids would take turns cranking it until it turned into ice cream. That would take about 45 minutes. Sometimes we called the neighbors over to visit and help eat the ice cream. We also made popcorn balls and crackerjack in the winter, with a recipe using sorghum molasses.

Dad always worked from daylight, or earlier, until dark. In the winter, when evenings were long, he used to sing to us after supper. He knew by memory the words to *Redwing, Little Indian Napanee, The Preacher and the Bear,* and other songs. We loved to hear them and asked him to sing them over and over.

Mother and Dad both liked to sing. When we visited friends with pianos, someone would play, and the adults would gather around and sing the old songs: *Long Long Ago; When You and I were Young, Maggie; My Wild Irish Rose*; *Believe Me, If All Those Endearing Young Charms; Seeing Nellie Home,* and others. We had a horse named Nellie, and when I was little, I thought they were singing about a horse. I always visualized someone leading a horse back to the barn.

Grandpa Kemp, Dad's father, who lived with us for a while, played the violin. He was sometimes called on to play for square dances. When a family moved into a new house, it was the custom to wax the floor and have a square dance before any furniture was moved into it. I remember going to these dances, watching Grandpa play the violin, and playing with the other kids while our parents danced.

Life was simpler in those days, but we never lacked things to do. When our city cousins came to visit, we made our own fun: running around the yard on summer evenings catching lightning bugs; playing "hyden-go-seek," as we called it; doing handsprings in the front yard; climbing up on the rafters in the barn and then jumping down on the hay; playing house in the corncrib; or making dolls out of corncobs, and doll houses out of cardboard boxes. We were never bored. When we didn't have jobs to do, we were happy to have free time for projects of our own. We enjoyed our childhood, and society did not push us to grow up before our time.

Fortunately, Mother and Dad did not lose their farm, as many farmers did. We went without many things, but we did not go hungry, though Mother used to say, with a laugh, that we ate potatoes and beans one day and beans and potatoes the next.

Mother did not like to talk about the depression years, but there is one incident that she did relate to us. When she and Dad realized they would not be able to make the next mortgage payment on the farm, they went together to tell the banker, fully expecting the bank to foreclose. Mother always remembered how the banker looked at Dad and said kindly, "Mr. Kemp, we are not going to take your farm. We know you are an honest man and, if you can just keep up the interest, we will trust you to pay the rest when you can." Mother was so relieved to hear these words, she cried.

Eventually, Dad paid off the mortgage. In 1951, after Bud, Mary, and I were married, he sold the farm. He, Mother, and Jackie, who was 11, moved to Florida. Mother began to take art lessons, and Dad joined a horseshoe club. They loved their life in Florida and lived to celebrate their fiftieth wedding anniversary with their children, grandchildren, and friends. Dad was almost 80 when he died, and Mother lived to be 92.

As for my siblings, Jack is still working, and the rest of us have retired. We have all been fairly healthy, successful in our chosen fields, and happy in our marriages. We realize now that growing up on the farm had advantages that were beneficial to us later in life, though we took them all for granted at the time.

(1) We had plenty of "togetherness," that important ingredient of family life which psychologists loudly bemoan the lack of in today's society. We ate together, worked together and played together.

(2) We did not lack role models. They were always with us. In our family, the girls helped Mother in the house, and the boys helped Dad on the farm. Bud was driving a tractor at the age of nine. When I was 11, Mother was sick for two or three weeks, and I did all the cooking.

(3) We had structure. Our home life was stable. We knew what was expected of us and what to expect from our parents. We felt safe and secure.

(4) Because we had to "make do" with what we had, we learned to be resourceful and creative.

Mother and Dad's attitude toward life in general was another plus: Do the best you can with what you have, and move on. Don't complain. Be honest and fair. Help people when you can. Find humor in every situation. Have fun along the way. Sing!

Boot Camp

It was 5:00 p.m. on May 15, 1943. There were seven of us, all young women, in that little Navy Recruiting Office in Cincinnati, Ohio. We stood tensely erect as a Navy officer read meaningful words in a deep monotone voice, pausing after every phrase and waiting for us to repeat it after him. We held up our right hands and solemnly swore to defend the United States of America against its enemies.

We were proud and starry-eyed with patriotism as the Commander shook hands with each of us and welcomed us into the United States Navy, Women's Reserve. In my mind's eye, flags were flying while a girl in Navy blue raised a white-gloved hand in salute.

A month later, I reported to Hunter College in New York City, the Navy "boot camp" for WAVES (Women Accepted for Voluntary Emergency Service) to which I had been assigned.

Once inside the gates of Hunter College, the severing of civilian ties was so abrupt and so complete that it is impossible for me to describe the rapid transition that took place. We quickly learned to "hit the deck" at 0445, to swab the decks on midnight watches, and to march endless miles in the hottest summer New York had seen in seventeen years.

First of all, we were given complete physical examinations and measured for uniforms and shoes. Then there were the shots, which made some of the girls sick, but I was amazingly healthy. I never missed a class, a drill, or a meal because of shots, a cold, or athlete's foot—the three most common reasons for reporting to Sick Bay.

One of the first Navy terms we learned was *muster*. It means: *Gather outside your barracks and get into platoon formation as soon as possible!* The first time we met to drill, our instructor arranged us in marching position, and that position never changed. We always knew exactly where we were supposed to stand when muster was called. We mustered in the mud and in the rain. We mustered in the bright June sun at midday, and in the darkness of 0500. There was no excuse for late muster or false muster. We mustered and marched to every activity on the station—to drill, to the Mess Hall and to classes. We mustered and hupped to chapel on Sundays and to Happy Hour every Monday evening.

It was the policy of the activity director that one night a week be spent in regulated recreation. This was called Happy Hour. Every Monday evening we mustered at 1930 and marched to the recreation hall to sing. We sang the traditional Navy songs and those that had been written especially for Waves. Under the direction of a perpetually smiling young Ensign, we sang and sang until we were hoarse, then mustered and hupped back to our barracks, singing as we marched. We fell into our bunks, weary in body, but renewed in spirit, happy to be serving our country and the U.S, Navy—at least, for another day!

Every day except Sunday, we had classes to learn how the Navy operates, from the Commander-in-Chief down to the lowly seaman. We learned the names, ratings, and symbols for the various Navy jobs held by enlisted personnel—Pharmacist's Mate, Yeoman, Storekeeper, Boatswain, etc.—and also the ranks of officers, their responsibilities, and how to salute them. We learned to identify the different kinds of Navy ships and planes, and memorized the Navy terms that were thrown at us helter-skelter: head, hold, gear, deck, ladder, bulkhead, galley, port, starboard, and many others. We quickly learned terms like "Pipe down!" and "Carry on!" We became accustomed to being addressed as "seamen" and came to love and admire our own beloved Captain McAfee.

Drilling took place on the drill field every day, rain or shine. A Marine sergeant barked orders at us, "*Hup*, two, three, four! *Hup*, two, three, four! *Hup*, right, *Hup!*" He was so gruff I used to wonder if he was angry because he was sent to train lady sailors instead of fighting the Germans overseas. He never smiled, but we were so afraid of him that we quickly learned what he wanted us to do. It was all very confusing at first, but as we got better at it, we came to appreciate the beauty of marching in step and moving in unison.

Another thing we learned was to eat the Navy way. This procedure is called, appropriately enough, Mess. We lined up for our meals, served on heavy, stainless steel trays which were always a little greasy, wet and hot from their recent dunking in hot water. Drinks were served in heavy white handleless mugs. We gulped our meals in 15 minutes in order to make room for the next platoon. Then we scraped what was left into the garbage barrel, swished our trays up and down a few times in the "dunking can" (a garbage can filled with soapy water), stacked it in a pile with the others, and hurried out to muster for the next class.

After about ten days into our training, our regulation gear came in—white blouses, Navy blue skirts and hats, black shoes and ties, and light cotton hose. We began to wear them immediately, and what a change it made, in our spirits as well as our appearance! Suddenly, it was a thrill to see a platoon practicing on the drill field in uniform, and know that I was part of the U.S. Navy. I was proud to be a Navy Wave and I felt ready to serve my country wherever the Navy sent me.

Then, surprisingly, we were allowed a day's liberty. We were all very excited to get outside the gates of Hunter College, to see New York City, and to appear in public in our new Wave uniforms! My four roommates and I stuck together the entire day. We crowded onto the subways, visited Radio City, the Empire State Building, and the Statue of Liberty. We rode on the top deck of a Fifth Avenue bus, viewed the city from the top of Rockefeller Center, and visited St. Patrick's Catholic Church, which made a lasting impression on me. Waves packed the buses going back that evening, and we had to run to get inside the gates before 2200.

Then one day we came back from drill to find orders posted on the quarterdeck bulletin board. Our training was coming to an end. My roommates and I would all be going to different locations, and I would be the first to leave. The Navy was sending me to Yeoman Training School in Stillwater, Oklahoma to learn how to do secretarial work the Navy way.

My loyal roommates got up with me in the pre-dawn darkness to see me off. We exchanged addresses, wished each other "smooth sailing" and promised to keep in touch. Then I joined the dark forms mustering outside with raincoats, havelocks, and duffle bags. There was a light drizzle and we talked in hushed whispers as we awaited further orders.

When the officer in charge arrived, we hupped down the hill to the subway station in platoon formation. No longer Apprentice Seamen, now Seamen Second Class, we were happy to be leaving boot camp behind, and very excited about our new assignments. Eager to move on to further training and new responsibilities, we boarded the subway to Union Station.

Rosemary

Rosemary was my Wave bunkmate when I was stationed in Washington, D.C. during World War II. Her humor was the corn-fed type, her conversation was filled with Missouri idioms, and her homely philosophy was nothing short of soul-building.

Rosemary's reasons for enlisting in the WAVES were twofold: to bring her husband back from Italy sooner, and to help President Franklin D. Roosevelt win the war. Her loyalty to these two never wavered. Even in the darkest days of near defeat, she knew that, with President Roosevelt at the helm and Charles in the Army, the Germans could never win.

Rosemary's loyalty to the Navy was unfailing; yet no uniform on earth could take away her femininity, and no amount of drilling could give her a military stride. She was short and curvaceous, with a round face, green eyes, and long eyelashes. Her thick brown hair was always a little longer and her skirt a little shorter than regulation. She had two vanities—her legs and her eyelashes—and she pampered them both.

Every morning, before going to work, Rosemary curled her eyelashes, holding the little metal gadget tight against her eyelid. The result of her untiring patience was a combination of a dewy-eyed Kewpie doll and a frightened rabbit. Her shapely legs she clothed in the sheerest hose. "Charles might come home at any time," she used to say, "and I want to look nice."

Rosemary clung hopefully to the idea that Charles might come home at any time. For three consecutive years, she believed with all her heart that her husband would be home for Christmas, and for three consecutive Christmases, Uncle Sam held him in North Africa, Germany and Italy. No wife was ever more faithful. We used to see her after taps, sitting out in the hall under the blue night light, in her pink pajamas with her hair up, writing her daily letter to Charles. Sometimes on Sundays, she would sit in her top bunk with a box of chocolates, curled up with her flowery stationary and two pillows behind her, to write the never-neglected letter. Writing every day was not a duty, Rosemary said, but a pleasure. She looked forward to it, because it was "like a little talk with him."

"Everything that happens," Rosemary used to say, "happens for the best, if you just wait long enough." And so she bought dainty underclothes and stored them in her closet in preparation for Charles' homecoming, and turned her eyelashes up each morning and let her hair grow as long as the rules would allow because Charles liked it long. She always talked as if he might arrive in the next day or two. I think God could not have allowed the enemy to harm Charles in the face of her shining optimism.

Rosemary loved pretty things, and our cubicle took on a festive air when she moved in—a lacy scarf, flowers on the windowsill, an embroidered pillow. She was always sweet-smelling. She sprinkled cologne in her hair, behind her ears, in her closet and her bureau drawers. Our cubicle looked and smelled like Rosemary.

Rosemary was by nature a happy, loving, outgoing person. She loved her husband and her family, loved her job in the Navy Department and loved life in general. She had a simple, childlike faith in the Bible and believed that the world is good and God is forgiving. She had a dream-child she called Joan (pronounced Jo Ann, she explained). Joan was the baby she would have when the war was over. "I'll tell Joan about this some day," she would say, or "I'll save this for Joan." Joan came to mean a symbol of peace—V-J Day, Charles, and a home of their own—all rolled into one.

The war is over now, and Charles is home. Rosemary is wearing house dresses in a little cottage in Independence, Missouri. Joan has not arrived yet, but Joan's older brother, Denny, is learning to walk. As Rosemary would say, "Everything that happens, happens for the best, if you just wait long enough."

—December, 1946

Honolulu

Honolulu sprawls low and lazy in the sun. Brown-skinned *kanakas* with bright shirts and white teeth gather on street corners and speak in soft pidgin English. Inside his little shop, an old Chinese gentleman sells fat jade Buddhas, ivory chopsticks, spicy incense and silver good luck charms. Down the side streets are the tattoo shops and the penny arcades. At the pier, native women in white *holokus* bargain for red salmon. The smell of Honolulu is the smell of fish and the bodies of too many people.

Dusk in Honolulu is cool, cool. The sun dips down behind the Pacific. The old Chinese gentleman carefully locks his shop and goes home to his wrinkled wife. Little brown children come out of red-tiled houses and sit on doorsteps—round-faced little girls with black bangs and solemn little boys with slant eyes and big teeth. The men come home from work. The women go indoors. Quiet are the streets of the city, quiet except for the narrow alleys where the rouged women live.

Night falls in Honolulu. The city sleeps. A great orange moon cuts a streak of silver across the sea. In the melting pot of the world, the white and the yellow, the brown and the black alike lie down. In their houses of thatch or stone or wood, in their huts, and beneath the red-tiled roofs, they all sleep. The *Pali* is black against the sky. Old Diamond Head stands guard over the island, gaunt and solemn in the moonlight.

The Burning Schoolhouse

School of my childhood days,
I shall never see thee more.
I view thy shattered ruins
And think of days of yore,

The days we spent together,
And the happy hours of play;
But the doors were closed forever
On the thirteenth day of May.

The cruel flames leap higher.
The crumbling ruins fall.
The shuddering crash that follows
The tottering high brick wall.

It is gone, but not forgotten,
The school we loved so well.
Now 'tis a mass of ashes,
For it burned, crumbled and fell,

A mingled mass of cinders,
A tumbling broken beam…
I would that I might wake again,
And find 'twas all a dream!

—*The Charlestown Courier*, May 1935,
Charlestown, IN

(This poem appeared anonymously in a local paper after our schoolhouse burned to the ground on the last day of school. I was a freshman then. Recently, a friend sent it to me, certain that I wrote it, so I include it here.)

Autumn

There is a stillness settled
On the earth today,
A gentleness that stirs
With every stirring breeze.
The noiseless wind
Treads softly now,
Softly through the trees.

Down the street
Walks, dreamy-eyed,
A solitary girl.
Upon my maple trees,
Gold leaves, withered, die,
And thin smoke wanders faintly
In a blue curl.

On Meeting Mrs. G.

I wish that I were 31
With black, braided hair,
And mascara,
And a sleek evening gown,
Smoking cigarettes,
Dignified and tall.

I wish I knew what to say at parties,
And how to play bridge,
And never blushed.

I wish I had a straight nose
And black eyebrows,
And no curls
And smiled slowly,
And laughed softly.

I wish I could be poised and sedate
Like Mrs. G.
And thirty-one
Instead of sixteen.

Sonnet

When I look above at night, won'dringly,
I think that it is comforting to know
A million people watch these stars with me.
I almost touch the moon, it hangs so low.
The Big and Little Dipper and the Bear,
The sparkling evening star I love the most,
The self-same stars that glow so brightly here
This night are shining on the western coast.

The gentle hand of God, who placed with care
Each silver star, the crescent moon, and sun
O'er-reaches woods and sea and desert air,
Embracing all the universe as one.
As this wide scope of blue brings peace of mind,
So God imparts his love to all mankind.

Spring

Little yellow buttercup,
Standing all alone,
Barest branches all around
Autumn leaves still on the ground,
Sign that winter's gone.

Summer Night

The pale green moon
Stands coldly aloof
Among the bright warm stars,
Like a proud mistress,
Haughty, majestic,
Observing the pretty young creatures
Lately come into her master's harem
Jealously.

The First Snow

When from his ivory palaces,
The good Lord bent his head,
The earth was drab and bare below.
The leafless trees stood dead.

Then long he sat in thought. "My work
Is not complete," he said,
"For there is something lacking
In this world that I have made."

He gently drew the wind aside
And bid it cooler blow.
He gathered raindrops from the clouds,
And wafted them below.

He looked upon the barren earth,
And watched his magic grow,
And then he smiled and was well pleased.
He had created snow!

All Through the Night

At 2200, when Taps I hear
Across the evening air,
I climb into my upper bunk
And slowly swelter there.

I roll my pink pajama legs
Way up above my knees,
And hang my head across the side
To get a little breeze.

I turn my pillow to and fro
To get the cooler side,
And close my eyes and feebly pray,
"Oh, Lord, with me abide."

To turn my mind to other things,
I conjugate *sit* and *set*,
And hup, 2, 3, 4, hup, 2, 3, 4
While I sweat and sweat and sweat.

At 2300, I decide
To pivot in my bed,
And so I place my weary feet
Where used to be my head.

At midnight, I am dreaming
Of Indiana hills.
At last, I'm snoring softly
And sweating off salt pills.

LOVE MAKES THE RIDE WORTHWHILE

So very peacefully I'm stretched
Across my upper bunk
When Shipmate gets off duty—
Clankety-clank, clunk, clunk!

Then once again I concentrate
On getting back to sleep.
I spend a weary hour
Counting Oklahoma sheep.

So now 'tis dawn and I'm awake.
The stifling night is past.
With morning breezes on my cheek,
I go to sleep at last.

But not for long, for Matey cries,
"Now all hands hit the deck!"
I hit with a resounding thud,
Seaman Second Class, total wreck!

—*Brightwork*, August 17, 1943
WAVE bi-monthly newspaper
U.S. Naval Training Station for Yeoman
Stillwater, Oklahoma

Plenty Papaya

Oh tell us, please tell us—
The question still remains—
What nutrients or vitamins
This yellow fruit contains,
That the Mess Hall's dietitians
And the Navy's best physicians
Insist and desiah
Our menus requiah
The daily papaya!

We have it for breakfast
In its natural size and form
With lemon, all mellow
And oozy and warm.
At lunch time, we get it
Cut up in dainty chunks,
At dinner, in fruit cups
In funny squares and hunks.
In Mess line, oh my-a,
I smell-a and sigh-a.
I smell-a papaya!

You may have your Hawaiian papaya.
I'll settle for a kiss and a lei.
May be something I've missed,
But I still will insist,
Whatever the natives may say,
That Princess Papuli
Was not so papuli
When she gave her papaya away!

The Lei Lady

Near a stretch of sandy beach
Under a banyan tree,
Not far from the Moana,
Down in Waikiki,

There's a brown wahini,
Wrinkled and little,
Stringing purple orchids
With a wooden needle.

What does she think of
All the day long,
Twining baby orchids
To sell for a song?

She's thinking of the lei she made
For a pretty miss.
She sells it to a sailor lad
Who trades it for a kiss.

Why does she sit and smile
All the long day?
She knows that if you buy her leis
You'll flip your heart away!

Mormon Temple in Hawaii

The temple is square and shining white,
And steps lead up to the hill it's on.
I lose myself in pure delight,
And fill my eyes ere the dream is gone.

Tiny flowers border the walk.
The grass is a rug of liquid green;
The tropical breezes seem to say,
"This spot is holy. This spot is clean."

Long cool pools in a stairstep row,
Are scrubbed as white as a whitewashed bowl.
Their crystal water beckons me
To take a dip and refresh my soul.

The Geode Speaks

Do not reject me
Because I am bumpy and ugly
On the outside.
You do not see how beautiful
I am on the inside.
If you break me open,
You will find clear crystals
That sparkle in the sun
Like diamonds.

The human brain
Is somewhat like me.
Within it are the capabilities
Of creating incredible beauty,
Of projecting ideas and visions
That are magnificent,
Deep and noble.

The human brain is complex
And impossible to duplicate,
An intricate creation,
Made according to Divine plan
And purpose,
Like the geode.

There is no other geode
In the universe
Exactly like me,
Nor will you find two human brains
Exactly alike.
Look upon us with awe
And treat us with respect.
We have been created
And perfected
By the hand of God

On Taking Psychology 101

Why does writing lines of verse
Fill my heart with great elation?
If it's not ability
It must be motivation!

Whatever from this brain of mine
In black and white emerges,
Springs forth, let me assure you,
From my deep creative urges.

What I used to think was *me*
And my own unique expressions,
I've learned are just an endless stream
Of wild impulses and repressions.

So now at night I shut my eyes,
And try to go on wishin'
When all the time I know that dreams
Are due to inhibition.

I always know, days in advance,
That if I lose or if I win,
There's nothing I can do about it.
It's the cycle that I'm in.

'Tis not a little sad to think
That man must do as mankind must
With his four-fold native traits—
Anger, fear, aggression, lust.

Oh, my days are dull and dreary
Since I've had Psychology.
I've no surprises left in life.
I always know what's wrong with me!

Poets Are Terribly Sensitive People (with Apologies to Ogden Nash)

Poets are terribly sensitive people
And they always want you to know it.
They go around saying how sensitive they are
Because they think that is what makes a great poet.

They do a lot of thinking
About philosophical things like why
God lets human beings live so many years
And lets the flowers die.

They never like to waste their time
On something simple, like a garden hose or a bonnet,
But let them get jilted
And right away they will come up with an ode or a sonnet.

LOVE MAKES THE RIDE WORTHWHILE

The death of a sweetheart is the inspiration
For dozens of manuscripts
To poets who have known it.
In fact, they almost wish for something tragic to happen to them
In order to bemoan it.

Poets are peculiar people
Who sleep with paper and pencil under their pillows at night
And lie awake waiting for an inspiration to strike them,
But they fascinate me because I've always wanted to be one,
And I guess that's the reason I like them.

—*Hill Thoughts*, 1949
Hanover College, Hanover, IN

To My Successor in Office

To you my files I leave, my dear,
With greatest pleasure. Do not grieve,
Though days may oft be dark and drear.
To you my files I leave. My dear,
Though you remain and struggle here,
I send my best regards and leave
To you my files. *I leave,* my dear,
With greatest pleasure. Do not grieve.

—*Hill Thoughts,* 1949
Hanover College, Hanover, IN

(This poem is a triolet, a very restricted verse form, originated by the French, which I experimented with in college.)

College Daze
(with Apologies to Ogden Nash)

When first I came to college,
I thought the purpose of education was learning.
I bought some books and a typewriter and a pair of glasses,
And my soul with ambition was burning.

Being gullible and a bit naïve,
It still amazes me to think that college
Is a place where a lot of other things
Take precedence over knowledge.

It is not enough that, in one week,
I must read 30 pages of Spanish,
And do a term paper and two days of Practice Teaching,
But I must also attend a pledging and a football game,
And decorate for a dance,
So that on Sunday I go to sleep in church
While the preacher is preaching.

It does not matter that my escort tells me
I am charming and bewitching.
I must be thinking of paying the orchestra,
And whether the lights will stay on,
And the punch hold out,
Till when I am home at last,
I go to bed with my tendons twitching.

JANE KEMP BAKER

Soon I will be leaving this place of learning
With my scrapbooks and my dead corsages,
My blue-and-white ribbons,
My black-and-white ribbons,
And my keys and gavels dangling.
If you hear of a vacancy in an English Department anywhere,
Please let me know, because I'm in such a state,
My nerves are all jangling.

—1949

Sonnet to a Friend

When this world's tribulations seemed to be
So suddenly too much for my young years,
I broke away and wept despairingly;
And when I rose to see, through countless tears,
Thy quiet face, I marveled wonderingly.
Why weep I here so miserably alone?
What child art thou that I can never be?
What gifts art thine that I can never own?

Teach me, O gentle one, thy ways of peace
Within the soul. Teach me to stand, like thee,
Serene and unafraid, though never cease
To weep with some poor sister tenderly.
Teach me and let me ne'er forget the art
Of reaching out to ease an aching heart.

Windy Days

Windy days are best for washing.
Pillowcases snap in the wind,
And bleached-white sheets billow and surge.
Colored clothespins stand in a row
Like sentinel birds snipping bites.

I fall into the rhythm of stooping,
Shaking, hanging, and pinning,
Loving the smell of the wet clothes
And the feel of the wind whipping my hair,
Hurrying me along, overturning my basket.

Clothes dry fast on a windy day.
As I take them down,
I crush the wind-dried towels
Against my face
To breathe in their freshness.

A windy day uplifts the spirit
By tossing and turning
And spinning and whirling
Till the chaff blows free.
Hanging up the wash on a windy day
Is good for the soul.

Rainy Days

Rainy days are good for ironing.
When the drops run down my window
In small rivulets,
And the back yard is only a blur
Of wet shrubbery and shallow puddles,
I stand at my ironing board, snug and dry,
Driving the hot iron over wrinkles and seams,
Savoring the toasty smell of fresh-ironed clothes.

Some days are better for doing,
Some for dreaming.
Rainy days are good for both.
My hands busy themselves
With the smoothing, the ironing, and the folding,
While my mind is leaping and cavorting,
Musing and remembering,
Now worrying, now planning, now hoping.

The sound of the rain
Swishing down the gutters
Is music to my ears
As I ponder and iron,
And worry and wonder
On wet drippy days.

Early Snowfall

The snow brings a strange stillness.
I wake in the early morning
To the chill pale light
That sifts through every window,
And slip downstairs
To look at the miracle
The snow has brought
Before even a footprint has marred it.

The children shout when they see it
And Daddy hopes the car will start.
There is much screaming and laughter
And bustling for boots.
With a rush of wind and snow at the door,
They hurry out to sweep the walk
And shovel the driveway.

Then they are back, red-faced and laughing
And dripping on the rug…
A quick breakfast, and off they go again
To work and to school
With their hooded coats and high boots,
Making footprints in the snow
And shouting to their friends.

LOVE MAKES THE RIDE WORTHWHILE

When all is quiet again,
The serenity of the snow surrounds me,
Casts its spell upon me.
A sense of peace engulfs the house
When the snow is deep around it.

Today is a day to do puttering, motherly things
Like finding the ice skates,
And mending the mittens,
Putting a log in the fireplace,
Making hot chocolate,
And filling the house with the smell
Of yeast bread baking.

Printed in the United States
57133LVS00004B/295

www.MCP

Professional

The internet site
that lets you
train on-line
for the
MCP exams

Test yourself

FREE
Demonstration
on the site

C++
programming language

All trademarks quoted are the property of their respective editors.

All rights reserved. No part of this publication may be reproduced, stored in a retrieval system, or transmitted, in any form, or by any means, electronic, mechanical, photocopying, recording or otherwise, without the prior permission of the publishers.

Copyright - Editions ENI - June 2000
ISBN: 2-7460-0983-8
Original edition: ISBN: 2-7460-0729-0

ENI Publishing LTD

500 Chiswick High Road
LONDON W4 5RG

Tel: 020 8956 2320
Fax: 020 8956 2321

e-mail: publishing@ediENI.com
http://www.eni-publishing.com

Editions ENI

BP 32125
44021 NANTES Cedex 1

Tel. 33.2.51.80.15.15
Fax 33.2.51.80.15.16

e-mail: editions@ediENI.com
http://www.editions-eni.com

Translated from the French by Andrew BLACKBURN
Author: Bruno DUBOIS
Collection directed by Joëlle MUSSET

Table of contents

Introduction — Chapter 1

A.	Origins of the C++ programming language . . .	**9**
B.	Going from C to C++	**9**
C.	"Object-oriented" programming	**10**
D.	Environment	**13**

Differences and similarities between C and C++ — Chapter 2

A.	Language elements	**17**
B.	Data types and data declaration	**18**
C.	New operators	**26**
D.	Functions	**36**

C++ programming language

Classes   Chapter 3

A.	Class definition syntax	**56**
B.	A first case study: the Rational class	**60**
C.	A second case study: the String class	**83**
D.	Other principles	**104**

Object-oriented programming   Chapter 4

A.	Deriving classes	**115**
B.	Polymorphism - Dynamic typing	**127**
C.	Multiple derivation	**150**

Streams — Chapter 5

- **A.** Standard input/output **157**
- **B.** Input/output with files **167**
- **C.** Input/output with memory **172**

Templates — Chapter 6

- **A.** Template functions **177**
- **B.** Template class **182**

Exceptions — Chapter 7

A. Introduction **193**

B. Propagating exceptions explicitly **197**

C. Acquiring resources **199**

D. Classes and exceptions **200**

E. Exceptions that are not caught **207**

Appendices

A. Full Rational class **211**

B. Full String class **217**

Index **224**

Chapter 1

Introduction

A. Origins of the C++ programming language 9

B. Going from C to C++ 9

C. "Object-oriented" programming 10

D. Environment 13

A. Origins of the C++ programming language

The C++ programming language was essentially developed by Bjarne Stroustrup of AT&T Bell Laboratories. The first version of C++ appeared in 1983. In 1989, the ANSI X3J16 committee was set up in order to standardize the language. The language has now been finalized.

C++ is largely based on the C programming language. In order to understand this book, **you need to be familiar with the concepts of the C programming language**. Simula67 also inspired the design of C++, particularly concerning the concepts of class, of derivation, and of virtual member functions.

The C++ concepts of templates and of exceptions are similar to those of the Ada and the CLU programming languages.

B. Going from C to C++

The C language was created in the 70s. It offers a number of advantages:
- it is a high level "procedural" language,
- it is suitable for system programming in general, and for UNIX programming in particular,
- it is portable,
- C compilers are generally very efficient.

However, C does have a number of drawbacks:
- C compilers are very lax when it comes to checking data types. This is often a source of problems that are difficult to fix.

– It is difficult to extend the language. For example, although you can define a "complex number" data type, you cannot redefine the arithmetical operators in order to handle these types of object.

Unlike the C compiler, the C++ compiler requires you to define your data types, clearly and precisely. You must define the type of each object (constant, variable or function) before you can use it.

The compiler checks data types thoroughly (by static analysis). However, you can still mix data types for certain "natural" conversions (for example from integer to float).

Thanks to a **function prototype**, your program must specify a **signature** for each of its functions:
– the number and the type of each argument,
– the type of the return value.

For example: `double cos(double)`

This strong typing allows you to **overload** functions. Overloading allows you to use the same name for different functions. The system is able to distinguish between these functions by their signatures.

C. "Object-oriented" programming

"Procedural" type programming languages, such as C and PASCAL, allow you to develop programs using structure mechanisms. These structure mechanisms include:
– **function** (or procedure).
– **user data type**
  With C, this concerns principally structures and enumerations.

- **module**
  This is a specific unit that groups together a set of data (which itself is linked together naturally) and a set of functions that allow you to handle it (with C, these functions are compiled separately).

Object-oriented programming provides the following concepts:

- **abstract data type**
  This is an enhanced user type that allows you to replace the module. It provides data access control and directly integrates functions that allow you to handle this data (with C++, this is the called the **class**).
  For an abstract type T, a type T **object**, is analogous to a type T variable. This is also called an **instance** of T.

- tree structure **of abstract types**
  Suppose that you want to handle different types of polygon. You could create the different abstract types and link them together as follows:

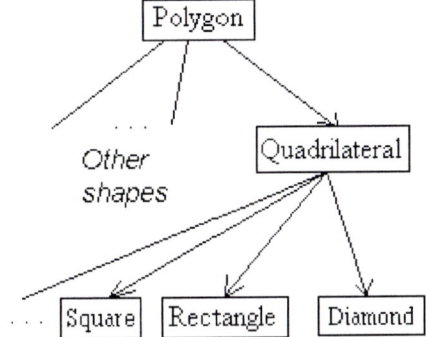

Square is said to be a **derived data type** (it is derived from Quadrilateral).
Quadrilateral is said to be the **base data type** (for Square, Rectangle and Diamond).
Square is also indirectly derived from Polygon, and Polygon is a base type for Square.

The data and the functions that are defined for `Polygon` are called **members** of `Polygon`. Thanks to the derivation process, these members are available automatically for `Rectangle` or for `Square`. This mechanism is called **inheritance**.
In general, you define specific new members for a derived type. However, you can also redefine inherited members.

> In the example above, the types are organized into a tree structure, because they derive from a single data type. This is called **single inheritance**. The first versions of C++ (AT&T compiler version 1.X) offered only single inheritance. Version 2.0 introduced **multiple inheritance**. With multiple inheritance a type can derive from several types. This produces a non-circular, network-type structure.

- **Polymorphism** or **dynamic typing**

    Suppose that you have a quadrilateral instance. How do you know if it is a rectangle or not? Polymorphism resolves such questions.
    In more general terms, suppose that `Tderive` is a data type that derives from the `Tbase` type (either directly or indirectly). Suppose also that `Tbase` has a member that is redefined in `Tderive`. Then, you can handle a `Tderive` type object via a `Tbase` instance, and when you access this redefined member, then the correct version of the member will be called (i.e. that which was redefined at `Tderive` level).

    For example, suppose that you define the `draw()` member that allows you to draw a Polygon. Then, this member is redefined in `Square`, in `Rectangle` and in `Diamond`. Thereby, you have a specific version of the `draw()` program for each particular Quadrilateral.
    Suppose that you have a Square type of object that you can access via the `Polygon` instance "p".

Although `p` seems to be a simple Polygon, when you call the `draw()` member for `p`, then the version that you defined for `Square` will run.
In the terminology of object-oriented languages, such a member is called a **method**. With C++, you implement a method using a **virtual member function**.

D. Environment

Examples that are set out in this book were tested using the *egcs 1.1.2* compiler on *Linux*.
You can call this compiler using the g++ command. A C++ source file can have a name extension of .C, of .cc, or of .cxx.

↓ personal notes ↓

Chapter 2

Differences and similarities between C and C++

A.	**Language elements**	**17**
	1. Comments	17
	2. Keywords	17
B.	**Data types and data declaration**	**18**
	1. Declaring, initializing and assigning	18
	2. Void type	20
	3. Enumeration types	21
	4. Anonymous union	21
	5. Declaring new type names	23
	6. Declaring constants	23
C.	**New operators**	**26**
	1. Overview of new input/output functions	26
	2. Managing the dynamic memory	29
	3. Explicitly converting the type	32
	4. Scope operator	32
	5. Operator priority	35

C++ programming language

D.	**Functions**		**36**
	1. Prototype		**36**
	2. Default argument values		**38**
	3. Inline functions		**40**
	4. Passing arguments		**41**
	5. Returning from a function		**47**
	6. Function overloading		**50**

Chapter 2

This chapter describes how C++ has extended the C language in a procedural programming context. Naturally, these new features are important, as they are widely used in C++ object-oriented programming.
This chapter will also illustrate the different results that the same programming code can have in these two programming languages.
In addition, this chapter will review certain aspects that are rarely used in C, but that are frequently used in C++, such as `const`.

A. Language elements

1. Comments

With C++, you can include comments in two ways.

You can use the classical C notation:
```
/* your comment can be composed of any text,
   and it can extend over several lines.
   The end of the comment is marked by */
```

Alternatively you can use a notation that is specific to C++:
```
// for a comment up to the end of the line
```

2. Keywords

Keywords are reserved words and you cannot use them as identifiers. In addition, as with C, you are strongly advised not to use identifiers that begin with a double underscore (_ _). This is because C++ uses such identifiers, particularly in its standard libraries.

Here is the list of C++ keywords. This list includes all the ANSI C key words. The keywords that are specific to C++ are shown in bold type.

asm	char	**delete**	extern
auto	**class**	do	float
break	const	double	for
case	continue	else	**friend**
catch	default	enum	goto
if	**public**	switch	**virtual**
inline	register	**template**	void
int	return	**this**	volatile
long	short	**throw**	while
new	signed	**try**	**operator**
sizeof	typedef	**private**	static
union	**protected**	struct	unsigned

B. Data types and data declaration

1. Declaring, initializing and assigning

Although this is often the case for the C programmer, as a C++ programmer you must not confuse initializing and assigning. Here are the different cases:

Declaring

```
int n;
```

Declaring with initialization

```
int k=10;
```

This is not equivalent to:

```
int k;
k=10;
```

in which you first declare the `k` object, and then you assign the value of 10 to it. From the point of view of the compiler, when you assign a value to it, then the object `k` exists. On the other hand, when you initialize it, then the object `k` is being created.
As this chapter will describe later, for a C++ abstract data type, you can define, and redefine the initializing and the assigning, and you cannot interchange these two operations.

> With a block of C code, when you start writing instructions, you cannot declare any new objects without opening a sub-block. With a block of C++ code, you can declare an object at any point, provided that your declaration appears before you use the object concerned.

```
void main ()
{
  int n;
  n=0;
  . . .
  you can use n here, but k does not yet exist
  . . .
  int k;
  k=0;
  . . .
  you can use n and k here
  . . .
}
```

In addition, you can declare an object in the initialization part of a `for` statement, and the scope of this object will be limited to the `for` statement:

```
void main ()
{
  int n;
  . . .
  for (unsigned i=0; i<MAX; i++)
  {
    // you can use i here
  }
  // the i variable no longer exists here
}
```

2. Void type

No object can have a `void` type. However, you can use this type in two ways:
- in order to declare a function that has no return value (such a function is equivalent to a procedure),
- in order to declare a generic pointer (`void *`) that is compatible with all other types of pointer.

C++ does not automatically convert from a void * pointer to a typed pointer.
For example, suppose you declare the following variables:
char s[10];
void *ps = s;
char *pc = ps;
Whereas these declarations will run as you want them to in C, with C++ the last initialization will cause an error (although with the egcs compiler it will simply provoke a warning). With C++, you must declare pc as follows:
char *pc = (char *) ps; // type conversion

3. Enumeration types

Thanks to the strong typing of C++, enumeration is a separate type.

```
enum Color {Red, Green, Blue};
Color c1=Red;
Color c2=1;
Color c3=Green+1;
```

The last two initializations will provoke errors with C++. This is because 1 is incompatible with the semantics of the type (moreover, carrying out arithmetic operations on colors may not always be very useful). Here again, you should convert the type if you want to make numbers compatible with colors, or if you want to do any arithmetic with your colors.

 With C, you must declare an enumeration variable as follows:
enum Color c;
With C++, the enum *keyword is optional when you declare a variable, a struct or a union.*

4. Anonymous union

When you have a structure that contains a variable part, then the syntax that you use in order to access a variable in the structure may not be very readable.

```
struct Person
{
  char name[20];
  enum {Married, Single, Divorced} marital_status;
  union
  {
    struct
    {
      char spouse[20];
      Date marriage_date;
      unsigned nb_children;
    } family;                         .../...
```

```
.../...
    // empty if single
    Date divorce_date;
  } information;
};

...

  someone.information.family.nb_children=3;
```

With C, if you want to access the number of children, then you must use the union name `information`. With C++, you can access the variable directly by specifying an **anonymous union**:

```
struct Person
{
  char name[20];
  enum {Married, Single, Divorced} marital_status;
  union
  {
    struct
    {
      char spouse[20];
      Date marriage_date;
      unsigned nb_children;
    } family;
    // empty if single
    Date divorce_date;
  };  // there is no name for the union
};

...

  someone.family.nb_children=3;   // more readable
```

5. Declaring new type names

In both C and C++, you can use the `typedef` declaration so as to define a new name as a **synonym** for an existing type. This technique does not entail strong typing. You can interchange the variables that you declare with either of the two names.

```
typedef double length;
typedef double area;
. . .
length l;
area a;
double add;


. . .

add=a+l;
// adding together an area and a length ???
```

6. Declaring constants

The `const` type modifier indicates that the object that you declare is a constant. When you declare an object in this way you must initialize it.

A simple example

```
const double PI=3.1415926;
```

`PI` is a constant.
Consequently, you cannot include the following line:

```
PI = 3.1415926;  //Error!
```

Pointer to a constant

```
const int *p;
```

*p is a constant.

In this case, only the object that you access via the pointer p is a constant. On the other hand, the object to which p points can be either a variable or a constant:

```
void f()
{
  int i=0;
  p=&i;
  i=10;
  i=*p-4; // i is now equal to 6 (as is *p)
  *p=1;   // error, because *p is a constant
}
```

Constant pointer

```
int i;
int *const p=&i;
```

*p is a constant (hence the initialization).
In this case, you can modify *p:

```
void f()
{
  int j;
  p = 4;   // i is now equal to 4
  p=&j;    // error, because p is a constant
  p++;     // error, because p is a constant
}
```

Constant pointer to a constant

The two cases above can occur simultaneously:
```
int i;
const int *const p=&i;
```

Both `p` and `*p` are constants.

In general

Suppose that you declare the following pointer of a pointer:
```
int *const *p;
```

In this case, `*p` is a constant. However, `**p` is not a constant, and neither is `p`.

The `const` modifier applies to the expression that appears immediately after it.

In addition, you cannot use a pointer in order to change the nature of a constant object:
```
const int i=1;
int *p=&i;    // error!
```

If the language allowed this last declaration, then you would be able to change the value of `i` by using the pointer `p`:
```
*p=0;
```
In order to obtain a pointer to `i`, you must declare your pointer, as a pointer to a constant:
```
const int *p=&i;    // OK
```

 As with ANSI C, a literal character string has the type: `const char *`. Consequently, you must declare your literal character string as follows:
`const    char    *s="literal    character string";` .
Also, you cannot change the value of the string using `s`.

C. New operators

1. Overview of new input/output functions

In order to maintain compatibility with C, the classical input/output functions use the stdio library. However, C++ provides a new library that is called iostream (stream input/output).
The advantage of this new library is that it allows you to carry out input/output operations using operators (these are the << and >> operators), rather than using the basic printf and scanf functions that cannot be extended so that they will function with new data types.
This section provides an introduction to C++ input/output that will be used later on in this book.

Here is an example of an output:

```
#include <iostream.h>

void main()
{
   cout << "a string \n";
}
```

This example produces the following output:
```
a string
```

cout is a variable, and it is an instance of a class. It is analogous to stdout of the stdio library. Similarly, C++ provides the variables cin and cerr, which are analogous to stdin and stderr respectively.

Consequently, to the left of the << operator you can also specify cout and cerr. To the left of the >> operator you can specify cin (in order to carry out an input operation). In addition, you can specify other variables in order to perform file input/output, or memory input/output. The section that concerns stream input/output will cover these techniques.

Chapter 2

To the right of these two operators, you must specify a literal constant or a variable. Thereby, you provide implicit information concerning the type. Consequently, the input, or the output, produces the required result automatically (you need only indicate the type using the % operator, for example).

```
#include <iostream.h>
void main()
{
  const char *s="Line\n";
  const void *p=s;
  int n=20;

  cout << s;
  cout << n;
  cout << '\n';
  cout << "Address of s (in hexadecimal): ";
  cout << p;
  cout << '\n';
  cout << "Address of s (in decimal): ";
  cout << (long)s;
  cout << '\n';
}
```

The above example will produce the following output:

```
Line
20
Address of s (in hexadecimal): 0x8049aa8
Address of s (in hexadecimal): 134519464
```

You can associate the operators << and >> with each other. Consequently you can string together << operators:

```
cout << "Address of s (in hexadecimal): " << p
     << '\n';
```

These operators function naturally with all the predefined types. However, with C++, you can also overload a function (and thereby an operator). This book will describe how you can make the following code:

```
Person someone;

. . .

   cout << someone;
```

produce the following output:

```
Dean
married on 10/12/99
```

by using the information that is stored in the `someone` variable.

Here is an input example:

```
#include <iostream.h>
void main()
{
  char s[20];
  int n;

  cout << "Enter a string: ";
  cin >> s;
  cout << "Enter an integer: ";
  cin >> n;
  cout << "Inputs: \"" << s << "\"and " << n
       << '\n';
}
```

As with C, C++ does not check the type of the input. If you enter non-numeric characters when the program prompts you to input an integer, then the program will simply assign this unexpected value to `n`.

Chapter 2

2. Managing the dynamic memory

As with C, you can manage the program *heap* using the functions `malloc` and `free`. However, this is not advisable. While the `malloc` function dynamically allocates memory, it does not manage the type (`malloc`'s sole argument is the size of the memory zone that must be allocated).
C++ offers two keywords that replace `malloc` and `free`. These keywords are `new` and `delete` respectively. As they are operators, the compiler recognizes them and is able to act according to the type of object that is concerned by the memory allocation.

Allocating

The argument of the `new` operator is the name of the type that must be allocated. The new operator returns a pointer to a zone of memory that can contain this type of object. You can call this operator using two syntaxes: one of the syntaxes must be used for an object, and the other syntax must be used with a table of objects:

```
int *p=new int;
Person *someone=new Person;

unsigned nb_people;

. . .

Person *several=new Person[nb_people];
```

When you allocate memory for basic types (such as `int` and `float`), for structures, or for unions, then the zone that is returned is not initialized. As this book will describe later, this need not be the case with C++ classes.

Although you can dynamically allocate multidimensional tables, `new` does not return a pointer to a pointer: the `new double[10][10]` type is `double (*) [10]`. Consequently, when you allocate memory for several dimensions, the system can evaluate only the first dimension at run time, and consequently only the first dimension can be a variable expression. The other dimensions must be constant expressions that the system must evaluate at compile time.

```
unsigned nb_lines;
. . .
char (*text)[255] = new char [nb_lines][255];
```

In addition, you must not hesitate to use a synonym for the type. This will improve readability, and it will also allow you to avoid repeating the second dimension constant:

```
typedef char Line[255];
Line *text = new Line[nb_lines];
```

Finally, as with `malloc`, the new operator returns `NULL` (0) if it is unable to allocate the memory that you request (this generally means that there is no more space left in the heap).

However, you can specify an error management function that must be used when `new` fails. In order to do this, you can use the `set_new_handler()` function that is declared in `<new.h>`. For example:

```
#include <stdlib.h>
#include <new.h>
#include <iostream.h>

void error_new(void)
{
  cerr << "new has failed: out of memory \n";
  exit(1);
}
                                              .../...
```

```
.../...
void main()
{   set_new_handler (new_error);
    char *p = new char[1024*1024*1024];
      // allocating 1 GB
      // (little chance of success)
    cout << "Allocation was successful \n";
}
```

This program will produce the following output:
`new has failed: out of memory`
and then it will stop (unless the machine has more than 1 GB of virtual memory!).
The argument for the `set_new_handler` function, must be a pointer to a function that does not have an argument, and that returns `void`.
Of course, this function can do much more than simply stopping the program. For example, you can use this mechanism in order to implement a *garbage collector*, so that you do not have to release the memory manually.

Releasing memory

When you apply the `delete` operator to the pointer value that is returned by new, then you release the memory storage that you allocated previously, without changing the pointer value. As with `new`, you can use two syntaxes with delete:
```
delete p;
delete [] several;
delete [] text;
```

You must note that when you release an array, you do not need to specify the size of the array (and you must not specify this size).

 The statement `delete 0` is correct, and has no effect. As will be described later, this technique is useful when you deal with virtual destructors.

3. Explicitly converting the type

With C++ you can use the conversion features of C, and indeed, these are widely used for converting between pointers. However, C++ also provides a new syntax:

```
int i=(int) 3.6;
    // the integer part of 3.6 is assigned to i
```
alternatively, you can use the following syntax:
```
int i=int(3.6)  //which has the same effect
```

4. Scope operator

Here is a C program:

```
struct A
{
  enum E {one, two;}
  struct B
  {
    int value;
  };
  Struct B value;
};

main()
{
  struct A a;
  struct B b;
  enum E e=one;
}
```

Although both the `struct B` type and the `enum E` type are defined within the definition of `struct A`, they have a global scope and could equally well have been defined externally.

You cannot compile this program with C++ because the definitions that are inside `struct A` do not have global scope.

You must specify the scope of the `struct B` type and the `enum E` type before you can use them (and before you can access the enumerated constant name, `one`).

C++ programming language

In order to specify the scope of one of these types you must use the scope operator (::). You must suffix the scope operator with the name of this type, and you must prefix the scope operator with the type that contains the definition of this type. Here is the C++ version of the above program:

```
struct A
{
  enum E {one, two};
  struct B
  {
    int value;
  };
  B value;
};

main()
{
  A a;
  A::B b;
  A::E e=A::one;
}
```

Of course, this mechanism is recursive. For example, suppose you have defined a `struct C` type within `struct B`, and that you wish to declare the variable `c` as a `struct C` type. Then, you must declare this variable as follows:

`A::B::C c;`

Since a class defines a type, it follows that this approach also applies to the definition of a class (indeed, a structure is just a particular sort of class).

In the anonymous union example that was set out earlier in this chapter (in section B.4), suppose that you want to access the `nb_children` field, only in the case where the `Person` type variable concerns a married person. In this case, you could set the nb_children field to 3 as follows:

```
if (someone.marital_status==Person::Married)
    someone.family.nb_children=3;
```

Suppose that you use the same name to identify two different objects, and that one of these objects has global scope, whereas the scope of the other object is local to a type. In this case you can access the object that has global scope by using the scope operator without a prefix.

Example:

```
struct B
{
   int v2;
};

struct A
{
   struct B
   {
      int v1;
   };
   B value1;
   ::B value2;
};

main()
{
   A a;

   a.value1.v1=1;
   a.value2.v2=2;
}
```

You can use the name of a function that has global scope as the name of a class. For example, for input/output, you can redefine the << global operator so that you can use it with instances of the cout class or the cerr class. These are two different functions that have the same name. If the argument types of both functions are identical (and in the same order), and if you want to call the global scope function from within the class function, then you must use the global scope operator (without a prefix) with the name of the function. Otherwise, your call will be recursive.

5. Operator priority

The following table lists all the C++ operators in order of priority. The lines are listed in order of decreasing priority, and the operators that appear on the same line have the same priority.

```
::
() [] -> .
! ~ ++ -- + - sizeof new delete (type) *variable
->* .*
* / %
+ -
<< >>
< <= > >=
== != &
^
|
&&
||
?:
= and all compound assigns
,
```

The unary operators and the assign operator are associated from the right, whereas all the other operators are associated from the left. For example, `a=b=c` means `a=(b=c)`, whereas `a+b-c` means `(a+b)-c`.
The operators `.*` and `->*` will be described later in this chapter.

D. Functions

With C++, a function can have two sorts of declaration:
- you can simply declare the function, thereby providing a **prototype**,
- you can **define** the function by specifying the body of the function (you specify the instructions that the system must execute when the function is called). This includes the prototype name as its **function definition header**.

The function prototype should always precede the function definition (for global functions, the function prototype may appear in the form of an include file). However, if this is not the case then the function definition will automatically imply a prototype declaration.

1. Prototype

With C, a function prototype may be simply the declaration of the function name and the type of its return value. For example:

```
double cos()
```

This means that there is a function that is called `cos` and that this function returns a double floating-point value. It does not say anything about the number of arguments (parameters) that `cos` may have, nor does it say anything about the argument types. On the other hand, the strong typing of C++ obliges you to specify this missing information (which you can also specify with C if you so wish). Thereby, with C++, this prototype becomes:

```
double cos(double)
```

This, then specifies that the `cos` function takes a single argument that is of the double type.

With C++, if a function does not take an argument then you should declare a single argument with the type void. However, if you do not specify an argument then the C++ compiler will also consider that your function does not have an argument. Thus, for the C++ compiler, the first declaration above (`double cos();`) is equivalent to:
`double cos(void);`

The above examples show only the type of the argument. However, you can also specify the name of the argument (as you do in the function definition header where the argument name is obligatory). If you do include an argument name in your prototype, then you include it only for information purposes. You are not obliged to use the same argument name in the function definition header.

Example:

```
ListElement element (List *,unsigned index);
// prototype
. . .
ListElement element (List *l,unsigned n);
// definition header
{
// body of your definition
...
}
```

For the prototype, specifying `unsigned index` is more readable than specifying simply `unsigned`, this technique allows you to provide a comment concerning the function of an argument.

With C, if you do not declare the function prototype, or the function definition, before you call the function, then the compiler will implicitly declare the function as a function that returns an `int` type value, and that takes any number of arguments that can have any types. Again due to its strong typing, C++ will not make such an implicit declaration and will raise a compile error in this case.

Consequently, you must always include the prototype, or the definition of a function, before you call it.

However, you can explicitly declare a function as taking any number of arguments that can have any types using (...):

```
void function (...);
int printf (const char *format, ...);
```

2. Default argument values

Both C++ and ANSI C allow you to specify a default value for one or more prototype arguments. You can do this as follows:

```
void error(int =0);
```

Thereby, you can call the `error` function, either without an argument, or with one argument (of type `int`):

```
error(); // this is equivalent to: error (0);
error(2);
```

This is a simple example, as the function has only one argument. When a function has several arguments then you must respect the following constraint: **only the last arguments in the list can have default values**.

Consequently, you cannot declare a prototype as follows:

```
int f(int,double =0, int, char ='a'); //Error!
```

However, if you have already declared a function by a first prototype, then you can declare default values for other arguments, provided that you respect the constraint that is specified above. For example:

```
int g(int, int =1);
   . . .
int g(int =0, int);
```

The second declaration concerns the same function (g) and specifies that you can also omit the first argument when you call this function later.
You must note this syntax (although it is confusing, it is portable): in the above example the second argument always has a default value of 1. However, you must not repeat this default value, even though some compilers, such as egcs, will allow you to do so.

This technique allows you to use your function in different scopes:

```
void f(int,int);

void scope1()
{
   int f(int,int =0);
   f(1);
}

void scope2()
{
   int f(int =0,int =0);
   f();
}
```

The system calculates the default argument expression, each time that the function is called, and this expression cannot access a local variable:

```
#include <iostream.h>

int a=1;

int f(int);

int g(int =f(a));

void main()
{
   a=2; //  ::a=2
   {
      int a=3;
      cout << g()<<'\n'; // calling g(f(::a))
      cout << g()<<'\n';
   }
}

int f(int n)
{ a++; return n;  }

int g(int n) { return n;}
```

This program will produce the following output:

2
3

3. Inline functions

Many functions that you call very often tend to have very short definitions. In order to avoid loss of performance due to the execution of the call sequence, C++ and ANSI C allow you to specify that the actual block of instructions that make up the function must replace a function call.
In order to specify this, you need only prefix the function definition (and the function prototype) by the `inline` keyword.

```
inline double average(double x, double y)
{
   return (x+y)/2;
}
```

This is a great improvement on the C preprocessor macros, as, unlike these macros:
- an `inline` function is strongly typed,
- an `inline` function has an address and can therefore be pointed to.

However, this declaration is only a suggestion to the compiler, which also has algorithms concerning the trade-off between inline expansion, and call sequences. This functioning is transparent to the user, even if the compiler decides to ignore the `inline` specification.

> In order to be able to expand an `inline` function, the compiler must have access to the instructions that make up the function.
> Consequently, before you call an `inline` function, you must define it in the same compile file. As with macros, you generally define `inline` functions in an include file (with a .h name extension).

4. Passing arguments

Formal parameters

These are the arguments that you use in the function definition header, and in the body of the function. These parameters are also called effective parameters.

```
int f(int i)
{
   int n;

   n=i+1;
   return n;
}                              .../...
```

```
.../...
    ...
void main()
{
   int k=10,n;

   n=f(k);
}
```

In the function `f()`, `i` is a formal parameter (and `n` is a local variable).

Real parameters

You use these arguments when you call the function.

In the example above, `k` is the real parameter that was used when the function `f()` was called.

 The real parameters and the formal parameters may have the same names, but they are not the same objects.

Passing arguments by value

When you call a function, if you pass the argument by its value, then the real parameter is assigned to the formal parameter, and the formal parameter acts as a variable that is local to the function.
Consequently, with this argument-passing mode, if you change the value of the formal parameter, you will not alter the value of the real parameter that is in the calling function.
This is the sole argument-passing mode of the C language.

Chapter 2

```
#include <iostream.h>

void inc(int n)
{
   n++;
}

void main()
{
   int k=10;

   inc(k);
   cout << k << '\n'; // displays 10
}
```

When this program calls `inc()`, this function acts as if it did not have an argument. In fact, it acts as if the local variable `n` were declared as the first line of the function, as follows:

`int n=k;`

However, in some cases, you may wish to modify the real parameter when you modify the formal parameter. C meets this need by allowing you to pass an argument by its address (by using a pointer):

```
#include <iostream.h>

void inc(int *n)
{
   (*n)++;
}

void main()
{
   int k=10;

   inc(&k);
   cout << k << '\n'; // displays 11
}
```

You are still passing the argument by its value: the address of `k` is copied as the value of the pointer `n`.

You can use this technique of passing an argument by its address so as to avoid having to copy the real parameter into the formal parameter. This can be useful if the object concerned is large, as it will improve call performance. In this case, you should declare the formal parameter as a pointer to a constant (if only so that you can pass a real parameter that has a constant type):

```
#include <iostream>

void print_person(const Person *p)
{
  cout << p->name << '\n';
  switch(marital_status)
  {
    case Married:
      cout << "married to " <<p->family.spouse
           << '\n';
      cout << "on " <<p->family.marriage_date
           << '\n';
      // I am assuming that the output (with
      // the << operator) has been defined for
      // the Date type
      cout << "children: " <<p->family.nb_children
           << '\n';
      break;
    case Divorced:
      cout << "divorced on " <<p->divorce_date
           << '\n';
      break;
    case Single:
      cout << "single\n";
  }
}

void main()
{
  Person me;
  . . .
  print_person(&me);
}
```

The above example copies the address of `me` as the formal parameter. If the program had not passed this argument by its address, then it would have had to copy all the fields of the `Person` structure as formal parameters.

C++ programming language

When you pass a scalar sort of argument by value, you do not need to declare it as a `const`. *However, if you do this, then you cannot modify within the function, the local variable that corresponds to the real parameter.*

Passing arguments by reference

Passing arguments by address is messy in C. You need to indicate that you are passing your argument by address in three places:
- in the function prototype (and in the function description header),
- in the function call (using the & operator),
- in the body of the function using the formal parameter with the indirection operator (either * or ->).

C++ allows you to pass your arguments by reference. This technique has the same effect as passing your arguments by address. However, you need only indicate that you are passing your argument by reference in the function prototype (and in the function description header).
This technique makes your program more readable and eliminates a source of error (that of forgetting the operator &, * or ->).

Here is the syntax for passing by reference: for a type T, then you denote the type reference to T, by T&.

```
#include <iostream.h>
void print_person(const Person& *p)
{
  cout << p.name << '\n';
  switch(marital_status)
  {
    case Married:
      cout << "married to " <<p.family.spouse
           << '\n';                    .../...
```

```
.../...
      cout << "on " <<p.family.marriage_date
           << '\n';
      cout << "children: " <<p.family.nb_children
           << '\n';
      break;
    case Divorced:
      cout << "divorced on " <<p.divorce_date
           << '\n';
      break;
    case Single:
      cout << "single\n";
  }
}

void inc (int& n)
{
  n++;
}

void main()
{
  int k=10;

  inc(k);
  cout << k << '\n'; // shows 11

  Person me;
  . . .
  print_person(me);
}
```

5. Returning from a function

A function can return any type except for an array (in this case you must return a pointer to the type of the array elements).
If your function returns a `struct` or a `union`, then a temporary object is created so that the copy can be made:

```
typedef char Name [20];
struct DOB
{
  Name surname,firstname;
  Date date_of_birth;
}

Date mk_date(unsigned year, unsigned month,
             unsigned day);

DOB mk_dob (const Name surname,
            const Name firstname,
            unsigned year,
            unsigned month,
            unsigned day)
{

  DOB res;
  strcpy(res.surname,surname);
  strcpy(res.firstname,firstname);
  res.date_of_birth = mk_date(year,month,day);
  return res;
}

void main()
{
  DOB me;
  me=mk_dob("Dawson","Bruce",1970,9,11);
}
```

When the program executes `return res`, then the program acts just as if it had assigned `res` to a global variable of type DOB, and then as if it had assigned this global variable to `me`:

```
DOB temporary;
DOB mk_dob( . . . );
{ . . .
   temporary=res;   / <=> return res;
}
void main()
{ . . .
   me=temporary;  // <=> me=mk_dob( . . . );
}
```

 The compiler considers the parameters of the type `const name` *to be of the type* `const char *`.

A function call is not an `lvalue` (an object to the left of an assign) unless the function returns a reference or a pointer:

```
int& f(int);

void main()
{
   f(2)=3;
}
```

Although this type of call may not seem to be of much use, it is very useful when you define the indexing operator.

In addition, if the function returns a pointer, then the `*` operator or the `->` operator allows it to be an `lvalue`:

```
struct List
{
   int value;
   list *next_element;
}; // classical linked list

List *element(List *l,unsigned n);
// accessing the nth element in the list l
                                           .../...
```

```
.../...
void main()
{
  List *list=NULL;
   . . .
  element(list,3)->value=10;
}
```

A function that returns a structure or a union with the selection operator (.) can also be an `lvalue`:

```
DOB person[NB_PEOPLE];

DOB element (unsigned index)
{
  return person[index];
}

   . . .

void main()
{
  element(3).date_of_birth = mk_date(2000,1,1);
}
```

However, this example will not produce the required result, as 2000,1,1 is assigned to the `date_of_birth` field of the temporary object, and then this temporary object is lost.

When a function returns a pointer or a reference, you can specify through the pointer or the reference, that the pointed (or referenced) object is a constant.
If the program had declared the `element()` function as follows:
```
const List *element(List *l,unsigned n);
```

then the call:
```
element (list,3)-value=10;
```

would have provoked a compile error.

Finally, you must remember that when a function that returns a pointer, or a reference, then the (pointed) object must continue to exist after you have called the function:

```
int& f(int n)
{
   int res;
   . . .
   return res;
/*
res will cease to exist after this call:
although there will be no compile error, you
will not obtain the result that you require when
you run this program
*/
}
```

The object that is pointed (or referenced) by the return of the function must belong either to the program's static data zone, or to the program heap.

6. Function overloading

Thanks to its strong typing, C++ allows you to overload function names (and also those of operators, which are merely functions with special names.

The compiler must be able to distinguish between several functions that have the same name (it does this using the **signature** of each of the functions).
This means that, when you call an overloaded function, the compiler is able to know which function must be called. This implies the following rule: no two functions that have the same name can have the same signature.

This signature corresponds to the number and to the types of the arguments. Consequently, the above rule rarely causes any problems. The return type of the function does not have any effect on this rule.
However, when you assign a value to a function pointer, then the type of the function pointer and the function (the return type and the signature) must correspond exactly.

```
void Error(const char *message, int number);
void Error(const char *message,
           const Person& to_be_notified);
Person me;
  . . .
  Error("Access denied",10);
  . . .
  Error("Security violation attempt", me);
```

The two `Error()` functions are obviously different here (even though they have a common part), and the signatures are different too. If you declare a further `Error()` function in the same program, as follows:
`int Error(const char * , int);`
then you will provoke a compile error, as you will be attempting to overload `Error()` with a function that has the same signature (even though the return types are different).

> If you use overloading and default values, be careful to avoid any ambiguity:
> `int Error(const char *message);`
> `void Error(const char *message, int number=0);`
> These declarations will not cause any problem because they have different signatures. However, suppose that your next call is as follows:
> `Error("Access denied");`
> Is this a call to the `Error()` function that has a single argument, or is it a call to the `Error()` function that has two arguments (with the second argument having the default value of 0)?
> The compiler will detect an ambiguity and will raise an error.

Finally, here is an example that illustrates the operation of the pointers of overloaded functions:

```
void f(int); // f1
void f(double); // f2

int g(int); // g1
int g(double); // g2

typedef void (*PF1)(int);
typedef void (*PF2)(double);

PF1 p1=f; // p1=f1
PF2 p2=f; // p2=f2

PF1 pe1=g;
  // Error: g1 does not have the right return type
PF2 pe2=g;
  // Error: g2 does not have the right return type
```

Chapter 3

A. Class definition syntax ... 56
1. Class members ... 56
2. Member access control ... 57

B. A first case study: the Rational class ... 60
1. First definition ... 60
2. Constructing a Rational class ... 64
3. Initializing and assigning a Rational class ... 67
4. Converting ... 67
5. Overloading operators ... 70
6. Incrementing/decrementing ... 78
7. Rational input/output ... 80

C. A second case study: the String class ... 83
1. Constructing and destructing ... 83
2. Table of instances ... 86
3. Initializing ... 87
4. Assigning ... 89
5. Compound assignments ... 91
6. Using the index operator to modify data ... 93
7. String input/output ... 94

Classes

C++ programming language

8.	Further points concerning operator overloading	94
9.	Resolving the overload	96
10.	Instance of a class that is a member of another class	101

D. Other principles 104

1.	Initializing references	104
2.	Pointers to overloaded functions	106
3.	Pointers to members of a class	107
4.	Overloading the -> operator	110

Chapter 3

A class is an implementation of an abstract data type that is defined by the programmer (user type).

The class is an extension of the C `struct`. You can define a class using the `class` keyword.

The class introduces three new features:
- You can store data fields in the C structure. This data is called **member** data. With classes, not only can you use such fields, but you can also declare functional fields, which are called member functions. A member function defines a method (set of operations) that must be allowed on objects of the class data type.
- Encapsulation: Encapsulation controls access to the structure members (data and functions). You can define members that are visible to the whole program (**public members**) and you can define other members that will be visible only for the member functions of the class (private **members** or protected **members**).
- You can create, initialize and delete data type objects that you defined previously (such an object is called an instance).

When you define a class, you are defining a new user data type. Internally, in the system memory, the class is merely a list of the underlying data representation is called an underlying C construct. This means you cannot access this structure directly because of the encapsulation, but you can access this structure indirectly via member functions. A classical C structure that defines no member functions is an underlying C structure of itself.

The member functions represent the operations that can be carried out on the object. The encapsulation defines the visibility of the members and of the operations.

A class defines a new data type (user type definition). Consequently you can create instances in any of your data constructions. You can also use pointers to your class, you can construct classes from other classes (use classes so as to define other classes, derived classes).

C++ programming language

A class instance has its own copy of the class's member data, and judging from the call syntax, you might imagine that the instance has a copy of the member functions. However, the system does not duplicate the code of these functions for each instance (it maintains a single copy of this code). In reality, the system applies member functions to an instance and the functions use the member data that belongs to the instance.

A. Class definition syntax

```
class Class_name
{
private:
// member declaration
protected:
// member declaration
public:
// member declaration
};
```

1. Class members

Member data

You must declare a field, using its type and its name.
For example:
```
unsigned nb_children;
```

Member functions

You must specify the prototype.
For example:
```
void married_to(Person);
```

Chapter 3

Alternatively, you can declare a full definition of the function by defining the body of the function instead of the prototype. In this case the system will consider it as an inline function.

2. Member access control

You can control access to members using the private, protected and public sections that are included within the class definition.

Private section
You can access members that are included in this section only from within a member function of the class (whatever the access control section of the member function).

Protected section
As with the private section, you can access members that are included in the protected section from within the member functions of the class. However, you can also access these members from within the member functions of derived classes.

Public section
You can access the members that are included in the public section from anywhere.

As a first access control application, you may wish to allow read-only access to functions that are not members of the class:

```
class control1
{
private:
  int private_value;
public:
  int value()
  { return private_value; }
  /* As you are in the body of a member function
     of control1, then you can access
     private_value.                          .../...
```

```
.../...
      In addition, as you have defined the body
      of this member function within the class
      definition, then this is equivalent to
      defining this member function externally
      with an inline prefix.
  */
};
```

Here is the declaration of an instance of `control1`:

```
void main()
{
  control1 instance;

  . . .

  cout << instance.value();
  // Displays the private_value member data
}
```

As this program demonstrates, the member function exists only via an instance. This is also true for the member data that you access via the fields of a structure.

This example does not cover the initialization of `private_value`. You can initialize this value only within a member function of `control1`. You will see later how you can initialize this value using the class constructor when you declare an instance.

The following example shows how you can constrain member data values (so that they must be between 0 and 10, for example):

```
class control2
{
private:
  int data;
public:
  void constraint_error();
  void set_data (int val)
  { if((n<=1)&&(n<=10)) data=val;
    else constraint_error();
  }
  int get_data() { return data; }
};
```

This example shows that a class declaration is similar to a structure declaration (moreover, as a class is a data type, a class declaration is the same as a class definition). In fact the following declaration:

struct structure_name
{
// field declarations
};

is equivalent to the following declaration:

class structure_name
{
public:
// declarations of member data
};

because the keywords struct *and* class *are optional when you declare a variable. Moreover, with C++, you can include member functions within a structure.*

B. A first case study: the Rational class

This example represents rational numbers in order to illustrate several ways in which you can define and use classes.

1. First definition

You can represent a rational number by a pair of integers (a numerator and a denominator). In C, this is represented as a structure that contains two integer fields.

In C++, you can use a class for which the underlying C structure contains these two fields.
Here is a first approach to defining this class:

```
class Rational
{
protected:
   int num;
   unsigned denom;
public:
   int numerator() const;
   unsigned denominator() const;
};
// Defining the member functions
int Rational::numerator() const
{
   return num;
}
int Rational::denominator() const
{
   return denom;
}
// Declaring and using the Rational object
void main()
{
   Rational r;
   int n;
   . . .
   n=r.numerator();
   . . .
}
```

Chapter 3

Here are a few remarks on this definition:

This example has set the access control level to `protected` for the two data items concerning the pair of integers `num` and `denom`. This is because they are not confidential fields. Consequently, if you want to use this class, then you can create a new class that is derived from it. You can then access these two items of member data from the member functions of your derived class.
Of course, the instruction `n=r.num;` in the `main()` function will provoke an error.

The two member functions allow you to read the values of the member data. You can call these functions by applying the structure selection operator.

You must note that you can call a member function only via an instance. A side effect of this rule is that, in addition to any parameters that it may have, each member function has a hidden parameter that points to the class:
`Class_name *this;`
You can refer to this pointer within the function. `this` simply points to the instance that you must use in order to call the function.

When you use the `const` keyword as a suffix to a member function prototype, you imply that you cannot modify any of the data members of the instance that you use in order to call the function. This has the same effect as declaring the hidden parameter as follows:
`const Class_name *this;`
This feature allows you to call the member functions for the constant instances of `Rational`. If you do not indicate the `const` suffix, then the following code will provoke an error:

```
void main()
{
  Rational r;
  const Rational cr=r;
  int n;
                                    .../...
```

```
.../...
   n=cr.numerator(); // Error!
}
```

You must remember that when you act in this way then you will change the constant nature of the `cr` object (via the `this` pointer).

Given the information above, here is the translation of the previous program into C:

```
struct Rational
{
   int num;
   unsigned denom;
};

// Defining the functions that use Rational
int numerator(const struct Rational *this)
{
   return this->num;
}
unsigned
   denominator(const struct Rational *this)
{
   return this->denom;
}

// Declaring and using the Rational object
void main()
{
   struct Rational r;
   int n;

   . . .
   n=numerator(&r);

   . . .
}
```

This example clearly shows that when you use a data member within a member function, then the data member is associated with the instance that you use in order to call the function.

Concerning the definition of the member functions, the syntax of the function header repeats the prototype that you declared when you defined the class. You must prefix the function name with the name of the class followed by the scope operator (::).

As far as the file organization is concerned, you can define the `Rational` class in the `Rational.h` file, you can define the member functions in the `Rational.C` file, and you can define the `main()` function in the `main.C` file. These two .C files must contain the following instruction:
`#include "Rational.h"`

As the bodies of the member functions are very simple (and very short), then you could insert them directly into the class definition without losing any readability:

```
class Rational
{
protected:
   int num;
   unsigned denom;
public:
   int numerator() const;
   { return num; }

   unsigned denominator() const;
   { return denom; }
};
```

They become inline functions. Consequently, you could write the `Rational.h` file as follows:

```
class Rational
{
protected:
   int num;
   unsigned denom;
                                           .../...
```

```
.../...
public:
  int numerator() const;
  unsigned denominator() const;
};

inline int Rational::numerator() const
{
  return num;
}

inline int Rational::denominator() const
{
  return denom;
}
```

Do not forget that when you write your programs in this way then you will need to recompile a lot of modules each time that you modify the body of a function (in fact, you will have to recompile all the modules that include `Rational.h`). On the other hand, if you separate the definition of the class from the definitions of the member functions, then when you modify the body of a function, then you will have to recompile only `Rational.C`, and then link all the programs that use the Rational class.

2. Constructing a Rational class

The Rational class definition that is set out above will allow you to declare the instances. However, these instances will contain a value that you cannot control because you do not have write access to the data members that are protected.

C++ allows you to construct and to initialize an instance using special member functions that are called **constructors**.

A constructor is simply a member function that bears the same name as the class and that does not have a return value. A constructor generally has public access control. You can define several constructors by using the overload technique.

You can use a constructor in order to enhance the `Rational` class as follows:

```
class Rational
{
protected:
   int num;
   unsigned denom;
public:
   int numerator() const;
   unsigned denominator() const;
   Rational(int =0,unsigned =1);
};

// simple constructor body
Rational::Rational(int n, unsigned d)
{
   num=n;
   denom=d;
}
```

You must note that the constructor is a function, and consequently you can take advantage of function declaration features such as overloading and parameter values by default. In the example above, the constructor has been designed so that it will define the rational number 0/1 when you call it without any parameters.
But how and when do you call a constructor?

The system creates a call to a constructor automatically when it creates an instance. In addition, there are three instance declaration cases in which the system creates objects at other times:
— when you declare static objects outside of all the blocks, then the system will create these objects when you launch the program,

- when you declare static objects in a block, then the system will create these objects when it starts running the block concerned,
- when objects must be allocated dynamically, the system creates them when it runs the `new` instruction.

You can specify the parameters of the Rational constructor as follows:

```
Rational r1(1,2);  // r1=1/2
Rational r2(2);    // r2=2/1
Rational *r3=new Rational(1,3); // *r3=1/3
```

If a class has a constructor without an argument then the default constructor will be called. In this case, the constructor has two parameters. However, as the parameters have default values, then the function is the same whether it has 0 or 1 arguments. The Rational *class has a constructor by default. This default constructor allows you to declare instances without specifying parameters:*
Rational r0;   // r0=0/1
Rational *p0=new Rational; // *p0=0/1
If a class has one or more constructors, but it does not have a constructor by default, then you must specify arguments when you create an instance.

Previously in this chapter, when this class did not have any constructors, then C++ simply created the underlying C structure and, in principle the member data values were unknown.

3. Initializing and assigning a Rational class

Remember that when you initialize an object, then you assign a value from an object that has a compatible type:

```
Rational r1(1,2);
Rational r_init=r;     // initializing
Rational r1;

r1=r; // assigning
```

When you declare `r_init`, then it will take the value 1/2 directly. On the other hand, the system will assign 0/1 to r1 when you declare `r1` (at the end of its construction). Then the system will modify its value so that it will be the same as that of `r`.

In this case, everything will run as you expect it to run, as, by default, instances of the same class will be initialized and assigned using a copy of the **underlying C structure**. This is a copy of all the member data whatever access control it may have. This is exactly what you must do in order to initialize or to assign a value to a Rational.

Sometimes however, this default mechanism does not produce the desired results. In this case you can dedicate one member function for initialization, and a second member function for assigning. You will see how to do this in the next class example.

4. Converting

It is useful to be able to convert from, or to, a class. You can do this with C++.

Converting to a class

A **constructor** that has a **single argument** automatically defines a conversion to the class of the type of this argument. In addition, this conversion is said to be implicit because you do not have to declare it before you use it.

In this case, again thanks to default values, the Rational constructor can have only one argument. This implies implicit conversion of `int` to `Rational`:
```
Rational  r=1;
```

Conversion is implicit, as you could have written:
```
Rational  r=(Rational)1;
```
or
```
Rational  r=Rational(1);
```

You must note from this last format that this conversion is clearly the result of a call by the constructor, which creates a temporary object that the system uses in order to initialize `r` (the same technique is used for assigning).

 The systematic, implicit conversion of a constructor that has only one argument is not always advantageous, as you cannot modify its behavior (although, in this case, this feature is very convenient).

Implicit conversion does not mean that you must forget to use explicit conversion. In fact, conversion is implicit only in the case of direct conversion to an instance that you have declared, and conversions do not nest implicitly:

```
class A
{
public:
  A(int); // constructor with one argument
};

class B
{
public:
  B(A); // constructor with one argument
};
                                          .../...
```

```
.../...
A a=0;
B b=a;
B error=0; // compile error!
B ok=A(0);
```

Converting from a class

In order to convert an instance to another type, you must define a member function with the following prototype:
`operator type_name() const;`
Note that `const` is used as a suffix so that you can convert a constant instance. Note also the use of the `operator` keyword, as, in this case, this conversion function is an operator.

The following example converts a Rational to a `double`:

```
class Rational
{
protected:
   int num;
   unsigned denom;
public:
   Rational(int =0,unsigned =1);
   // constructor by default
   // plus int->Rational conversion
   operator double() const;
   // Rational-double conversion
   int numerator() const;
   unsigned denominator() const;
};

Rational::operator double const
{
   return double(num)/denom;
}

Rational r(1,3);

double x1=double(r);
// double x2=r.operator double();
double x2=r;
// you can use the conversion implicitly
```

A conversion operator never has an argument (the instance that you use in order to call it is sufficient). In addition, you must never specify its return type as this is naturally the type to which the conversion is made.

Note that `num` is converted to `double` within the operator body so as to carry out the division on floating-point values and not on integers.

5. Overloading operators

You may wish to carry out classical arithmetic operations in your `Rational` instances. Of course, you can always define addition and subtraction functions, for example. However, it is more convenient, and more readable to use the standard operators: +, -, *, and /. With C++ you can do this using the `operator` keyword: this technique is known as overloading operators.

Overloading by member functions

The unary minus operator and multiplication operator will be used in this example (see the appendix for the other arithmetic operators):

```
class Rational
{
protected:
  int num;
  unsigned denom;
public:
  Rational(int =0,unsigned =1);
  // constructor by default
  // plus int->Rational conversion
  operator double() const;
  // Rational->double conversion
  int numerator() const;
  unsigned denominator() const;
  // arithmetic operators
  Rational operator -() const;
  Rational operator *(Rational) const;
};                                             .../...
```

```
.../...
Rational Rational::operator -() const
{
   return Rational (-num,denom);
}

Rational Rational::operator *(Rational r) const
{
   return Rational (num*r.num, denom*r.denom);
}

void main()
{
   Rational r1(1,2), r2(1,3),r;

   r=-r1;
   // < = > r=r1.operator-();
   // => r=-1/2;
   r=r1*r2;
   // < = > r=r1.operator *(r2);
   // => r=1/6;
}
```

As its name indicates, the unary minus operator has only one operator. Naturally, since it is a member function, this argument is the instance through which you call `operator-()` (the hidden parameter or the this pointer). Because of this there is no explicit parameter in the prototype of `operator-()`.

The multiplication operator has two arguments. However, as the first argument is the hidden parameter, you need specify only one argument (the second argument) in the prototype of `operator*()`.

Here is the member function prototype of binary minus:
`Rational operator-(Rational)const;`

Naturally, the return type of these functions is Rational. Thereby, in the body of these functions you can return directly a call to the constructor. The following body definition will function in the same way and may be clearer.

```
Rational Rational::operator-() const
{
  Rational result(-num,denom);
  return result;
}
```

You must note that the member function is called `operator-()` without any space between the operator keyword and the - sign.

Finally, in the body of `operator *()`, you must note that you can directly access the member data of the `r` parameter, even though it is protected (and you would still have access to the member data even if they were declared as private). This is because you are in a Rational member function and therefore you can access the non-public members of the hidden parameter. You can also access any other instance of Rational.

Suppose that you did not define the conversion operator from `Rational` to `double`. In this case, because of the implicit conversion of `int` to `Rational`, you can write:
`r=r1*2; // simple and readable`
the compiler will interpret this line as follows:
`r=r1.operator *(Rational(2));`
*The conversion operator from `Rational` to `double` will be ambiguous for the compiler, which will find two signatures of the * operator: the rational signature (thanks to implicit conversion) and the signature that is integrated in the language, and that has the following prototype:*
`double operator *(double,double);`
This means that the compiler can understand this instruction as follows:
`r1=double(r1)*double(2);`
In this case, you must note that the overload resolution rule that runs according to the signature clearly illustrates that the function return type has no effect on this signature.

In this case, you do not have `Rational` to `double` conversion. Consequently, if you write the instruction:
`r=2*r1; // simple and readable`
then the compiler will never be able to understand the instruction:
`r=2.operator *(r1);`
This is because the `int` type is not a class and consequently you cannot define a * member operator overload for it.

When you re-integrate the `rational` to `double` conversion into your class, then you must modify the two previous simple instructions so that they will run correctly:
`r=r1*Rational(3);`
`r=Rational(3)*r1;`
This complicates the program and forces the user of the class to specify the conversion explicitly.

Overloading non-member functions

Up until this point, this chapter has defined only functions that are members of a class. However, as a class is a type (according to the C meaning of the term) you can define classical C functions that accept class type parameters, and that return a class instance.
You can define such a function as an operator overload.

In this way, you can define your arithmetic operations as non-member functions:

```
Rational operator -(Rational);
Rational operator *(Rational,Rational);
```

In this case, the prototypes are not declared in the class. You must note that the unary minus operator has an explicit parameter, and the multiplication has its two parameters.

The bodies of these functions are simply:

```
Rational operator-(Rational r)
{
   return Rational(-r.numerator(),
                   r.denominator());
}

Rational operator*(Rational r1, Rational r2)
{
   return
     Rational(-r1.numerator()*r2.numerator(),
              r1.denominator()*
              r2.denominator());
}
```

However, the instruction:
`r=r1*2;`
is again is ambiguous for the compiler because of the `Rational` to `double` conversion operator.
On the other hand, if the `Rational` to `double` conversion operator does not exist, then the following instruction will be perfectly clear to the compiler:
`r=2*r1;`

To conclude therefore, if you have a commutative binary operator, and you use this operator with other types that have implicit conversion, then you should define the overloading using non-member functions.
In this case, it is best to define the unary minus (and the unary plus) as member functions, and to define all the other binary arithmetic operators as non-member functions.

Chapter 3

So as to be free from any trouble that may be caused by the `Rational` to `double` conversion operator, you must define the following non-member functions:

```
Rational operator*(Rational r,int n)
{
   return r*Rational(n);
}

Rational operator*(int n,Rational r)
{
   return Rational(n)*r;
}
```

You can write:
```
r=r1*2;
r=2*r1;
```

Unfortunately, this approach is not very practical as you must write the functions above, and you must also write functions for the other binary arithmetic operators.

Friend functions

Up until this point in this chapter, the operators used the protected member data access functions `numerator()` and `denominator()`.

Such functions are not always available for a given class. Nevertheless, you may need to write a non-member function that must access private or protected members.

You can do this by declaring in the class definition that this (non-member) function is a **friend** of the class. Thereby, this friend function will have read/write access to the private and to the protected members of the class.

The following example illustrates this mechanism by re-writing the * operator of the `Rational` class:

```
class Rational
{
protected:
  int num;
  unsigned denom;
public:
  Rational(int =0,unsigned =1);
  // constructor by default

  operator double() const;
  // Rational->double conversion

  int numerator() const;
  unsigned denominator() const;

  // arithmetic operators
  Rational operator -() const;
  friend Rational operator *(Rational,
                             Rational);
};

Rational Rational::operator -() const
{
  return Rational (-num,denom);
}

Rational operator*(Rational r1,Rational r2)
{
  return Rational(r1.num*r2.num,
                  r1.denom*r2.denom);
}
```

The * operator is clearly not a member function, as its name in the body header does not have a `Rational::` prefix, and its declaration includes two parameters (whereas the member function version would have only one).

In addition, only the class has the right to choose its friends. You declare in the class definition, the prototype of the function that the class will accept as its friend (by simply prefixing the `friend` keyword).

In addition, a class can declare another class as a friend:

```
class Pal;

class Principal;
{
private:
    . . . // private members
protected:
    . . . // protected members

   friend class Pal;
};

class Pal
{
  . . .
 // Pal members
};
```

All the member functions of the `Pal` class can access all the members of the `Principal` class (via an instance of `Principal`).

Note the first declaration, which indicates that there is a class that is called `Pal`, and which you have not yet specified. This is analogous to a function prototype declaration. When you declare:

```
friend class Pal;
```

then the compiler is aware that this class exists.

In this case, if you insert the body of `Principal` function members directly into the specification, then you will not have access to the members of the `Pal` class. The compiler will not find out about these `Pal` class members until later on.

Note that the "friendship" is not reciprocal. The `Pal` class did not declare the `Principal` class as its friend. Consequently, the member functions of the `Principal` class can access only the public members of the `Pal` class.

6. Incrementing/decrementing

You can define the incrementation and the decrementation of a `Rational`. This section will deal only with incrementation, as decrementation is identical.

There are two sorts of incrementation: **prefix** and **postfix**. Here is a C example as a reminder of these two types:

```
void main(void)
{
  int i,j;

  j=0;
  i=++j; /* prefix => j=1 and i=1 */
  i=j++; /* postfix => j=2 and i=1 */
}
```

Note that incrementation is a function that returns a value. C++ allows you to implement these two types with all data types, such as Rational for example.

Incrementation can be a member function or a non-member function (incrementation is generally a member function, as in this case where it will be used so as to modify the `num` and the `denom` data members). The following example introduces the **prefix incrementation operator**, which must **return an lvalue**, and therefore a reference, so as to implement and use the `++(++r);` instruction.

```
class Rational
{
   . . .
  Rational& operator++();
}

Rational& Rational::operator++()
{
  num+=denom;
  return *this;
}
```

The above example defines the prefix incrementation. If you call the incrementation postfix at this stage, the compiler will warn you that the postfix incrementation does not exist and that it will use the prefix incrementation instead. This form of incrementation is enough to allow the code to run, although it will not necessarily do what you want it to do (programmers often call postfix incrementation simply, without using an assign operation, in which case it will have the same effect as a prefix incrementation).

However, you may want to implement postfix incrementation so as to take full advantage of its functioning mode. In this case, **the postfix incrementation must not return an lvalue**. The postfix incrementation signature must be different from the prefix incrementation signature. When the operator++ function takes an additional, integer type argument, then it implements postfix incrementation. Upon each call to this function, this argument equals 0 automatically and is not used.

```
class Rational
{
  . . .
  Rational& operator++();    // prefix
  Rational operator++(int); // postfix
}

Rational& Rational::operator++()
{
  num+=denom;
  return *this;
}

Rational Rational::operator++(int n)
{
  Rational r=*this;
  num+=denom;
  return r;
}

void main()
{
  Rational r0(1,2),r1,r2;              .../...
```

```
.../...

  r1=++r0;  // <=>r1=r0.operator++();
  r2=r0++;  // <=>r2=r0.operator++(0);
  cout<<"r0="<<r0<<'\n';  // r0=5/2
  cout<<"r1="<<r1<<'\n';  // r1=1/2
  cout<<"r2="<<r2<<'\n';  // r2=5/2
}
```

7. Rational input/output

The Rational class will now allow you to handle rational numbers conveniently. You might want to display the value of an instance in a simple way.
There are several ways of doing this:

You can use a member function, or a non-member function, as you can call the access functions numerator() and denominator() that call the C function printf:

```
void Rational::print()
{
  printf("%d/%d",num,denom);
}

void main()
{
  Rational r(3,2);

  r.print();  // displays 3/2
}
```

However, it is better to use the iostream library. In this case, when you define the prototype of operator<< as an output operator for a class, then it is always the same, apart from the name of the class.

This is a non-member function. It must be a friend for the classes that do not have member functions with access to non-public members:

```
ostream& operator <<(ostream& out,Rational r)
{
   out<<r.numerator()<<'/'<<r.denominator();

   return out;
}

main()
{
   Rational r(1,3);
   cout<<r;
   cout<<'\n';
   cout<<"Value of r: "<<r<<'\n';
}
```

When you call `cout<<r;`, `cout` is the real parameter, and `out` is formal parameter, of the `operator<<` function. `cout` and `out` are the instances of the `ostream` class that are supplied by the `iostream` library. This function must return its format output parameter so that the operator will keep its associative nature. In reality, the line:
`cout<<"Value of r: "<<r<<'\n';`
calls `operator<<` three times:

```
(((cout<<"Value of r: ")<<r)<<'\n');
((        cout          <<r)<<'\n');
(             cout          <<'\n');
```

The innermost brackets return the modified value of `cout` (the value is modified, as there is an output). The system uses this modified value in order to run the second level, and so forth. This mechanism explains why the formal parameter `out` must be a reference, and why it must be returned.

Given that `cin` is an instance of the `istream` class, then definition of a Rational input must be immediate:

```
class Rational
{
   . . .
   friend
      istream& operator >>(istream&,Rational&);
}

istream& operator >>(istream& in,Rational& r);
{
   in>>r.num>>r.denom;
   return in;
}
```

The objective is clearly to modify the `Rational` that is passed as a parameter. Consequently, the formal parameter `r` is a reference. Also, as you must modify its protected member data, then the function must be a friend.

Using the `Rational` example, this chapter has now covered the features of a class. As an exercise, you can develop this class in the following ways:
- develop a more sophisticated constructor that will store a rational number in canonical format (the declaration `Rational r(2,4);` must store 1 and 2 in r.num and in r.denom),
- develop the class so that it will cover all the arithmetic operations,
- develop the class so that it will cover the relational operators:
  operator==,   operator!=,   operator>, operator>=, . . .

You must note that defining the operators == and does not allow you automatically to define the operator >=. You must define this operator completely (in general you can do this simply by calling the first two operators).

C. A second case study: the String class

This example concerns a class that requires you to manage memory dynamically (as is frequently the case). This is a study of the `String` class.

As its name indicates, this class handles character strings. The objective is to create a class that will handle strings more conveniently than the standard functions of the C library do.

The internal representation of String (the underlying C class) is an array of characters that you must allocate dynamically. As with C, you will use a null terminated array so that you can use the standard functions on this internal format. In addition, you will store string length information so that you do not need to recalculate it every time that you need it.

1. Constructing and destructing

You will use several constructors. Each of these constructors will allocate memory in order to store the string.
In this way, you will automatically implement the dynamic memory allocation when you declare an instance. You can, and must, do this automatically by specifying the **destructor** of the class.

```
void f()
{
   String s;
   // handling s
}
```

Each time that you call `f()`, the system will allocate the underlying C structure for String. It will then call the String default constructor. When the system reaches the closing brace of the function, it will invoke the inverse mechanism: it will call the String destructor (if it exists) for the instance `s`, and then it will de-allocate the underlying C structure for `s`. Consequently, you must specify the de-allocation of the character array in this destructor.

A class can have only one destructor (whereas you can have several constructors for a class thanks to the overloading mechanism). The destructor is a public member function without a parameter. The name of this function is the name of the class prefixed with the tilde (~) character.

Here is a definition of the `String` class:

```
class String
{
protected:
   // internal format
   char *s;
   size_t len;
public:
   // Constructors, destructor
   String(const char * =0);
   String(char);
   ~String(); // Destructor
   // Access function
   size_t length() const { return len; }
   // Converting to const char *
   operator const char *() const { return s; }
};
```

The `size_t` type is the return type of the standard function `strlen()`.

The first public constructor is a constructor by default (thanks to its value by default). It defines the conversion of `char*` to `String`, whereas the second public constructor defines the conversion of `char` to `String`.

You can declare the following instances:

```
String s;
String s1("string");
String s2="Another string";
String s3('a');
String s4='b';
```

You convert to `const char*` so that you cannot modify the real contents of a String when you carry out a conversion.

The specification of a class is the most important step in the development and analysis in C++. If you implement this step in a suitable way, then you will have done 80% of the work. The rest of the work consists of developing the member functions. This approach produces a program that is more modular (as it runs via a class), more readable, and overall, quicker to produce. It requires an analysis phase, which some C programmers carry out in parallel to the development phase (at the risk of having to revise their data structures).

Here is an example implementation of the member functions:

```
String::String(char c)
{
  len=1;
  s=new char[2];
  s[0]=c;
  s[1]='\0';
}
String::String(const char *str)
{
  if(str==0)
  {
    len=0;
    s=new char(0);
  }
  else
  {
    len=strlen(str);
    s=new char[len+1];                    .../...
```

```
.../...
   strcpy(s,str);
   }
}

String::~String()
{
   delete [] s;
}
```

This chapter has already covered the cases when the system calls a class constructor. In a symmetrical way, the system calls the class destructor at the end of the lifetime of the instance. This can be:
− at the end of the program (for static objects),
− at the end of a block (for automatic objects),
− upon the call to `delete` (for a dynamically allocated object).

In addition, as with all function members, you can call the destructor explicitly, by specifying the name of the class:

```
void trial()
{
  String s;
  String *ps = new String;

  . . .

  s.~String();
  ps->~String();
}
```

2. Table of instances

What happens when an instance table is declared or when an instance table is dynamically allocated? This section also concerns the `Rational` class.

```
String ts[10];
String *ps=new String[10];
```

In order that this will run correctly, the construction mechanism of a class instance must have the following constraint: you must be able to declare an instance without a parameter. This means that, either the class does not have a constructor, or that the class has a constructor by default. Both the `Rational` class and the `String` class meet this constraint.

What happens at the end of the instance's lifetime?

For `Rational`, there is no class destructor. Consequently, a `Rational` table is deleted, cleanly, in the same way as a Structure table. However, when you run the following instruction:
```
delete [] ps;
```
then the `String` destructor is called for each element of the `ps` table (10 times) and it is called once again at the end of the lifetime of `ts`.

3. Initializing

As this chapter has already indicated, the initialization by default is the copy of the underlying C structure. Consequently, when the system runs the following instructions:
```
String s1="abcd";
String s2=s1; // s2 is initialized with s1
```

the data member `s` from the instance `s1` points to the same memory zone as the data member `s` from the instance `s2`! This will certainly not produce the required result.

When you have implemented the mechanism that will modify the contents of a `String` (and that will also modify the dynamically allocated character array), then you will not want to affect `s1` when you modify `s2` (C++ provides the concepts of pointer and of reference so that you can avoid this sort of problem).

You want the member `s` of the `s2` instance to point to its own area of memory. In order to achieve this, you must define a specific initialization for the class. You can do this using a new member function. When you carry out an initialization, you declare the instance. Consequently, the object does not yet exist at this point. This is why the initializer of a class is a constructor (and therefore its name is that of the class). This constructor always has the same prototype. For a class that is called `T`, the initialization member function is as follows:

```
class T
{
public:
  T(const T&); // initializing
};
```

This is also called the **copy constructor**.

Here is a definition of the copy constructor for String:

```
String::String(const String& s0)
{
   len=s0.len;
   if(len==0)
      s=new char(0);
   else
   {
      s=new char[len+1];
      strcpy(s,s0.s);
   }
}
```

Thereby, when you make the following initialization:
`String s2=s1;`

then effectively, you implement the following declaration:
`String s2(s1);`

You must note that the system calls the initialization constructor in three cases:
— when you declare an instance with an initialization (as in the previous example),

— when you pass an argument by value:
```
void f(String);
f(s1);
```
C++ initializes the formal parameter of the `f()` function with the value of the real parameter `s1`,
— when you make a function return by value (as opposed to a function return by pointer or by reference:
```
String error_message(int error_code);

String err1=error_message(1);
```

In the final example above, note that the initialization constructor is invoked twice. Upon return from `error_message()`, the system creates a temporary object and initializes it with the result. Then, the system constructs `err1` using this temporary object.

4. Assigning

As with initializing, when you assign values, then by default, C++ copies the underlying C structure. Consequently, when you run the following instructions:

```
String s1="abcd";
String s2;

s2=s1; // s2 is assigned to s1
```

the data member `s` from the instance `s1` points to the same memory zone as the data member `s` from the instance `s2`! Again, this does not produce the desired effect.

Here again, you must define a member function that will manage the assignment in a suitable way.
This function is called `operator()` and for a class that is called `T`, its prototype must be as follows:
```
T& operator=(const T&);
```

Here is a definition of this function for the `String` class:

```
String& String::operator=(const String& s0)
{
  delete [] s;

  len=s0.len;
  if(len==0)
    s=new char(0);
  else
  {
    s=new char[len+1];
    strcpy(s,s0.s);
  }

  return *this;
}
```

Note that between the first and the last instruction, the body of this function is exactly the same as that of the initialization constructor. This is the case for most classes that dynamically allocate one of its data members when it is constructed.

The first instruction is present because the instance that must be assigned already exists, and therefore you must de-allocate the member `s`.

However, this assignment definition is a bit clumsy, as it is unnecessary systematically to de-allocate the memory in order to ensure that you re-allocate the correct size. You could check first whether or not the memory zone that is already allocated is suitable in order to receive the contents of the assignment. This approach is more efficient.

Here is the explanation for the last instruction:
```
return *this;
```

With C, an assignment is an expression. This means that it returns a value. Because of this, you can string assignments together:

```
int a,b,c;

a=b=c=1;
```

The compiler interprets this statement as follows:

```
a=( b=(c=1) );
```

Consequently, the expression `c=1` must return the value of c.

The assignment operator must return an instance of `String` that is the value of the current instance after assignment. This is the reason for the final instruction in this function.
As `*this` continues to exist after the output of `operator()`, its return type is a reference.

5. Compound assignments

Although this is not yet the case, you can consider that you can concatenate `String` using the binary addition operator `operator+()`. This lets you write the following instruction:

```
String s,s1="ab",s2="cd";

s=s1+s2;  // s="abcd"
```

Moreover, as the assignment exists, can you apply the compound assignment += ?
Unfortunately, this compound assignment is not defined automatically, because of the definitions of `operator=()` and of `operator+()`.
This is the case for all compound assignments.

Here is a quick and simple way of defining += for a class (the class T) on which operator+() is defined:

```
T& operator+=(const T& instance)
{
   return *this = *this + instance ;
}
```

This form is suitable, provided that the assignment for T is suitable (either the default assignment or the explicit assignment).

However, this is not always the most efficient form. It is sometimes preferable to define this operator in a more advanced way so that you can take advantage of the efficiency of the += arithmetic operator. This is a suitable definition for the String class. However, if you implement a Compound class (for compound numbers) then your += operator will be more efficient in the following form:

```
class Compound
{
protected:
   double re,im;
public:
   // Constructor
   Complex(double x =0,double y =0)
   { re=x; im=y; }
   // Access function
   double Re() const
   { return re; }
   double Im() const
   { return im; }
   // Compound += assignment
   Compound& operator+=(const Compound&);
};

Compound& operator+(Compound, Compound);

Compound& Compound::operator+=(const Compound& z)
{
   re+=z.re;
   im+=z.im;
   return *this;
}                                          .../...
```

```
.../...

Compound operator+(Compound z1,Compound z2);
{
  return
    Compound(
      z1.Re()+z2.Re(),
      z1.Im()+z2.Im());
}
```

 The addition operator `operator+()` *is neither a member function of the Compound class, nor is it a friend function of the Compound class. It works very well as it is.*

6. Using the index operator to modify data

In this section, you must designate a character in the string that is contained in a `String` instance using the index operator. For example, you could write the following instructions:

```
String s="abcd";
char c=s[3]; // c='d'
```

However, you want this operator to provide you with write access to a specific character, for example:

```
s[0]='z'; // s="zbcd"
```

In order to achieve this effect you can use function return **by reference**. As this chapter has specified earlier, when a function returns a reference, it returns an lvalue. This property is a useful one in this context.

Here is a definition of the index operator for `String`:

```
char& String::operator[] (size_t i)
{
   return s[i];
}
```

This version does not manage access-errors if `i>=len`.

However, there is one more detail that must be clarified. What will happen with the following instructions?
```
const String sc="abc";
char *c;

c=&sc[0];
```
The compiler will raise an error upon the assignment of `c`, as you are accessing a constant element via a (non-constant) pointer. All the constraint checks are OK.
In order to make all of this work, you must declare the c variable as the type: `const char *`.

7. String input/output

Concerning the output of a String instance, you need do nothing further thanks to the conversion operator: `String to const char *`.

8. Further points concerning operator overloading

C++ defines a certain number of standard operators:

+	-	*	/
%	^	&	|
~	!	,	=
<	>	<=	>=
++	--	<<	>>
==	!=	&&	||
+=	-=	*=	/=
%=	^=	&=	|=
<<=	>>=	[]	()
->	->*	new	delete
..	..	.*	?:
sizeof			

Here are the constraints that are associated with the overloading of these operators:

You can overload all the operators in this list except for those that are underlined. You cannot define a new operator (such as `operator#()`). You cannot modify their priority, nor can you modify their associativity.

The following operators must be member functions:
= [] () ->
You can overload the other operators as friend functions.

You cannot modify the number of parameters for an operator. On the other hand, you are free to change the types of these parameters (for example you do not have to use an integer parameter for the index operator).

On this subject the function-call operator `operator()()` is a special case. There is no constraint on the number of parameters for this operator. By overloading this operator, you can specify any number of parameters (including no parameters).
For example, you can specify a substring extractor for the `String` class as follows:
```
String operator()(size_t start,size_t finish);
```

Then, you can write:
```
String s="1234567890";
String ss;

ss=s(2,6); // => ss="34567"
```

If you redefine an operator then your operator must have at least one parameter that is a user type (`class`, `struct`, `union` or `enum`).

Thereby, you can define a concatenation as follows:
```
String operator+(const String&,const String&);
```

which can be a friend function of the `String` class.
```
String s,s1="abc",s2="de";
```
```
s=s1+s2;
```

However, the following expression is unsuitable:
```
s="abc"+"de";
```

as the compiler will attempt to add together two `char *` types. It will not carry out implicit conversion to `String` on the two operands. In order to achieve the result that you require you must explicitly convert one or both of these operands:
```
s=String("abc")+"de";
```

9. Resolving the overload

When you overload a function (or an operator) and an instruction calls this function, then the compiler will use the following method in order to decide which function it must call:
- Collect information on the number and the type of call parameters (remember that the return type plays no role in this context).
- Search for a function definition signature (with the same name as the function that is called) that corresponds exactly.
- If the above search fails, then the compiler will repeat the same search after carrying out a single conversion that leads to an exact correspondence.

Concerning this conversion, it must be stressed that the compiler has a set of ordinary conversions (these conversions are defined by the language such as `int` to `double`), and it will also use the conversions that have been defined by the user (including those that are defined for a class such as `String` to `char *`). The compiler then, will carry out all the ordinary conversions that it can. It will then carry out the user conversions that it can then combine with its ordinary conversions.

Here are a few examples:

```
class Convert1
{
public:
   // Converting Convert1 to int
   operator int() const;
};

class Convert2
{
public:
   // Converting Convert2 to Convert1
   operator Convert1() const;
};
void f();
void f(int);

void trial()
{
   Convert1 object1;

   f(object1);
}
```

The (user) conversion for the instance `object1` from the type `Convert1` to the type `int` is carried out automatically upon the call to `f()`.

If the instructions that follow the definition of these two classes are as follows:

```
void f();
void f(double);

void trial()
{
   Convert1 object1;

   f(object1);
}
```

then the compiler is able to call `f()` thanks to the combination of the user conversion, `Convert1` to `int`, and the ordinary conversion, `int` to `double`.

On the other hand, if these instructions are as follows:

```
void f();
void f(int);
void f(double);

void trial()
{
   Convert1 object1;

   f(object1);
}
```

Then the instruction `f(object1);` will call the `void f(int);` function without any ambiguity as the compiler will use only the user conversion (the user conversion will be combined with an ordinary conversion only if the user conversion is insufficient). In this case, the compiler will be satisfied with the conversion from `object1` to `int`.

Suppose that you write the following instructions:

```
void f();
void f(int);

void trial()
{
   Convert2 object2;

   f(object2); // Compile error!
}
```

In this case the compiler will not be able to convert `object2` from the `Convert2` type to the `int` type using a single user/ordinary conversion. However, as the conversions from `Convert2` to `Convert1`, and from `Convert1` to `int` exist, you can write the call to `f()` as follows:

`f(Convert1(object2));`

Thereby, you explicitly convert `object2` to `Convert1`, and the compiler will implicitly convert the result of this conversion to `int`.

Naturally, if you define `f()` as:
`void f(double);`
instead of:
`void f(int);`
then the call `f(Convert1(object2));` will still work correctly as the compiler will combine the implicit user conversion with the ordinary conversion of `int` to `double`.

Here are a few remarks concerning pointer or reference type pointers, and their association.

In terms of overload resolution, C++ cannot distinguish between a parameter that is passed by value and a parameter that is passed by reference when the function is called:

```
void f(String);
void f(String&);

String s;

f(s); // Error: ambiguity!
```

However, the compiler can distinguish between a pointer (or a reference) and a constant pointer (or a constant reference):

```
void f(String&);        // f1
void f(const String&);  // f2

void g(const String&);

String s;
const String EmptyString;
const String sc="constant string";

f(s);  // call to f1
f(sc); // call to f2
g(s);
g(sc);>g(s);
```

The compiler will resolve the calls `f(s)` and `f(sc)` and `g(s)` by exact correspondence. The compiler will resolve the call g(sc) thanks to the **ordinary** conversion of `String&` to `const String&`.
In fact, for any type `Type` (either user-defined or language-defined) then the conversion `Type*` to `const Type*` and the conversion `Type&` to `const Type&` are ordinary conversions.

Finally, note that in its definition, the `EmptyString` object is not explicitly initialized even though this object is a constant. In this case the compiler will still initialize this object (as it must initialize all constants) because there is a default constructor for `String` (which assigns an empty string to the constructed instance).

C++ programming language

10. Instance of a class that is a member of another class

Suppose that you want to represent information concerning a person (for example the first name and the surname of the person). One immediate method would be to create a structure that contains two fields with a character string type. You could use the `String` class as the type for these two fields.

```
struct Individual
{
   String firstname;
   String surname;
};

void trial()
{
   Individual me;

   me.firstname="andrew";
   me.surname="blackburn";

    . . .
}
```

What happens when you create an instance of `me`?

The system allocates the members (or the fields) `surname` and `firstname`. Remember that with C++, a structure is a class in which all the members are public members. Consequently, a structure can have function members, and it can also have constructors.

```
struct Individual
{
   String firstname;
   String surname;
   // Constructor
   Individual(String f,String s)
   {
      firstname=f;
      surname=s;
   }
};                                          .../...
```

```
.../...

void trial()
{
   Individual me("andrew","blackburn");

   . . .

}
```

Here again, when the system creates the `me` instance, it allocates two items of member data (String construction by default). Then the system assigns these members to their respective values (de-allocation and re-allocation of the String member s). This approach is not really very efficient (this is not a problem with this example, but it could become one with a class in which the constructors require long execution times). It would be very useful to have a mechanism that allowed the system to call a member data constructor when it allocated this member.

Naturally, C++ allows you to do this. Here is the syntax concerned:

```
struct Individual
{
   String firstname;
   String surname;
   // Constructor
   Individual(String f,String s);
};
Individual::Individual(String f,String s)
   : firstname(f), surname(s)
{ }
```

When the system creates an instance of an `Individual`, it does not call the default constructor, but it calls the constructor that has a single parameter of type `char *` (in the case of `String` this is the same constructor). Of course, although each constructor must have a body, the `Individual` constructor need do nothing. This allows you to specify an empty body for this constructor.

This technique can do more than simply optimizing execution. Firstly, although a class does not need to have a default constructor, this technique provides you with a data member for the class. Secondly, this technique can become essential when you want to construct a derived class, as this chapter will describe later on.

Note that the `Individual` default initialization and assignment mechanisms are suitable. The initialization rule for the data members of a class is as follows:
- if the class has an initialization constructor, then this constructor has full responsibility for the initialization of its data members (notably, this constructor can call the initialization constructors of these items, provided that these initialization constructors exist),
- if the class does not have an initialization constructor, then the system uses the initialization mechanism that belongs to each of the data members of the class.

The assignment rule for the data members of a class is the same.

```
void f()
{
   Individual me("andrew","blackburn");
   Individual namesake=me;
. . . }
```

Therefore, when the system initializes `namesake`, it calls the `String` initialization structure for both data members.

 You would normally use this syntax for applications such as that which is shown in this example. However, you can also use it to initialize any data member of a class (or of a structure). Notably, you can use this syntax with standard type member data. For example:

```
struct Individual
{
   String firstname;
   String surname;
   unsigned age;                        .../...
```

```
.../...
  // Constructor
  Individual(String f,String s, unsigned a);
};

Individual::Individual
        (String f,String s,unsigned a)
        : firstname(f), surname(s), age(a)
{ }
```

In this case, if you had written this constructor body as follows:

```
Individual::Individual
        (String f,String s,unsigned a)
        : firstname(f), surname(s), age(a)
{
  age=a;
}
```

then your program would run in exactly the same way.

D. Other principles

1. Initializing references

Although a reference acts in the same way as a pointer as far as the generated code is concerned, the compiler distinguishes between these items with respect to their initialization.

You must initialize a reference.

```
int i;

int & ri=i;  // OK
int & ri0;   // Compile error!
```

If you initialize a reference with a constant, or with an expression, or if the compiler needs to convert your initialization, then the compiler will create a temporary object, and it is this temporary object that the compiler will reference.

```
int & ri1 = 3;
int & ri2 = i+j
double & rd = 1;  // conversion: rd=(double)1
```

The first case is equivalent to the following instructions:
```
int tmp=3;
int & ri1 = tmp;
```

Also, you can write similar instructions for the next two cases.
The lifetime of this temporary object is the same as that of the reference.

Concerning this subject, the following example shows that you must be careful of this peculiarity:

```
void inc(double & r)
{
   r++;
}
void trial()
{
  double x=3.0;
  int i=1;

  inc(x);  // => x=4.0
  inc(i);  // => i still equals 1
}
```

In fact, when this sequence runs, the formal parameter `r` is a reference that the system initializes each time that `inc()` is called. Consequently, upon the second call, the system creates a temporary object that has a double type. It initializes this temporary object to 1.0, and then it increments it. Finally, the system destroys this temporary object when it finishes execution of the function.

2. Pointers to overloaded functions

When you point a function pointer to an overloaded function, you do not have any problems. This is because the pointer knows the signature of the function that you want to call. Furthermore, the function that you want to call must have a corresponding signature.

However, you must note that the signature is not the only thing that must correspond to the type of the function pointer. In addition, the **return type of the function must correspond to that of the function pointer**.
This is the only case in which the compiler checks the return type of the function, irrespective of whether the function is overloaded or not.

```
int f(int);              // f1
String f(String);        // f2

int (*pf1)(int)=f;       // pf1=f1
String (*pf2)(String)=f; // pf2=f2

void (*pf3)(String)=f;   // Compile error!
```

In this last case, even though the signature of `f2()` corresponds to that of `pf3()`, the compiler will reject this initialization because these two functions have different return types.

3. Pointers to members of a class

With C, you can have a pointer (or a reference) to a function or to an object. With C++, functions and data items can be members of a class. As with C, you can have a pointer to either of them, but you must use a different syntax.

Suppose that you have the following class that defines the processing that an interrupt must carry out (in the context of the development of an operating system):

```
class Interrupt
{
. . .
public:
   void zero_divide();
   void memory_fault();
   void overflow();
. . .
};
```

In an operating system, an interrupt generally corresponds to a level. Consequently, you must set up a correspondence between an interrupt level and the function that the system must call.

With C, you can implement this using an array of function pointers (in which case the functions `zero_divide()`, `memory_fault()` and `overflow()` will not be class members, but will be ordinary functions).
With C++, you can implement this using an array of **member function pointers**.

The problem is to know the type of the `Interrupt` member functions. These functions cannot be `void (*)()` type functions (without arguments and without return values), as a member function always has a hidden parameter (`this`). These functions are therefore member functions of the Interrupt class, without arguments and without return values.

You must access a member function using the scope operator:

```
void (Interrupt::*pf)()=
                  Interrupt::zero_divide;
```

Here then, is your pointer array:

```
typedef void (Interrupt::*PF();
PF level[]={

  Interrupt::zero_divide;
  Interrupt::memory_fault;
  Interrupt::overflow;
};
```

Finally, you can use the new operators .* or ->* so that you will be able to call your functions via a pointer. Of course, an `Interrupt` type object must exist. You can call these functions only through an instance.

```
Interrupt i;

void trial()
{
  Interrupt & ri=i;
  Interrupt * pi=&i;

  i.*pf();
  ri.*pf();
  pi->*pf();

  i.*level[0]();    //zero_divide()
  ri.*level[1]();   //memory_fault()
  pi->*level[2](); //overflow()
}
```

C++ programming language

Chapter 3

It is easier to access a pointer to an instance data member:

```
class A
{
public:
   double x;
};

void trial()
{
   A a;
   double *pa=&a.x;

   *pa=1;
}
```

In addition, you can use these two new operators on data members of a class, provided that you **define the type as a pointer to a data member of a class**.

```
void trial2()
{
   A a;
   A *p=&a;
   double A::*pointer_to_member= &A::x;
   /* Defining the pointer_to_member type as a
      pointer to the data member x
      of the class A
   */

   a.*pointer_to_member=0.2;
   p->pointer_to_member=1.2;
}
```

You can point to static members of a class in an ordinary way. In fact, a static data member is unique, however many class instances that you have, and it is not associated with any instance. A static member function does not have any hidden parameters.

```
class A
{
public:
  static double x;
  static int f(double);
};

void trial()
{
  double *p1=&A::x;
  int (*pf)(double)=A::f;

  A a;
  double *p2=&a.x; // => p1==p2
}
```

4. Overloading the -> operator

Remember that you cannot overload this operator as a friend function.

Although this operator acts as a binary operator when you use it, you must overload it as a unary operator (its sole parameter is the call parameter that is placed to its left: this is the hidden parameter `this`).

You must call this operator via an instance or via a reference. **If you use this operator with a pointer, then you will call the standard -> operator (access to a field)**.

The return type of the -> operator can be a pointer to a class with a member that has the same name as that which you wrote to the right when you called the operator. Alternatively, the return type of this operator can be an instance of a class that itself defines operator->().

```
class A
{
public:
   int val;
   A(int i) : val(i) {}
   double f() { return val*2.7; }
};

class B
{
protected:
   A a;

public:
   B(int i) : a(i) {}
   A * operator->()
   {
      return &a;
   }
};

void main()
{
   B b(10);
   cout<<b->val<<'\n';
   cout<<b-f()<<'\n';
}
```

This means that you can access the members of the member `a`, via an instance of `B`.

Chapter 4

Object-oriented programming

A.	**Deriving classes**	**115**
	1. Derived class constructors	118
	2. Types of derivation	119
	3. Converting with public derived classes	121
	4. Constructing a derived class	126
	5. Initializing and assigning derived classes	127
B.	**Polymorphism - Dynamic typing**	**127**
	1. Virtual functions	130
	2. Internal implementation of C++ virtual functions	132
	3. Exceptions to dynamic typing	135
	4. Abstract classes	136
	5. Functions that you can convert into virtual functions	147
C.	**Multiple derivation**	**150**

C++ programming language

Chapter 4

The previous chapter described the features of this new C++ data structure, the class. However, the operations that the previous chapter carried out on these classes are still in the domain of procedural programming.

You start doing object-oriented programming when you define a hierarchy of classes (by deriving classes) and when you implement polymorphism via this class hierarchy tree (by defining virtual functions).

A. Deriving classes

Suppose that you want to implement a program in order to manage the people who are employed in a company.

You could represent an employee using the following simplified class:

```
class Employee
{
protected:
  String Fname;
public:
   Employee(String s)  : Fname(s) {}
   String surname()
   { return Fname; }
};
```

Suppose now that you want to represent a type of employee that has specific data: the manager.
This specific data could be simply the employees for whom the manager is responsible. As a manager is also an employee, then the manager must also have all the information that concerns an employee.

The classical C approach that is used in order to express the fact that a manager is also an employee is to provide the `Manager` type with a member data item that has the `Employee` type:

```
class Manager
{
public:
  Employee info;
  Manager(String s) : info(s) {
  Employee *list;
  unsigned nb_employees_list;
};
```

The data member `list` points to a table of employees, and the number of elements in this table is stored in `nb_employees_list`.

This approach has two drawbacks. Firstly, you must go through the `info` member in order to access the employee information that relates directly to the `Manager`. Secondly, and more importantly, you cannot handle the `Manager` simply, in the same way as you would handle an `Employee`. In other words, a pointer to `Employee` cannot point directly to a `Manager`.

C++ provides a mechanism that allows you to declare that one data representation is compatible with another data representation and that it includes this other data representation. This mechanism is called class derivation (or class inheritance). The following syntax specifies that `Manager` derives from `Employee`:

```
class Manager : public Employee
{
public:
  Manager(String s);
  Employee *list;
  unsigned nb_employees_list;
};
```

`Employee` is said to be the **base class** and `Manager` is said to be the **public derived class**.

A derived class **inherits** from all the members of its base class. This means that the data member `Fname` exists in `Manager`.

This is the practical application of the encapsulation that previous chapters described. Only the member functions of `Manager` can access `Fname` (which is protected), via an instance of `Manager`.

A derived class can have can have its own members with any level of access control.

A derived class can redefine a member function of its base class (by changing its access level and its signature). The redefined function masks the initial function, which you can still access thanks to the scope operator.

```
struct Base
{
  void f(); //f1()
};

struct Derived:Base
{
  void f(); //f2()
};

void trial()
{
  Base b;
  Derived d;

  b.f();         // f1()
  d.f();         // f2()
  d.Base::f();   // f1()
}
```

In this case, a `Manager` constructor has been added with the same signature as that of the `Employee`. It seems obvious that this constructor must act in the same way as `Employee` (it must initialize `Ename` correctly). However, you still have to define the body of this constructor.

You must carry out this latter step because **a derived class does not inherit the constructors of its base class**. However, the initialization constructor is an exception to this rule.

Since the members of a base class are present in one of its derived classes, it follows that the underlying C structure of a derived class is the underlying C structure of its base class, plus the data members that are specific to the derived class.

```
sizeof(Employee)=sizeof(Fname);
sizeof(Manager)=sizeof(Employee)+sizeof(list)+
               sizeof(nb_employees_list);
```

Naturally, you can use a derived class as a base class for another derived class. In this way, you can construct a consequential class hierarchy.

Essentially, this chapter will deal with the case where a class derives from a <u>single base class</u>. This type of derivation is called **single derivation**.
You can also have **multiple derivation**.

1. Derived class constructors

As the previous section indicated, when you construct a `Manager`, then you simply construct the base `Employee`. The syntax that allows you to call the `Employee` constructor from within the body of `Manager` is analogous to that which allows you to initialize a member:

```
Manager::Manager(String s) : Employee(s) {}
```

Although the body of the constructor is empty in this example you can use it to specify certain processing that will provide a more concrete implementation of these two classes (with many more data members).

2. Types of derivation

In the declaration syntax for derivation that is set out above, you will have noticed the presence of the `public` keyword. This implies that you can also use the other two keywords: `private` and `protected`. Consequently, there are three types of derivation.
These types define the access level in the derived class, for members of the base class.

In the derived class, you cannot access the private members of the base class, whatever the type of derivation.

Public derivation

```
class Derived : public Base
{
  . . .
};
```

- the `Base` **public members remain public in** `Derived`.
- the `Base` **protected members remain protected in** `Derived`.

Protected derivation

```
class Derived : protected Base
{
  . . .
};
```

- the `Base` **public members become protected in** `Derived`.
- the `Base` **protected members remain protected in** `Derived`.

Private derivation

```
class Derived : private Base
{
    . . .
};
```

or

```
class Derived : Base
{
    . . .
};
```

– the `Base` public members and the `Base` protected members become private in `Derived`.

Important note
If you do not specify the type of derivation, then the compiler will assume private derivation by default. Consequently, you must not forget to specify the type of derivation that you require (especially since you will generally require public derivation).

 As a structure is a class that does not have access control, you can derive your structures. This derivation is necessarily a public derivation and you do not need to specify it.

```
struct SBase
{
    . . .
};

struct SDerived : SBase // Public derivation
{
    . . .
};
```

3. Converting with public derived classes

Thanks to inheritance, a `Manager` is also an `Employee`. C++ reinforces this concept by allowing you to assimilate a derived class into a base class using automatic ordinary conversions.

You can make the following conversions:
- you can convert a derived class object to a base class object,
- you can convert a pointer that points to derived class object, to a pointer that points to a base class object,
- you can convert a reference to derived class object, to a reference to a base class object.

```
void trial()
{
  Employee e("Druley"), *pe;
  Manager m("Popgood");

  pe=&r;
  e=r;

  Manager pr=new Manager("Pat");
  e=*pr;
  delete pr;
  . . .
}
```

When you assign `pe`, although you cannot access the members `list` and `nb_employees_list` via `pe`, these members still exist (as `pe` is a pointer, it contains the memory address of a `Manager`).

On the other hand, these members do not exist as far as `Employee` is concerned, and consequently you do not copy them when you assign `e=r`.
In the rest of the function, when you delete `pr`, you also delete its specific members. Consequently, you can no longer access them, even though you previously assigned `e=*pr`.

These conversions are defined only in the case of a public derivation*.*
*From a practical viewpoint, public derivation is the most frequently used, and the most useful. In fact, when you use the other two types, you generally want to simulate **class composition**, whereby a class type object is a member of another class. When the conversions are no longer applied, derivation is of only limited use.*

Naturally, this conversion principle is recursive. If you have a deep class hierarchy you can convert any object that it contains, either to the root of the class hierarchy, or to another of the object's base classes.

 *Concerning friends: only the class concerned can choose its **friends**. Therefore, a class does not inherit friends and it does not transmit its friends to its parent classes.*
However, in the case of public derivation, ordinary conversion of a derived class to its base class allows you to use the friends of the base class.

```
class A
{
  friend void f(A);
  . . .
};

class B : public A
{
  . . .
};


void trial()
{
  B b;
  f(b); // conversion: f(A(b));
}
```

The explanation of the previous example stressed the fact that even though `pe` points to a `Manager`, it does not provide access to the specific members of `Manager` because `pe` is a pointer to `Employee`.

However, it is often useful to be able to handle an object via a pointer to one of the object's base classes (this is particularly convenient when the pointer is a function parameter that is of general use). In addition, it may be useful to be able to see this pointer as its real type, or as any other class that is situated between its real type and the class of the pointer in the class hierarchy, so that you will be able to access specific members of the object. You can achieve this using an inverse conversion: by converting from base class to derived class. However, C++ does not carry out this conversion automatically. You must use the generic function **dynamic_cast** (for a discussion of generic functions see the section that covers templates).

Here is an example that illustrates the use of dynamic_cast:

```
class Root
{

};

class Level1 : public Root
{
public:
   void f1();
   { cout<<"Calling f1\n"; }
};

class Level2 : public Level1
{
public:
   void f2();
   { cout<<"Calling f2\n"; }
};
                                      .../...
```

```
.../...
void general1(Root *object)
/* object might point to an instance of Level1
   and in this case you may want to call f1()
*/
{
  Level1 *l1;
  l1=dynamic_cast <Level1*>(object);
  if (l1!=0) l1->f1();
  else
    cout<<"general1: Dynamic_cast failure\n";
}

void general2(Root *object)
/* object might point to an instance of Level2
   and in this case you may want to call f1()
   and f2()
*/
{
  Level2 *l2;
  l2=dynamic_cast <Level2*>(object);
  if (l1!=0)
  {
    l2->f1();
    l2->f2();
  }
  else
    cout<<"general2: Dynamic_cast failure\n";
}

void trial()
{
  Level1 l1;
  general1(&l1);

  Level2 l2;
  general2(&l2);

  general1(&l2); // OK
  general1(&l1);
  // will cause dynamic_cast to fail
  // l1 does not have a Level2 type
}
```

This program will output the following:

```
Calling f1
Calling f1
Calling f2
Calling f1
general2: Dynamic_cast failure
```

Note that this program caries out a test before it calls `f1()` and `f2()`. In fact, the `dynamic_cast` function allows you to convert from a base class pointer to a derived class pointer but the base class pointer can also point to another derived class that is incompatible with the class that you would like with for your conversion. This is the case when the program calls `general2(&l1)`. In this case `dynamic_cast()` returns NULL.

 Unfortunately, the egcs compiler will allow you to use `dynamic_cast()` only if either the base class from which you want to convert is an abstract class, or one of its base classes is an abstract class (this concept is discussed later on in this chapter). Other compilers, such as that of C++ Builder 4 allow you to use `dynamic_cast()` without this constraint.
Here are the class declarations in the form that you must specify them so that the last example will work with all compilers (this virtual function definition implies that `Root` is an abstract class):

```
class Root
{
  virtual void f()=0;
};
class Level1 : public Root
{
  void f() {}
public:
  void f1();
};                                     .../...
```

```
.../...
class Level2 : public Level1
{
public:
   void f2();
};
```

4. Constructing a derived class

So as to create an instance of a derived class you must construct the following items in this order:
– the base class(es),
– the members that are specific to the derived class,
– the class itself (possibly the body of the derived class constructor).

You must apply this rule recursively by moving up the class hierarchy.

If a derived class has a constructor then this constructor will be entirely responsible for the construction (notably, it may need explicitly to call the constructor of its base class, as it may need explicitly to call the constructor of `Manager`).

If the derived class has no constructor, then the compiler will construct the base class and/or the members using the default constructor. If there is no default constructor then the compiler will make a bit-to-bit copy of these items.

5. Initializing and assigning derived classes

Initializing derived classes

If a derived class defines an initialization constructor, then this initialization constructor will be entirely responsible for the initialization of the base class and of the derived portion.

If a derived class does not define an initialization constructor, then the compiler will initialize the base class according to its specific characteristics, and it will initialize the derived portion by bit-to-bit copy.

Assigning derived classes

If a derived class defines its assignment operator then this operator will be entirely responsible for the assignment of the base class and for that of the derived portion.

If a derived class does not define its assignment operator, then the compiler will initialize the base class according to its specific characteristics, and it will initialize the derived portion by bit-to-bit copy.

B. Polymorphism - Dynamic typing

Polymorphism and **dynamic typing** are two identical concepts that C++ implements thanks to the **virtual function** concept.

Suppose that you want to be able to find out the real type of an `Employee` at any time (notably, when you have access to a `Manager` via a pointer or via a reference).

In order to achieve this objective by applying the techniques that you have seen up until now, you must create a type member at `Employee` class level. The compiler will then correctly initialize each of the constructors in the class hierarchy.

Thereby, you can implement your class hierarchy as follows:

```
#include "string.h"

class Employee
{
public:
  enum Type { Emp,Resp };

protected:
  String Fname;
  Type Ftype;

public:
  Employee(String s) : Fname(s) { Ftype=Emp; }
  String surname()
  { return Fname; }
  Type type() { return Ftype; }
};

class Manager : public Employee
{
public:
  Manager(String(s) : Employee(s) { Ftype=Man; }
  Employee *list;
  unsigned nb_employee_list;

};

void try()
{
  Manager r{"Popgood"};
  Employee &re=r;
                            .../...
```

```
.../...
  switch(re.type())
  {
    case Employee::Emp :
      cout << "Employee\n";
      break;
    case Employee::Man :
      cout << "Manager\n";
      break;
  }
}
```

When this program calls `try()` then it displays `Manager`.

However, this is not a modular approach, as if you need to add a new class to the hierarchy (a class that is derived from `Employee` or from `Manager`), then you will have to modify the enumeration in order to add a new type (indeed, you may have only the `.h` include file that defines the two classes `Employee` and `Manager`, and in this case you will no longer be able to modify the enumeration).

The only truly dynamic solution would be to define a member function for `Employee` that you must still call `type()`, and that simply returns a string that identifies the type (this could be the name of the class, for example):

```
#include "string.h"

class Employee
{
protected:
  String Fname;

public:
  Employee(String s) : Fname(s) {}
  String surname()
  { return Fname; }

  String type() { return "Employee"; }
};
                                                       .../...
```

```
.../...
class Manager : public Employee
{
public:
  Manager(String(s) : Employee(s) {}
  Employee *list;
  unsigned nb_employee_list;

  String type() { return "Manager"; }
};

void try()
{
  Manager r{"Popgood");
  Employee &re=r;

  cout<<re.type()<<'\n';
}
```

Unfortunately, when the program calls the `try()` function it outputs `Employee`. This is because, via `re`, the program sees the `Manager` as an `Employee`. Consequently, the program calls the `type()` member function of `Employee`.

1. Virtual functions

C++ can help you to solve this problem. The C++ dynamic typing means that when you call a function via a pointer, or via a reference to an object, then the compiler must call the "right" function that you have redefined in the class hierarchy. The "right" function is that which corresponds to the real type of the object.

The compiler is able to implement this mechanism thanks to virtual functions. In order to stipulate that a member function is a virtual function, you need only prefix its prototype with the `virtual` keyword in the first base class in which you declare this prototype.

Chapter 4

Because of this, you need only declare the `Employee` class as follows:

```
class Employee
{
protected:
  String Fname;

public:
  Employee(String s) : Fname(s) {}
  String surname() { return Fname; }

  virtual String type() { return "Employee"; }
};
```

When you declare your `Employee` class in this way then the `try()` function will run as you want it to and will return `Manager`.

 In the `Manager` class, you can prefix the `type()` prototype with `virtual`. However, this is optional as you have already declared `type()` as a virtual function in one of the `Manager` base classes (in this case this program made this declaration in the root of this simple hierarchy: in `Employee`).

You must note that C++ implements the **dynamic typing mechanism only via a pointer or via a reference**.

In fact, if you declare the `re` of the `try()` function as follows:

```
Employee re=r;
```

then the compiler will create an object of type `Employee` and it will initialize it with the members of `r` (this operation will truncate your data since it will not recopy the specific members of `Manager` into an object of the type `Employee`). However, the type of `re` stays as `Employee`, and when the program calls `type()` it will return the string "Employee".

2. Internal implementation of C++ virtual functions

Dynamic typing means that the system will decide which function it must call when it runs the program. The compiler simply generates the instructions that the system requires so that it can make this choice.

This section will describe how polymorphism works in C++.

For each class that has a virtual function, the compiler constructs a **virtual functions table** for this class, and includes this table in the executable program. This table contains only pointers to the virtual function bodies. There is a table entry for each virtual function of the class.

For example, for the following two classes:

```
class Base
{
   . . .
public:
   virtual void f1();
   virtual void f2();

   . . .
};

class Derived : public Base
{
   . . .
public:
   virtual void f3();
   . . .
};

void Base::f1()
{ . . . }

void Base::f2()
{ . . . }

void Derived::f1()
{ . . . }                                       .../...
```

```
.../...
void Derived::f2()
{ . . . }

void Derived::f3()
{ . . . }
```

then the compiler will create two virtual function tables as follows:

Each instance of each of these classes has a pointer to its virtual function table. This pointer is situated in the first field of the underlying C structure.

The system can then access the "right" function by consulting the virtual function table.

Suppose that you have an instance d of Derived. Then, its underlying C structure will be as follows:

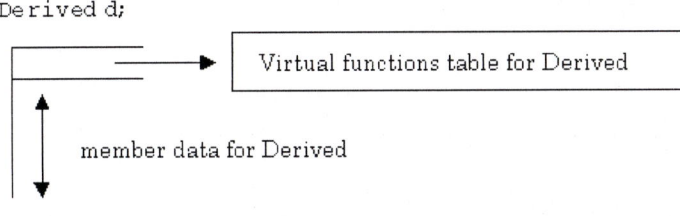

When the system runs the following instructions:

```
Derived d;
Base *pd=&d;

pd-f2();
```

then `pd` points to `d`, which has a pointer to the virtual functions table for `Derived`. Thereby, in order to call `f(2)`, the system need only consult the second entry in this table.

If the `Derived` class does not redefine `f1()`, then the entry for `f1` in the `Derived` virtual functions table will still exist, and will point to `Base::f1()`.

This approach is not expensive in terms of machine resources, but it does have one drawback. In order to understand this drawback you must remember that the `"sizeof"` for a class that has virtual functions is the sum of the `"sizeof"` of each item of member data, plus the `"sizeof"` for a pointer.

As this pointer is always situated in the first field of the underlying C structure, if your class must be used as a read mask (with a cast) in a buffer, then you must take this first field into account (an example of such a buffer is a network frame buffer that you want to avoid copying to another area of memory for performance reasons).

In this case, the best approach is to have a data member that contains a pointer to a structure that represents the mask itself (remember that deriving a structure is a useful technique in many different circumstances):

```
char *frame // buffer

struct Frame
{
   . . .
   // fields that represent a network frame
};
                                              .../...
```

```
.../...
class HandleFrame
{
   . . .
// defining one or more public virtual functions
public:
   Frame *t;
};

void try()
{
   HandleFrame mask;

   mask.f=(Frame *)frame;

// handling the frame via the mask instance
   . . .
}
```

3. Exceptions to dynamic typing

C++ does not implement dynamic typing in three cases:
− when you call the function via an instance.

```
Employee e("me");
cout<<e.type()<<'\n';
```

− when the scope operator explicitly specifies the function version that the program must call.

```
Manager *m=new Manager("someone");
r->Employee::type();
```

− when you call the function from a class constructor.

In all of these cases, the compiler will decide which function version the program must call.

In the last case above, the compiler determines this function statically. This is because the instance does not yet exist during construction and therefore the `this` pointer does not yet exist either.

On the other hand, if a virtual function is called by any other function that is in the same class, then C++ will implement dynamic typing by means of `this`.

4. Abstract classes

This section will deal with a new example.

Suppose that you want to represent arithmetic expressions. For the moment, this example will handle only integer constants and will use only the following arithmetic operators:

```
+ , -         unary operators
+ , - , * , / binary operators
```

You can represent such arithmetic expressions by a tree in which the nodes are the operators, and the leaves are the constant integers. Incidentally, this is how all compilers interpret such expressions when they read them in the source code (the leaves can be either constants or variables):

Here is an example of such a tree structure:

This is the tree that is associated with the following expression:

```
-(1+1)-4+2*(3-5)
```

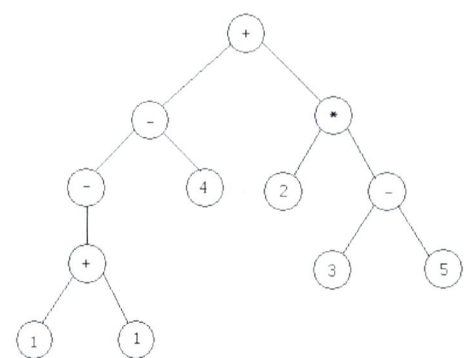

Chapter 4

This tree contains three types of expression:
− expressions that are reduced to a constant (the leaves),
− unary expressions,
− binary expressions.

Using a C approach, you can represent this tree by a structure that contains the type of the expression and a union.

```
struct Expr
{
  enum type
  { Constant,Unary,Binary };

  enum UnaryOp
  { Uplus,Uminus };

  enum BinaryOp
  { Plus,Minus,Mult,Div };

  type t;

  union
  {
    int val;

    struct
    {
      UnaryOp op;
      Expr *e;
    } unary;

    struct
    {
      BinaryOp op;
      Expr *e1, *e2;
    } binary;
  };   // anonymous union
};
```

Naturally, with this structure, the evaluation function of an expression is recursive:

```
int eval(const Expr *e)
{
  switch(e->t)
  {
    case Expr::Constant :
      return e->val;
    case Expr::Unary :
      switch(e->unary.op)
      {
        case Expr::Uplus :
          return +eval(e->unary.e);
        case Expr::Uminus :
          return -eval(e->unary.e);
      }
    case Expr::Binary :
      switch(e->binary.op)
      {
        case Expr::Plus :
          return eval(e->binary.e1)+
                 eval(e->binary.e2);
        case Expr::Minus :
          return eval(e->binary.e1)-
                 eval(e->binary.e2);
        case Expr::Mult :
          return eval(e->binary.e1)*
                 eval(e->binary.e2);
        case Expr::Div :
          return eval(e->binary.e1)/
                 eval(e->binary.e2);
      }
  }
}
```

A syntax analyzer can take an arithmetic expression in infix format (a mathematical notation) and generate the corresponding tree in the above form.

In order to test the `eval()` function, you can construct the tree "manually":

```
void try()
{
  // Constructing the tree that represents
  // the expression:
  // -(1+1)-4+2*(3-5) == -10
  Expr *expression,*ss_expr1,*ss_expr2,*ss_expr3;

  ss_expr1=new Expr;
  ss_expr1->t=Expr::Constant;
  ss_expr1->val=1;

  ss_expr2=new Expr;
  ss_expr2->t=Expr::Constant;
  ss_expr2->val=1;

  expression=new Expr;
  expression->t=Expr::Binary;
  expression->binary.op=Expr::Plus;
  expression->binary.e1=ss_expr1;
  expression->binary.e2=ss_expr2;

  ss_expr1=new Expr;
  ss_expr1->t=Expr::Unary;
  ss_expr1->unary.op=Expr::Uminus;
  ss_expr1->binary.e=expression;

  ss_expr2=new Expr;
  ss_expr2->t=Expr::Constant;
  ss_expr2->val=4;

  expression=new Expr;
  expression->t=Expr::Binary;
  expression->binary.op=Expr::Minus;
  expression->binary.e1=ss_expr1;
  expression->binary.e2=ss_expr2;

  ss_expr1=new Expr;
  ss_expr1->t=Expr::Constant;
  ss_expr1->val=3;

  ss_expr2=new Expr;
  ss_expr2->t=Expr::Constant;
  ss_expr2->val=5;
                                .../...
```

```
.../...
  ss_expr3=new Expr;
  ss_expr3->t=Expr::Binary;
  ss_expr3->binary.op=Expr::Minus;
  ss_expr3->binary.e1=ss_expr1;
  ss_expr3->binary.e2=ss_expr2;

  ss_expr1=new Expr;
  ss_expr1->t=Expr::Constant;
  ss_expr1->val=2;

  ss_expr2=new Expr;
  ss_expr2->t=Expr::Binary;
  ss_expr2->binary.op=Expr::Mult;
  ss_expr2->binary.e1=ss_expr1;
  ss_expr2->binary.e2=ss_expr3;
  ss_expr1=expression;

  expression=new Expr;
  expression->t=Expr::Binary;
  expression->binary.op=Expr::Plus;
  expression->binary.e1=ss_expr1;
  expression->binary.e2=ss_expr2;

  cout<<eval(ss_expr1)<<'\n';
  cout<<eval(ss_expr2)<<'\n';

  cout<<eval(expression)<<'\n';

}
```

Naturally, when his program calls `try()`, it displays -10.

The major drawback with this approach is that it is not modular. For example, if you want to add the binary operator `modulus`, then you must modify the structure and you must also modify the `eval()` function.

An object-oriented approach to this problem would be to represent the three different types of expression in the following class hierarchy:

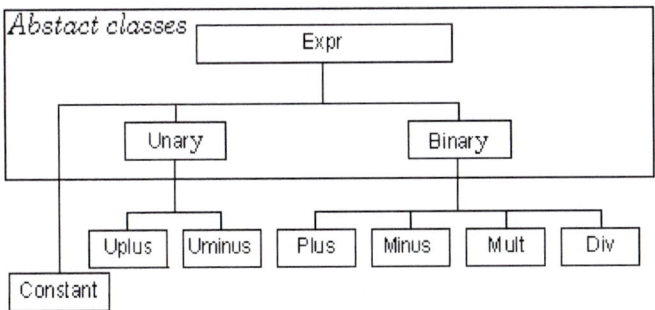

Expr is the root of this hierarchy (this must therefore represent an expression). This class has all the common properties of an expression. Clearly, all that you know about an expression is that you can evaluate it.

The directly derived classes of this hierarchy represent the three types of expression. The members of these classes are the properties that are common to a given type: a Constant has a value; a Unary expression has a single operand (of Expr type); and a Binary expression has a two such operands.

From Unary and Binary, you must derive the classes that correspond to the operators.

The three classes Expr, Unary and Binary will never have instances. You must declare only pointers or references to this type of object. This is why they are called abstract classes (on the other hand the other classes, or concrete classes, can have instances).

C++ allows you to declare that a class is abstract.

In practice, a pointer (or a reference) of type Expr* will point to an instance of one of the concrete classes.

As this section indicated earlier, all you can do with an `Expr` is to evaluate it (hence the `eval()` function). Clearly then, real evaluation is carried out in the concrete classes. Consequently, `eval()` must be a virtual function.

In addition, at `Expr` class level, the body of `eval()` is difficult to determine (as there is no instance of this class). In fact, rather than being empty, this body must not exist. C++ allows you to **declare that a virtual function does not have a body**. Such a function is called a **pure virtual function**.

Finally, when a class has at least one virtual function, then C++ considers it as an abstract class, and the compiler does not allow you to declare an instance of such a class.

In order to take all of these aspects into account, you must declare `Expr` as follows:

```
class Expr;
{
public:
  virtual int eval() const =0;
};
```

Note that you need only add a suffix to the prototype of `eval()` in order to declare it as a pure virtual function. Subsequently, the `Expr` class is abstract.

Here are the other two abstract classes:

```
class Unary : public Expr
{
protected:
  Expr *e;
public:
  Unary(Expr *expr) : e(expr) {}
};

class Binary : public Expr
{
protected:
  Expr *e1, *e2;                           .../...
```

```
.../...
public:
  Binary(Expr *expr1, Expr *expr2)
    : e1(expr1),e2(expr2) {}
};
```

As this section indicated previously, each of these two classes has only one property: the first of these classes must have one expression and the second of these classes must have two expressions.

This is why these expressions are data members that are initialized by the constructor.

 Repeating the `eval()` prototype in these classes is optional. These classes automatically inherit from the pure virtual function. Consequently, they become abstract classes.
If you repeat the prototype, then the suffix `=0` is compulsory so as to specify that the abstract classes and the `eval()` function do not have bodies. On the other hand, the virtual prefix is always optional.

Now, you can specify the concrete classes without any problem:

```
class Constant : public Expr
{
protected:
  int val;
public:
  Constant(int n) : val(n) {}
  int eval() const;
};

class Uplus : public Unary
{
public:
  Uplus(Expr *e) : Unary(e) {}
  int eval() const;
};
                                  .../...
```

```
.../...
class Uminus : public Unary
{
public:
  Uminus(Expr *e) : Unary(e) {}
  int eval() const;
};

class Plus : public Binary
{
public:
  Plus(Expr *e1,Expr *e2) : Binary(e1,e2) {}
  int eval() const;
};

class Minus : public Binary
{
public:
  Minus(Expr *e1,Expr *e2) : Binary(e1,e2) {}
  int eval() const;
};

class Mult : public Binary
{
public:
  Mult(Expr *e1,Expr *e2) : Binary(e1,e2) {}
  int eval() const;
};

class Div : public Binary
{
public:
  Div(Expr *e1,Expr *e2) : Binary(e1,e2) {}
  int eval() const;
};
```

On the other hand, in this case the body of `eval()` must exist for each of these concrete classes. Consequently, you must repeat the prototype without the prefix =0. In fact, each time that you repeat the prototype, you redefine the member function.

When you have suitably defined the hierarchy, then the `eval()` bodies are simple:

```
int Constant::eval() const
{
   return val;
}

int Uplus::eval() const
{
   return +e->eval();
}

int Uminus::eval() const
{
   return -e->eval();
}

int Plus::eval() const
{
   return e1->eval()+e2->eval();
}

int Minus::eval() const
{
   return e1->eval()-e2->eval();
}

int Mult::eval() const
{
   return e1->eval()*e2->eval();
}
int Div::eval() const
{
   return e1->eval()/e2->eval();
}
```

Finally, as with the non-object oriented implementation, here is a test function:

```
void try()
{

  Expr
    *e=new Plus(
          new Minus(
            new Uminus(
              new Plus(
                new Constant(1),
                new Constant(1))),
            new Constant(4)),
          new Mult(
            new Constant(2),
            new Minus(
              new Constant(3),
              new Constant(5)))));
// e= -(1+1)-4+2*(3-5)

  cout<<e->eval()<<'\n';
}
```

The fact that this `try()` function is simpler and more readable than the previous `try()` function, is not one of the advantages of this implementation. This function constructs a tree manually. The code that is associated with a real syntax analyzer is very clear in both cases.

The main advantage of this implementation is that it is modular. The analysis and the hierarchy construction are the most complex phases. However, when you have completed these specifications, then you can add the `modulus` operator very easily. You can even create ternary operators, and in all these cases you need only the include file, and a library, for this hierarchy.

5. Functions that you can convert into virtual functions

Friend functions cannot be virtual functions.

All member functions can be virtual functions except for constructors and assignment operators.

Notably, a destructor can be a virtual function, and destructors that belong to abstract classes generally are virtual functions.

For example, the last `try()` function that this chapter described made a large number of memory allocations. This example should have freed this memory space.

Given the expression that constructs the tree for the assignment of the variable `e`, the only way that this program can free this memory space is by adding the following instruction at the end of the `try()` function:

```
delete e;
```

Unfortunately, `*e` has the type `Expr`, and consequently the delete operator frees simply the memory space that the program allocated for the pointer to `Expr`. The size of the space is `sizeof(Expr)=sizeof(void *)`. This is because this class does not have a data member but it has a virtual function. Consequently, its underlying C structure has only a pointer to the virtual functions table of `Expr`.

Clearly, this approach will not free the memory space completely.

Using the class specification techniques that this book has covered so far, in order to free all the memory, you must have a different `Expr *` pointer for each of the calls to `new` that you make. You must construct the tree structure using these pointers. Then, when you want to free the memory, you must apply `delete` to each of these pointers.

However, this approach is not very easy to implement.

However, when you apply delete to a class pointer, then the program will call the destructor for this class, if this destructor exists. The solution to this problem is therefore to define a destructor for the `Expr` class.

But, what must this destructor do?

As `Expr` has no member data, there is nothing in `Expr` that you can destroy.

In addition, `Expr` is abstract. Consequently, you cannot create instances of `Expr`, and similarly, the compiler will refuse an expression such as `new Expr`.

In fact, the real type of an `Expr` pointer is always a concrete class, and the real type of the `e` pointer is `Plus`.

The complete solution then is to call the destructor for the real type of an `Expr` pointer. For this reason, the `Expr` destructor must be a virtual destructor (and it must do nothing):

```
class Expr
{
public:
  virtual ~Expr() {}
  virtual int eval() const =0;
};
```

Now, all you have to do is to define the destructors for the concrete classes.

In theory, a class does not inherit a destructor (whether the destructor be virtual or not). However, if you derive a class that has a non virtual destructor and you do not declare a destructor for this `derived` class, then the compiler will generate a destructor by default. This destructor calls the destructor of the base class and that of the members of the derived class.

The destructor for the `Constant` class has nothing to do and consequently you do not need to redefine it.

The destructors for all the other concrete classes need only apply `delete` to data members of the type `Expr *` that are inherited from their Unary and Binary base classes.
A simpler way of implementing this approach is to redefine the destructors at Unary and Binary abstract class level.

Firstly, the data members are declared at this level.
Secondly, if you do not redefine the destructor at Unary and Binary derived class level in the virtual functions table of the classes Uplus, Uminus, Plus, Minus, Mult and Div, then the entry that corresponds to the virtual destructor will point to the destructor that is defined in their base class.

Now, all you have to do is to complete the specifications of Unary and Binary as follows:

```
class Unary : public Expr
{
protected:
  Expr *e;
public:
  Unary(Expr *expr) : e(expr) {}
  ~Unary() { delete e; }
};

class Binary : public Expr
{
protected:
  Expr *e1, *e2;
public:
  Binary(Expr *expr1,Expr *expr2)
    : e1(expr1),e2(expr2) {}
  ~Binary()
  {
    delete e1;
    delete e2;
  }
};
```

Although the Expr destructor is virtual, in order to redefine it in its derived classes, you must not declare a function that is called ~Expr(). You compose the name of a class destructor by prefixing its name with a tilde (this prefix is simply a convention that denotes "class destructor").

This section demonstrates that object oriented programming is simple to implement when compared to the technique that you would need to use in order to free the memory that was allocated for the first version of the tree (this required a specific, recursive release function that must run through the tree).

C. Multiple derivation

So far, this chapter has described single derivation. Many object-oriented languages implement only this type of derivation (such as Smalltalk for example). C++ also supports multiple derivation. With multiple derivation, a derived class can have several direct base classes.

Here is an example of multiple derivation:

```
class A
{
    . . .
};

class B
{
    . . .
};

class Multiple : public A , public B
{
    . . .
};
```

As with simple derivation, for each of the base classes, you must declare the derivation type that you require (public, protected or private).

You can specify the base classes in any order. The order in which the compiler will allocate memory for the base classes will depend on how you configure your compiler.

You cannot specify a class as a direct base class more than once. However, you can specify a class as an indirect base class several times.

```
class A { . . . };

class Multiple : public A, public B
{
   . . .
}
// Error!
```

However:

```
class Root { . . . };

class A : public Root { . . . }

class B : public Root { . . . }

class Multiple : public A , public B
{
   . . .
};
// OK
```

In this example, an object of the `Multiple` class will have two sub-objects that are of the `Root` class.

Consequently, every time that you access the member data of `Root`, in an instance of `Multiple`, you will reference one of these sub-objects. You will not know which of these two sub-objects that you are accessing, but you will always access the same one.

However, this means that for the other object you will be occupying memory to no purpose. Furthermore, if a class derives from both `Multiple` and from `A`, then the class will have three sub-objects in the `Root` class. The system may not see any assignments that `Multiple` member functions make to `Root` data members, when the program accesses the same `Root` data members from an instance of this derived class (via this instance, the program may access a third sub-object that does not exist in `Multiple`).

In order to resolve this problem, you must declare that, for such a derivation, each base class of `Multiple` will inherit and share only one sub-object.

You can implement this approach thanks to **virtual multiple derivation**. Example:

```
class Root { . . . };

class A : virtual public Root { . . . }

class B : virtual public Root { . . . }

class Multiple : public A , public B
{
   . . .
};
```

In this case, an object of the `Multiple` class will have only one sub-object of the `Root` class.

`Root` is a **virtual base class**.

It is a pity that this sort of multiple derivation is not automatic.

Constructing virtual base classes

C++ calls the constructors of the virtual base classes before it calls any of the constructors of non-virtual base classes.

If the class hierarchy contains several virtual base classes then the system will call their constructors in the order that you declare the classes.

The system then constructs all non-virtual base classes before it calls the constructor of the derived class.

If a virtual class derives from a non-virtual base class then it will appear first so as to ensure that the virtual base class will be correctly constructed.
For example, for the following instructions:

```
class A
{
public:
   A() { . . . }
   . . .
};

class B
{
public:
   B() { . . . }
   . . .
};

class Multiple : public A ,virtual public B
{
public:
   Multiple() { . . . }
   . . .
};
```

the system will call the constructors in the following order:

```
B(); // constructing the virtual base class

A(); // constructing the non-virtual base class

Multiple(); // constructing the derived class
```

Whenever you are thinking of specifying a class hierarchy with multiple inheritance, you must always ask yourself whether you can produce the same result using a well-designed simple inheritance. You will often find that you can.

Multiple inheritance is most commonly used in order to integrate software components that have been developed separately.

A concrete and practical example of multiple inheritance is the MFC hierarchy of Microsoft Visual C++. This application implements distributed application development using the `Interface` class.

Chapter 5

Streams

A.	Standard input/output	**157**
	1. Input	**158**
	2. Output	**161**
	3. Stream states	**162**
	4. Formatting	**163**
B.	Input/output with files	**167**
C.	Input/output with memory	**172**

C++ programming language

Chapter 5

As with C, the C++ language does not offer any native input/output instructions. However, C++ does offer the input/output stream library. This library provides a method with security by typing that allows you to manage standard types. In addition, its flexibility allows you to extend its application to user types (this book provided an example of this technique with the `Rational` class).

Essentially, the <iostream.h> file provides the interface for this library. Apart from input/output with the keyboard and the screen, this chapter will describe how you can handle the memory and files (moreover, for all Unix systems, the keyboard and the screen are just two specific files).

A. Standard input/output

This book briefly touched on input/output when it covered standard types. You must note that the `istream` class defines input functions, and the `ostream` class defines output functions. These two classes derive from the `ios` class.

More generally, the `ios` class controls the association of one of its instances with a buffer. As all stream I/O operations use either an instance of `ios`, or an instance of classes that are derived from `ios`, these operations use buffers.

The `ios` class defines enumeration functions and constants that this chapter will describe.

1. Input

The `istream` class redefines `operator >>()` (which means "read from ...") for all the standard types. Here is the specification for this type:

```
class istream : virtual public ios
{
   . . .
public:
  istream& operator>>(char *);
  istream& operator>>(char &);
  istream& operator>>(short &);
  istream& operator>>(int &);
  istream& operator>>(long &);
  istream& operator>>(float &);
  istream& operator>>(double &);

  istream& get(char &);
  istream& get(char *buf,int size_buf,
              char terminator ='\n');

  istream& putback(char);
  istream& unget(char);
   . . .
};
```

All the overloads for `operator>>()` skip space. "Space" is defined by the `isspace()` function of the `<ctype.h>` file (it includes space characters, tabs, newlines, page breaks, carriage returns and end of file characters). In fact these functions consider space to be a read separator between one instance and the next.

```
void main()
{
  int i,j;
  char s1[50],s2[50];

  cin>>i>>j;
  cin>>s1>>s2;
}
```

When you run this program, if you enter the following lines:
```
1 2
several words on the line
```

then the variables `i` and `j` will receive the values 1 and 2, respectively, and `s1` and `s2` will receive the values "several" and "words" respectively. Finally, "words on the line" will stay in the input buffer awaiting the next call from `cin` to an input function.

In particular, with the instructions:
```
char c;
cin>>c;
```

the `c` variable would never receive a "space" value.

In addition, when you run `cin>>i>>j;` and you enter non-numeric characters, then `i` and `j` will receive arbitrary values, and the system will raise no error.

For this reason, the `istream` class defines two overloads of the `get` function, which reads all the characters.

The first overload gives a value to a character type variable. Thereby, with the following instructions
```
char c;
cin.get(c);
```

`c` could receive a "space" value.

The `istream::get` function that has three arguments, it reads a maximum of `size_buf -1` characters and it stores them in `buf` (it reads `size_buf -1` characters because a C++ character string is always terminated by `'\0'`). The third argument defines the end-of-read character. Typically, you can read this function in order to read a full line.

```
void main()
{
  char s[50];
  char c;

  cin.get(s,sizeof(s));
  if(cin.get(c)  && c!='\n')
  {
    // the input string is too long for
    // the buffer

    cin.putback(c); //for example

    . . .
  }
}
```

When you run this program, if you enter:

`several words on the line`

then `s` will receive the string "`several words on the line`".

Note the purpose of the test that follows the read for `s`. When the program has finished calling the three-argument version of `istream::get()`, the read buffer will not be empty. It will contain at least the terminator character. If this is not the case, then it means that the read was not completed because the storage buffer was too small. You can then act accordingly.

Finally, the function `istream::putback()` is equivalent to the function `istream::unget()`. These functions allow you to put back into the read buffer, the character that you pass to them as a parameter.

Remember that C++ implements the input for a user type `T`, thanks to an overload of `operator>()` that is not a member of the class `T`, but that may be a friend of the class `T`:

`istream& operator>>(istream &,T&);`

2. Output

The ostream class redefines `operator <<()` (which means "write to...") for all the standard types. Here is the specification for this type:

```
class ostream : virtual public ios
{
  . . .
public:
  ostream& operator<<(const char *);
  ostream& operator<<(char);
  ostream& operator<<(short);
  ostream& operator<<(int);
  ostream& operator<<(long);
  ostream& operator<<(float);
  ostream& operator<<(double);

  ostream& operator<<(const void *);
    // for the value of a pointer

  ostream& put(char);

  . . .
};
```

This book has already dealt with the overloading of `ostream::operator<<()` on these types.
The `ostream::put()` function is equivalent to `ostream::operator<<(char)`, and it was defined in order to provide a function that is symmetrical to `istream::get()`.

Finally, remember that C++ implements the output for a user type `T`, thanks to an overload of `operator<()` that is not a member of the class `T`, but that may be a friend of the class `T`:

```
ostream& operator<<(ostream &,const T&);
```

3. Stream states

Each input or output stream has a **state** associated with it. You can consult this status using the functions that are defined in the `ios` class:

```
class ios
{
  . . .
public:

  int eof() const;
  // the end of file has been reached

  int fail() const;
  // the next operation will fail

  int bad() const;
  // the steam is corrupt

  int good() const;
  // the next operation "can" be successful

  enum io_state
  { goodbit=0,
    eofbit=1,
    failbit=2,
    badbit=3
  };

  typedef int iostate;
  iostate rdstate() const;
  // returns a set of io_state bits

  . . .
};
```

The `ios::rdstate()` function allows global access to the state of a stream, whereas the functions `ios::fail()`, `ios::bad()` and `ios::good()` allow you to find out the state bit values for a stream.

4. Formatting

Up until this point, this book has illustrated outputs without formatting. Formatting features are implemented in <stdio.h>. These features cover C++ streams.

The `ios` class allows you to specify and to read formatting information:

```
class ios
{
   . . .
public:

   int width(int);
   // indicates the length and
   // returns the former length value
   int width() const;
   // reads the length

   char fill(char);
   // defines the fill character and
   // returns the former fill character
   char fill() const;
   // reads the fill character

   int precision(int);
   // defines the precision of floats
   // returns the former precision defined
   int precision() const;
   // reads the precision of floats

/***
Enumeration constants that allow you to control
formatting flags
***/
   enum
   {
     skipws,
     // skips separators for an input
     // Justification
     left,  // fills after the value
     right, // fills before the value
     internal,
        // fills between the sign and the value
                                    .../...
```

```
.../...
   // Base
   dec,oct,hex,
   showbase, // displays the base

   showpoint,
      // displays zeros after the decimal point

   uppercase, // ex: E and X instead of e and x

   showpos, // displays + pour positive values

   scientific, // .dddd Edd notation
   fixed,      // dddd.ddd notation

   initbuf,    // empties the output buffer
               // after each output operation

   stdio       // empties the output buffer
               // after each character
};

long flags(long);
// sets formatting flags and
// returns their former values
long flags() const;
// reads the values of formatting flags

long setf(long flag);
// sets a formatting flag and
// returns its former value
long unsetf(long flag);
// unsets a formatting flag and
// returns its former value

   . . .
};
```

Here are some formatting examples.

The formatting functions that do not manage the flags take effect only upon the next I/O operation. The following instructions:

```
cout.width(4);
cout<<'('<<12<<')'<<'\n';

cout.fill('#');
cout<<'('<<12<<')'<<'\n';

cout.width(4);
cout.fill('#');
cout<<'('<<12<<')'<<'\n';
```

will output the following:

```
(  12)
(12)
(##12)
```

The function `ios::width(int)` sets the **minimum** number of characters that the program must output. If the program needs to output more characters than this minimum number then the program will output them. By default, you use `ostream` with `width(0)`. This means that your programs will output as many characters as necessary.

The meaning and the enumeration of the flags are simple. You can set and unset flags as follows:

```
const int io_options=
  ios::left|ios::oct|ios::showpoint|ios::fixed;
cout.flags(io_options);
```

`ios::flags(long)` sets all the formatting flags. If you want to set a single flag, then you can use `ios::flags()` as follows:

```
cout.flags(cout.flags()|ios::hex);
```

You can do this in a simpler way as follows:

```
cout.setf(ios::hex);
```

These instructions are essentially used for outputs. However, this approach means that for a single output operation, you must include one or more formatting instructions before the output instruction itself. In contrast to this approach, the C function `printf()` allows you to carry out the whole operation in a single instruction. Therefore, this technique is not very elegant, nor is it very readable.

Historically, programmers carried out formatting in this way when streams first appeared. Then, the `<iomanip.h>` library was developed (from an idea that Andrew Koenig introduced). As with `printf()`, the `<iomanip.h>` library allows you to specify the formatting and the output in a single instruction. Consequently, you should use the following approach, as it will make your programs more readable.

This section will focus on the use of these manipulators, rather on the details of their implementation. Note simply that after you have studied this library, you will be able to define new manipulators. A manipulator can be either a function that takes an argument of the type `ostream&`, `istream&` or `ios&`, and that returns a reference of the same type as the argument. Alternatively, a manipulator can be an instance of `omanip`, `imanip` or `smanip` (these classes are defined in `<iomanip.h>`).

Here are the standard manipulators:

`dec`	decimal notation
`hex`	hexadecimal notation
`oct`	octal notation
`endl`	add '\n' and flush the stream.
`ends`	add '\0' and flush the stream.
`flush`	flush the stream.
`ws`	skip the input separators.
`setbase(int)`	output in the specified base. If you do not specify 8, 10 or 16, then `setbase()` has no effect and your program will output in base 10.
`setw(int)`	defines the width.

`setfill(int)`	defines the fill character.
`setprecision (fint)`	defines the precision of a floating-point value.
`resetiosflags (long)`	unsets the flags that you specify in the parameter.
`setiosflags (long)`	sets the flags that you specify in the parameter.

You can use these manipulators as follows:

```
cout<<hex<<setw(2)<<setfill('0')<<
     setiosflags(ios::uppercase)<<10<<endl;

cout<<10<<endl;
  cout<<setbase(10)<<setw(4)<<setfill('#')
     <<'('<<12<<")\n";
cout<<setprecision(4)<<12.34567<<endl;
cout<<setprecision(4)<<1.234567<<endl;
cout<<1.234567<<endl;
```

The above instructions will produce the following output:

```
A
(##12)
12.35
1.234
1.234
```

B. Input/output with files

The standard streams `cin`, `cout` and `cerr` are nothing other than instances of `istream` or `ostream`. You must note that there is another standard stream, which is called `clog`. The clog stream acts like the `cerr` stream. The only difference is that every output from `clog` is automatically flushed (the system calls the `flush()` function systematically), whereas this is not the case with `cerr`.

You can use the classes `istream` and `ostream`, so as to handle the streams that are physically associated with disk files.

In order to associate a stream with a file, you need to use additional classes. These classes are `ofstream` (output stream), `ifstream` (input stream), and `fstream` (input and output stream).

The file `<fstream.h>` specifies these classes, which derive in a multiple way from `ostream` and/or `istream`.

Some of the members that `ostream` and `istream` define are especially useful for streams that are associated with disk files:

```
class ostream : virtual public ios
{
  . . .
public:
  ostream& flush();
  // flushing the output stream

  ostream& seekp(streampos);
  // absolute placing of the position pointer
  // in the stream

  ostream& seekp(streamoff,seek_dir);
  // relative placing of the position pointer
  // in the stream

  streampos tellp();
  // returns the position
  // of the position pointer

  . . .
};
```

Generally, the `streampos` type is a synonym for unsigned long, and the `streamoff` type is a synonym for long (although this depends on the architecture of the target machine).

Chapter 5

The `ios` class defines the type `seek_dir`:

```
class ios
{
  . . .
public:
  enum seek_dir
  {
    beg, // from the beginning
    cur, // from the current position
    end  // from the end
  };
  . . .
};
```

In a stream, the initial position of the stream pointer is 0.

```
class istream : virtual public ios
{
  . . .
public:
  int peek();
  // returns the next character that is in
  // the output stream without affecting
  // the position pointer

  istream& putback(char);
  // places the character that is passed
  // as a parameter, in the read buffer.
  // Consequently, the next read
  // will return this character

  istream& seekg(streampos);
  // absolute placing of
  // the position pointer in the stream.

  istream& seekg(streamoff,seek_dir);
  // relative placing of
  // the position pointer in the stream.

  streampos tellg();
  // returns the position of
  // the position pointer

  . . .
};
```

In order to demonstrate how you can associate a stream with a file, here is a C++ implementation of the UNIX command `cp` (this command copies the contents of one file into another file).

```cpp
#include <fstream.h>
#include <stdlib.h> // so as to use exit()

void error(char *s1,char *s2 ="")
{
  cerr<<s1<<' '<<s2<<'\n';
  exit(1);
}

int main(int argc,char **argv)
{
  if(argc!=3)
    error("Wrong number of parameters");

  ifstream source(argv[1]);
  if(!source)
    error("cannot open source: ",argv[1]);

  ofstream dest(argv[2]);
  if(!dest)
    error("cannot open destination: ",argv[2]);

  char c;

  while(source.get(c))
    dest.put(c); // or dest<c;

  if(!source.eof() || dest.bad())
    error("a strange error has occurred");

  return 0;
}
```

By default, the system opens one instance of `ofstream` in write mode, and one instance of `istream` in read mode. However, as with an instance of `fstream`, the constructors of these classes (and therefore the instance declarations) take a second parameter of the type `open_mode` that specifies the opening mode (this second parameter is simply a default value for `ofstream` and for `ifstream`):

```
class ios
{
   . . .
public:
  enum open_mode
    {
    in,   // open as an input
    out,  // open as an output
    ate,  // open and go to the end of the file
    app,  // open in append mode
    trunc, // empty the file if not already
    nocreate, // fail if file does not exist
    noreplace,// fail if file exists
    binary // open in binary mode
         // otherwise open in text mode
  };

  . . .
};
```

You can use these enumeration constants with the `binary` or operator |.

Consequently, you open a file in read mode and in write mode. This is why the positioning functions have two separate names: `seekg()` and `seekp()`. The stream manages two separate pointers: one for reading and the other for writing.

You may have noticed that the program above does not include an explicit function that closes the file. In fact, the class constructor of the stream opens a stream, and its class destructor closes the stream. However, the classes `fstream`, `ifstream` *and* `ofstream` *have a member function that is called* `close()`. *You can call this function explicitly for a stream that is associated with a file, if you must close this file before the end of the scope for which you declared the stream.*

C. Input/output with memory

Just as you can associate a stream with a disk file, you can associate a stream with an area of memory (with a table of characters). This feature replaces the C functions `fprintf()`, `sprintf()`, `fscanf()` and `sscanf()`.

In an analogous way to `<fstream.h>`, the `<stsstream.h>` interface specifies the classes `strstream`, `istrstream` and `ostrstream`.

The constructors of these three classes take at least two parameters.

The first parameter is of the type `char *` and indicates the beginning of the memory zone that you wish to use.

The second parameter is of the type `int` and indicates the size of this memory zone.

The constructors of the classes `strstream` and `ostrstream` take a third parameter that is of the type `open_mode`. This parameter indicates the opening mode. It specifies whether you want to open the file in read mode or in write mode. Each constructor has a default value of `ios::out`.

```
char buffer[500];

strstream stream(buffer,sizeof(buffer));
```

The above instructions associate `stream` with `buffer`.

You do not have to worry about any overflow of your buffer as the stream manages this aspect. If you exceed the buffer size then the stream will go into `fail` state.

For this type of stream, the '\0' character is equivalent to the end-of-file character.

Chapter 6

Templates

A. Template functions 177

B. Template class 182

Chapter 6

Templates are also known as *models* or *generic types*. They allow you to construct a family of functions, or a family of classes, without concerning yourself with certain data types. In fact, the type becomes a parameter of the function or of the class.

A. Template functions

Suppose you have a function called `max(x,y)` that returns the greater of its two arguments. These two arguments, x and y, can be any type, and they can be an ordered pair. However, as C++ is strongly typed, you must declare the types of the x and y parameters when you compile your program. If you do not use a template, then you must use numerous overloaded versions of the `max` function. You will need one overloaded version for each data type that your function must support, even though the function code is identical for each of them. Each of your versions must compare the two arguments and then return the value of the greater one.

You can get round this problem by using the following macro:

```
#define max(x,y) (((x) (y)) ? (x) : (y))
```

However, if you use `#define` then you will also bypass the type control mechanism, which is a C++ improvement with respect to C. In fact with C++, this usage of macros is almost obsolete. The objective of `max(x,y)` is to compare types that are compatible with each other, whereas this macro would allow you to compare types that are incompatible with each other, such as an `int` and a `struct`.

Moreover, if you use a macro you could substitute values where you might not wish to do so. On the other hand, if you use a template, you can define a structure for a family of associated, overloaded functions, by including the data type as a parameter.

In order to specify a function that has one or more types as parameters, you must prefix your function as follows:

```
template <class T1,class T2>
// so as to include two types as parameters
```

In this way, you can declare as local variables, objects of type `T1` or `T2` as function parameters or as function return types (you can also specify `T1*` or `T2&` in this way).

 You must use the class keyword even if you use a standard type for `T1` or for `T2` (such as `int` or `char *`, for example).

You must declare `max(x,y)` as follows:

```
template <class T>
T max(T x, T y)
{
   return (x > y) ? x : y
}
```

Then, you can call your function as follows:

```
Rational r,r1(1,2),r2(1,3);
int n;
double x;

n=max(1,2);
x=max(1.0,2.0);
r=max(r1,r2);
```

But what code will the compiler generate?

When you define the body of the `max()` template function, the compiler will not generate any code. It will consider this function body as a "declaration".

Chapter 6

When you call `max()` for the first time, passing integer arguments, the compiler will generate the specific code for this function, in which it will "replace" `T` with `int`.

Upon your second call to this function, the compiler will generate further code for `max()`, in which it will "replace" `T` with `double`.

When you call `max()` for the third time using `Rational` values, then the compiler will deal with your call in a similar manner.

On a practical level, the compiler will generate an overload for `max()` automatically, each time that it needs to do so. The template is said to be **instantiated**.

The strong typing of C++ means that you cannot call `max()` with two parameters that have incompatible types. This feature illustrates a first constraint for this function.

What will happen if you write the following instruction?

```
double x=max(1 , 2.0);
```

In this case, the compiler will raise an error, as it will not find the prototype for `max(int,double);`. The template specifies that the two `max()` parameters must be of the same type and the compiler will make no implicit conversion in order to satisfy this constraint.

In order to solve this problem you could specify the template as follows:

```
template <class T1,class T2>
T2 max(T1 x, T2 y)
{
   return (x   y) ? x : y;
}
```

With this template, all the calls that you will have made up to now will work correctly. However, if you decide to switch the order of the parameters in the last call, as follows:

```
double x=max(2.0 , 1);
```

then the compiler will warn you that you might lose precision because of the conversion from `double` to `int`. This will not be a problem in this case, but in general you would effectively lose precision.

Consequently, this is not a satisfactory solution, as it privileges only one of the two data types for the return value of the function.

Unfortunately, you cannot introduce a third type as a parameter for the return type of `max()`, as follows:

```
template <class T1,class T2,class T3>
T3 max(T1 x, T2 y)
{
   return (x > y) ? x : y;
}
```

because the compiler cannot generate the code for all the calls to `max()`, as the function return type is not part of the function signature.

The only way round this problem is to keep the first version of `max()` and to make an implicit conversion when you call it:

```
double x=max(double(1), 2.0);
```

A further constraint with `max()` is that your definition of `operator()` must be "consistent" with the type that you use when you call the `max()` function. For example, if you use the following instructions:

```
const char *s, *s1="code",*s2="cone";
s=max(s1,s2);
```

although the compiler will not raise an error, the program will test `(s1>s2)`. Thereby it will compare the memory addresses of `s1` and of `s2`, which is not really what you want it to do.

C++ programming language

Chapter 6

In order to solve this problem you can define an explicit overload on `max()` for the type const `char *`:

```
const char *max(const char *s1,const char *s2)
{
   return strcmp(s1,s2)0 ? s1 :s2 ;
}
```

Then, as there is an explicit overload on `max` for the type `const char *`, the compiler will not generate a new one using the template. The compiler will use the template in order to produce a function that corresponds to a given prototype, only as a last resort.

Here is a second example of a simple template function. The objective of this function is to exchange the values of two variables:

```
template <class T>
void swap(T& v1 , T& v2)
{
   T tmp;
   tmp=v1;
   v1=v2;
   v2=tmp;
}
```

The constraint in this case is that you must define `operator()` "consistently" for all the types that you use in order to call this function.

You could not have implemented this generic function using a macro.

To conclude, you must implement a template function whenever its algorithm is independent of the types that you use.

B. Template class

You can use this parameterized types mechanism in order to define a class. As with template functions, in order to do this you need only prefix your class specification with template <....>

Suppose that you want to create a class that will implement a data list. Whatever the type of the data that is concerned, you will carry out the same operations on the data list (inserting, deleting, indexing, and so forth). In addition, as a user of this class, you will not have to concern yourself with the internal implementation of this list, even though you may be able to view this organization in the private and in the protected parts of the specification. As a user, you will be interested only by the public operations (in this case a simple linked list will be used).

```
template <class T>
class List
{
protected:

  struct list
  {
    T val;
    struct list * next;

    list(T,v) : val(v) {}
  };

  list *start;
  unsigned len;

  list *last();
  list *next_but_last;
  // member data is updated upon each call
  // to last()                              .../...
```

```
.../...
public:
List()
  {
    start=0;
    len=0;
  }

  ~List();

  unsigned length() const
  { return len; }

  // 2 add functions in the list:
  // the second add function adds an element
  // to the end of the list.
  // the first add function adds an element
  // at a precise position in the list.

  void add(const T&,unsigned position);
  void add(const T& val)
  { add(val,len); }

  void del(unsigned index);
  void clear();

  T& operator[](unsigned) const;
};
```

This specification illustrates a constraint on the parameterized type. The constructor for the list private structure requires a "correct" initializer for the type T.

When you implement template classes, it is useful if you ensure that all the constraints on the parameterized types appear clearly. In order to do this, you can insert the bodies of the member functions directly in your specification (however, in this case you do not need to indicate the constraint with a comment as well). Alternatively, you can omit the member function bodies from the specification and you can indicate the constraints that these absent member function bodies imply, using a comment. As a user can generally access only the class interface (the .h file), then the user will not see these constraints.

In general, you should indicate all the constraints as comments in the class interface.

You can declare an instance of an integer list (for example) as follows:

```
List<int> l;
```

Then, you can handle `l` as follows:

```
l.add(0);

. . .

l[0]=12;

. . .

l.del(0);

. . .

l.clear();
```

An instance of a template class cannot be generic. You must specify the type(s) with which this instance runs.

You must note that the `List` symbol appears in its specification, and as it is a template, it must now always appear as follows:

```
List<type>
```

`type` can be a parameterized type (this book will discuss this point further, later on).

The instances of a given type are compatible with each other. For example, you can assign instances.

```
List<int> l1;
List<int> l2;
List<double> l3;

    . . .

l2=l1; // OK

l3=l1; // Error!
```

Naturally, in order to enable the first assignment to run correctly, you must define the assignment operator correctly for the template class `List`.

As with template functions, when you declare an instance, the compiler will generate the class definition for the type concerned (if it has not already done this). Consequently, the `l1` and `l2` type is `List<int>` and the `l3` type is `List`. As these are not the same symbols, they are not the same types.

The member function bodies of template classes are template functions. Consequently, you must prefix them with template <...>, even if the function does not use the parameterized type(s).

```
template <class T>
List<T>::~List()
{
   clear();
}
```

Naturally, this class needs a destructor, since the internal implementation by linked list implies that each list element will be allocated dynamically. Consequently, you must release the memory at the end of the instance's lifetime.

Even though this function is not concerned about whether or not there is a parameterized type, it is still a template function. In addition, you must remember that the `List` symbol must no longer appear as such. However, in order to indicate that this function is a member of the `List` class, you must prefix the function name with `class_name::`. Then, you have to place something between the `<` and the `>`. You include simply a parameterized type that is declared in the `template` specification.

As a syntax example, here is an (artificial) specification of a template class that has two parameterized types:

```
template <class T1,class T2>
class A
{
   void member();
}

template <class T1,class T2>
void A<T1,T2>::member()
{
   . . .
}

A<int,double> a;
```

Here is the `List` class example, completed with the bodies of its other member functions:

```
template <class T>
void List<T>::clear()
{
   list *current,*next;
   for(current=start;current!=0;current=next)
      {
         next=current->next;
         delete current;
      }
   len=0;
   start=0;
}
template <class T>
List<T>::list * List<T>::last()
{                                      .../...
```

C++ programming language

```
.../...
  if(start==0)
    {
      next_but_last=0;
      return 0;
    }
  list *current=start;
  while(current->next!=0)
    {
      next_but_last=current;
      current=current->next;
    }
.../...
  return current;
}

template <class T>
T& List<T>::operator[](unsigned n) const
{
  if(n>=len) exit(1); // fatal

  list *current;
  unsigned i;

  for(i=0,current=start;i!=n;i++)
    current=current->next;

  return current->val;
}

template <class T>
void List<T>::add(const T& val,unsigned position)
{
  if(position>len) exit(1); // fatal

  list *newl=new list(val);

  if(position==0)
    {
      list *former_start=start;
      start=newl;
      newl->next= former_start;
    }
  else if(position==len)
    {
      last()->next = newl;
      newl->next = 0;
    }                                      .../...
```

```
.../...
  else
  // then the list has at least 2 elements
     {
        list *before,*after;
        unsigned i;

        for(i=0,after=start;i!=position;i++)
           {
              before=after;
              after=after->next;
           }
        before->next=newl;
        newl->next=after;
     }
  ++len;
}

template <class T>
void List<T>::del(unsigned index)
{
  if(index>=len) exit(1); // fatal

  if(index==0)
     {
        list *former_second=start->next;
        delete start;
        start=former_second;
     }
  else if(index==len-1)
     {
        delete last();
        next_but_last->next=0;
     }
  else
  // then the list has at least 3 elements
     {
        list *before,*current;
        unsigned i;

        for(i=0,current=start;i!=index;i++)
           {
              before=current;
              current=current->next;
           }
        before->next=current->next;
        delete current;
     }
  --len;
}
```

Note the header of the `last()` member function. Its return type is `list *`. However, as this structure is internal to the `List` class, you must use the scope operator in order to specify the return type for this function.

This program calls the `exit()` function three times. It calls this function when tries to access an element that does not exist, or when it tries to create an element beyond the end of the list. This is a basic error-management technique. This book will shortly indicate how you can provide a user with an error recovery mechanism using exceptions. In addition, if the user of the class does not use this mechanism, then the program will stop all the same.

Now that this program has fully defined the `List` class, when you use this class in a function (as a parameter or as a local variable), or when you use this class as a member of another class, then you must specify the type concerned (either an existing type, or a parameterized type). If you specify a parameterized type, then the function or the class will become a template. For example:

```
template <class T>
ostream& operator<<(ostream& out,const List<T>& l)
{
  for(unsigned i=0;i<l.length();i++)
    out<<l[i]<<'\n';
  out<<'\n';
  return out;
}

template <class T>
class Pile
{
protected:
  List<T> pile;
public:

  int IsEmpty()
  { return pile.length()==0; }

  void push(T val)
  { pile.add(val); }              .../...
```

```
.../...
  T pop();
};

template <class T>
T Pile<T>::pop()
{
  if(IsEmpty()) exit(1); // fatal

  T res=pile[pile.length()-1];
  pile.del(pile.length()-1);
  return res;
}
```

Similarly, you can derive a template class. In this case the derived class will not be a template, provided that you specify the type(s) for the template class that you enumerated in the derivation list (this is the case for the `Derive2` class that follows).

```
template <class T>
class Derive1 : public List<T>
{
  . . .
};

class Derive2 : public List<String>
{
  // therefore, this is a template class
  . . .
};

template <class T>
class Derive3 : public List<int>
{
  // Using the parameterized type T only
  // internally to the Derive3 class
  . . .
};
```

Chapter 7

Exceptions

A.	Introduction	193
B.	Propagating exceptions explicitly	197
C.	Acquiring resources	199
D.	Classes and exceptions	200
E.	Exceptions that are not caught	207

Chapter 7

The author of a software component such as one or more classes in a library can detect runtime errors but does not generally know what the program should do about these errors. The user of a software component may know how the program should manage runtime errors but he/she cannot detect them. The exception concept is provided in order to deal with this sort of problem.

A. Introduction

The basic principle of an exception is as follows: when a function meets a problem that it does not know how to handle, it **throws** an exception hoping that its caller (either its direct or indirect caller) will be able to deal with it.

A function that wants to manage this sort of problem must indicate that it would like to **catch** the exception.

If an exception is not caught, then the program will call abort().

A function throws an exception using the throw keyword, followed by an item of data that can be of any type:

```
void f(int n)
{
  if(n==0) // this is an error!
    throw "Exception";
  cout<<"f() OK\n";
}
```

The calling function indicates that it wants to catch an exception using a **try** block, which contains one or more function calls (the calling function might not have called f() directly; it might have called a function that called f()).

The calling function catches an exception using a **catch** block, which is also called an exception handler. The catch block must specify the type of the data that is thrown as an exception. It can also specify a name that stores the value of this type so that it can use this value in the catch block.

The catch block(s) follow the try block.

```
void main()
{
  try
  {
    f(10);
    f(0);
    f(20);
  }
  catch(char * s)
  {
    cout<<s<<'\n';
  }
  // normal sequence
  cout<<"End of main()\n";
}
```

This program outputs the following lines:

```
f() OK
Exception
End of main()
```

The call to f(10) runs normally. A call to f(0) follows, which raises an exception. The program flow is interrupted at this point.

The exception is communicated to the calling functions (in this case main() is the only calling function) until one of them indicates that it wants to catch the exception (call in a try block).

Then, this function tries its exception handlers in the order that it has defined, so as to find a `catch` block for the type that is raised by the exception (in this case, this type is `char *`). The function then runs the instructions that are contained in this `catch` block.

If the type that is indicated in the catch block had not been `char *`:

```
void main()
{
  try
  {
    f(10);
    f(0);
    f(20);
  }
  catch(int n)
  {
    cout<<n<<'\n';
  }
  // normal sequence
  cout<<"End of main()\n";
}
```

then, the calling program will not be able to catch the exception and will transmit the exception to its calling functions. In this case it does not have any, so the program will close.

This version of this program will output the following line:

```
f() OK
```

The call to `f(0)` provokes an error that stops the program.

In no case (whether the exception is caught or not) will this program ever call the `f(20)` function.

Here is an example of the exception mechanism via several calling functions. This example keeps the same `f()` function, and it introduces the `g()` function, plus a new version of `main()`:

```cpp
void g()
{
   f(10);
   f(0);
   f(20);
   cout<<"End of g()\n";
}

void main()
{
   try
   {
      g();
   }
   catch(char * s)
   {
      cout<<"main() exception handler\n";
      cout<<s<<'\n';
   }
   // normal sequence
   cout<<"End of main()\n";
}
```

Here is an alternative version of this program:

```cpp
void g()
{
   try
   {
      f(10);
      f(0);
      f(20);
   }
   catch(int n)
   {
      cout<<n<<'\n';
   }
   // normal sequence
   cout<<"End of g()\n";
}
                                        .../...
```

```
.../...
void main()
{
  try
  {
    g();
  }
  catch(char * s)
  {
    cout<<"main() exception handler\n";
    cout<<s<<'\n';
  }
  // normal sequence
  cout<<"End of main()\n";
}
```

These programs output the following lines:

```
f() OK
main() exception handler
Exception
End of main()
```

B. Propagating exceptions explicitly

When it has finished dealing with an exception, an exception handler may decide to propagate the same exception to its calling functions. The exception handler may take such action if it decides that it was not able to deal with the problem fully, and that its calling functions must take over this task.

In order to do this, the program need only specify a `throw` instruction.

```
void g()
{
  try
  {
    f(10);
    f(0);                                    .../...
```

```
.../...
    f(20);
  }
  catch(char * s)
  {
    cout<<"g() exception handler\n";
    cout<<s<<'\n';
    throw;
  }
  // normal sequence

  cout<<"End of g()\n";
}

void main()
{
  try
  {
    g();
  }
  catch(char * s)
  {
    cout<<"main() exception handler\n";
    cout<<s<<'\n';
  }
  // normal sequence
  cout<<"End of main()\n";
}
```

This program will output the following lines:

```
f() OK
g() exception handler
Exception
main() exception handler
Exception
End of main()
```

In some cases, you might wish to catch an exception, whatever its type. You can do this by indicating an ellipsis (...) as the catch "parameter".

If you define `g()` as follows:

```
void g()
{
  try
  {
    f(10);
    f(0);
    f(20);
  }
  catch(...)
  {
    cout<<"g() exception handler\n";
    throw;
  }
  // normal sequence
  cout<<"End of g()\n";
}
```

then this program will output the following lines:

```
g() exception handler
main() exception handler
Exception
End of main()
```

C. Acquiring resources

When a function obtains a resource (when it opens a file or when it allocates memory for example), then it is important that you release this resource, whatever happens. You can ensure this by using the elements that this chapter has described previously:

```
void memory_allocation()
{
  double array=new double[10000];

  try
  {                                      .../...
```

```
.../...
    // using the array
    . . .
  }
  catch(...)
  {
    delete [] array;
    throw;
  }
  delete [] array;
}
```

Thereby, you will release the memory allocation for your array whether the try block raises an exception or not.

D. Classes and exceptions

As this chapter has indicated, exceptions are raised with a data type value.

This data type can be a class, which provides you with all the advantages that classes offer (such as constructors and inheritance, for example).

In this case, a `catch` block for a class type is **the exception handler for this class and also for all its derived classes (either its directly derived classes or its indirectly derived classes)**.

In this case also, the order in which you indicate the `catch` blocks is important, as you must specify the block that is relative to a derived class before you specify the block that is relative to the base class. If you do not specify these blocks in this order, then the base class block will run and the block that is specific to one of its derived classes will not run.

In fact, as soon as the program finds an exception handler that corresponds to the type of an exception, then the program will use this exception handler and it will skip those that follow.

Example:
```
class GeneralException
{};

class Exception1 : public GeneralException
{};

class Exception2 : public GeneralException
{};

void f()
{
  try
  {
    . . .
  }
  catch (Exception1& e)
  {
    // processing
    . . .
  }
  catch (GeneralException)
  {
    . . .
  }
}
```

The first exception handler will deal with the exceptions of `Exception1`, and the second exception handler will deal with the exceptions of `GeneralException` and those of `Exception2`.

If you change the order of these two exception handlers, then the first exception handler will deal with the exceptions of `GeneralException`, of `Exception1` and of `Exception2`. In this case, the second exception handler will never run.

In the definition of the `List` class template that appeared in the previous chapter, all the calls to `exit()` should raise an exception for a local class type of the `List` class. You could write the following sequence:

```
template <class T>
class List
{
protected:

  struct list
  {
    T val;
    struct list * next;

    list(T v) : val(v) {}
  };

  list *start;
  unsigned len;

  list *last();
  list *next_but_last;
  // member data that is updated upon each call
  // to last()

public:
  List()
    {
      start=0;
      len=0;
    }

  ~List();

  unsigned length() const
  { return len; }

  // 2 adding functions in the list:
  //    the 2nd adds an element at
  //    the end of the list.
  //    the 1st adds an element at
  //    a precise position in the list.
  void add(const T&,unsigned position);
  void add(const T& val)
  { add(val,len); }                           .../...
```

C++ programming language

```
.../...
  void del(unsigned index);
  void clear();

  T& operator[](unsigned) const;

  class BadIndex
  {
  protected:
    const char *Function_Fname;
    unsigned Findex;
    unsigned Fsize;
  public:
    BadIndex(const char *s,unsigned i,unsigned l)
      : Function_Fname(s),Findex(i),FSize(l) {}

    const char *function_name()
    { return Function_Fname; }

    unsigned index()
    { return Findex; }

    unsigned size()
    { return Fsize; }
  };
};
```

You can also modify the body of `operator[]()` as follows:

```
template <class T>
T& List<T>::operator[](unsigned n) const
{
  if(n>=len) throw BadIndex("[]",n,len);

  list *current;
  unsigned i;
  for(i=0,current=start;i!=n;i++)
    current=current->next;

  return current->val;
}
```

You can replace the other calls to `exit()` in a similar manner.

In the same way, the following program:

```
void main({
  List<int> l;

  l.add(1)
  try
  {
    l{1}=0;
  }
  catch(List<int>::BadIndex& e)
  {
    cout<<"Calling "<<e.function_name()<<
          "with the value of index "<<e.index()<<
          "for a list of size "<<e.size()<<'\n';
  }
}
```

will output the following line:

```
Calling [] with the value of index 1 for a list of
size 1
```

 Note that the `e` instance of the `catch` block is a reference. Each time that you want to get the value of an exception then you must declare (for the exception handler) either a pointer, or a reference.

When you program exceptions, the best approach is to make the type of your exceptions a class (if possible with a name that does not have global scope).

Moreover, the ANSI is currently studying a proposal of class hierarchies (and of their associated members) for standard exceptions.

For example, part of this class hierarchy could well be as follows:

```
class Exception
{
   . . .
};

class MathError : public Exception

{
   . . .
};

class ZeroDivide : public MathError
{
   . . .
};

class SystemError : public Exception
{
   . . .
};

class MemoryFault : public SystemError
{
   . . .
};
```

This complete hierarchy would be specified in a standard interface (in `<exception.h>` for example).

When you work with exceptions, then the runtime environment of your C++ programs needs to interact with the operating system. In fact, divisions by zero and memory access errors that provoke a core dump, are generally handled by the system (indeed they are called system exceptions). The system then stops the program that generated such errors. In order to be able handle these errors from your C++ program, the compiler that you use must take account of the target operating system.

C++ compilers for Windows environments implement such exception hierarchies: for example, the *C++ Builder* compiler, and the Visual *C++* compiler. Although, the exception hierarchies of these two compilers function in a similar way, they do not necessarily use the same class names (as a standard has not yet been established in this field). This is a pity. However, these programs are able to interact with the exceptions that the system detects.

Similarly, certain libraries in the UNIX environment provide exception hierarchies. Not only are these exception hierarchies not necessarily the same ones, but also they do not generally interact with the system (consequently a core dump is still inevitable).

It is highly desirable that a standard will rapidly be published in this field, and that the compiler vendors will follow its recommendations (this will require these vendors to carry out a great deal of work in order to implement system exceptions).

Thereby, every correct `main()` function must have the following framework:

```
void main({
  try
  {
    . . .
  }
  catch(Exception& e)
  {
    // Display as much as possible of the
    // information that is supplied by e
    . . .
  }
}
```

In the meantime, if you develop a standalone software component, then your exceptions may be totally independent from each other (indeed only some of them may participate in a class hierarchy). For the moment, you cannot derive them from a root exception class, as nothing has yet been standardized in this field.

If you develop a complete program, then you should implement at least one root exception class (that has global scope), from which all the other exceptions should derive (although your derived exceptions need not necessarily have global scope). In order to do this, you can use as an example the implementation of `String` that is in the appendix.

E. Exceptions that are not caught

This chapter indicated earlier, that when you throw an exception and your exception is not caught, then the program calls the `abort()` function.

In fact, this is not strictly the case. In reality, the program will call the `terminate()` function, and this function will then call the `abort()` function by default.

Alternatively, you can specify that `terminate()` must call different function, using the `set_terminate()` function as follows:

```
typedef void (*PF)();
PF set_terminate(PF);
```

`set_terminate()` returns the pointer of the function that was previously passed to `set_terminate()`. When your program calls `set_terminate()` for the first time, it will receive a pointer to `abort()`.

Your program will also call `terminate()` when your exception handling mechanism detects that the stack has changed. It will also call `terminate()` when your program is running the stack that has been provoked by an exception and calls a destructor that tries to close by using an exception.

Your program will call `terminate()` as a last resort. It is particularly useful in order to implement fault tolerance, as you can use it so as to re-initialize this system, and/or so as to stop a process, for example.

Appendix

A. Full Rational class **211**

B. Full String class **217**

Appendices

A. Full Rational class

rational.h file

```cpp
#include <iostream.h>

#ifndef RATIONAL_H

#define RATIONAL_H

class Rational
{
protected:
  int num;
  unsigned denom;
public:
  // Constructor
  Rational(int =0,unsigned =1);

  // Converting Rational-double
  operator double() const;

  // Access functions
  int numerator() const;
  unsigned denominator() const;

  // Arithmetic operators
  Rational operator +() const; // unary
  Rational operator -() const; // unary

  Rational& operator++();
  Rational operator++(int);
  Rational& operator--();
  Rational operator--(int);

  Rational& operator+=(Rational);
  Rational& operator-=(Rational);
  Rational& operator*=(Rational);
  Rational& operator/=(Rational);

  // input to Rational
  friend
    istream& operator >>(istream&,Rational&);
};                                              .../...
```

```
.../...

/*
****************************************************
This program presents, function prototypes that
are neither members nor friends of the class.
Access functions are sufficient in order to
implement these functions.
****************************************************
*/

// output from Rational
ostream& operator >(ostream& out,Rational r);


// Other arithmetic operators
Rational operator +(Rational,Rational);
Rational operator -(Rational,Rational);
Rational operator *(Rational,Rational);
Rational operator /(Rational,Rational);


// Relational functions
int operator==(Rational,Rational);
int operator!=(Rational,Rational);
int operator<(Rational,Rational);
int operator<=(Rational,Rational);
int operator>(Rational,Rational);
int operator>=(Rational,Rational);


/*
****************************************************
Inline implementation
****************************************************
*/

inline int Rational::numerator() const
{
  return num;
}

inline unsigned Rational::denominator() const
{
  return denom;
}
                                            .../...
```

Appendix

```
.../...

inline Rational Rational::operator+() const
{
  return *this;
}

inline Rational Rational::operator-() const
{
  return Rational(-num,denom);
}

#endif
```

rational.C file

```
#include "rational.h"

static unsigned pgcd_rec(unsigned a,unsigned b)
{
  unsigned remain=a%b;
  return (remain==0) ? b : pgcd_rec(b,remain);
}

static unsigned pgcd(unsigned a,unsigned b)
{
  return (a<b) ? pgcd_rec(b,a) : pgcd_rec(a,b);
}

static unsigned abs(int n)
{
  return (n<0) ? -n : n;
}

Rational::Rational(int n,unsigned d)
{
  unsigned p=(n==0) ? 1 : pgcd(abs(n),d);
  num=n/p;
  denom=d/p;
}                                       .../...
```

```cpp
Rational::operator double() const
{
  return double(num)/denom;
}

Rational& Rational::operator++()
{
  num+=denom;
  return *this;
}

Rational Rational::operator++(int n)
{
  Rational r=*this;
  num+=denom;
  return r;
}

Rational& Rational::operator--()
{
  num-=denom;
  return *this;
}

Rational Rational::operator--(int n)
{
  Rational r=*this;
  num-=denom;
  return r;
}

Rational& Rational::operator+=(Rational r)
{
  *this=*this+r;
  return *this;
}

Rational& Rational::operator-=(Rational r)
{
  *this=*this-r;
  return *this;
}

Rational& Rational::operator*=(Rational r)
{
```
.../...

```cpp
.../...
  num*=r.num;
  denom*=r.denom;
  return *this;
}

Rational& Rational::operator/=(Rational r)
{
  num*=r.denom;
  denom*=r.num;
  return *this;
}

istream& operator >>(istream& in,Rational& r)
{
  in>>r.num>>r.denom;
  return in;
}

ostream& operator <<(ostream& out,Rational r)
{
  out<<r.numerator()<<'/'<<r.denominator();
  return out;
}

Rational operator +(Rational r1, Rational r2)
{
  return
    Rational(
      r1.numerator()*r2.denominator()+
      r2.numerator()*r1.denominator(),
      r1.denominator()*r2.denominator());
}

Rational operator -(Rational r1, Rational r2)
{
  return r1+(-r2);
}

Rational operator *(Rational r1, Rational r2)
{
  return
    Rational(
      r1.numerator()*r2.numerator(),
      r1.denominator()*r2.denominator());
}                                            .../...
```

```cpp
.../...

Rational operator /(Rational r1, Rational r2)
{
   return
     Rational(
       r1.numerator()*r2.denominator(),
       r1.denominator()*r2.numerator());
}

int operator==(Rational r1,Rational r2)
{
   return
     (r1.numerator()==r2.numerator()) &&
     (r1.denominator()==r2.denominator());
}

int operator!=(Rational r1,Rational r2)
{
   return !(r1==r2);
}

int operator<(Rational r1,Rational r2)
{
   return
     r1.numerator()*r2.denominator()<
     r2.numerator()*r1.denominator();
}

int operator<=(Rational r1,Rational r2)
{
   return
     r1.numerator()*r2.denominator()<=
     r2.numerator()*r1.denominator();
}

int operator>(Rational r1,Rational r2)
{
   return !(r1<=r2);
}

int operator>=(Rational r1,Rational r2)
{
   return !(r1<r2);
}
```

You can implement `operator==()` *in the same way that this example implements* `operator<()`, *by replacing* < *with* ==. *However, as in this example you can be sure that the rational values are irreducible (thanks to the calculation in* `pgcd`*), the implementation shown is preferable because it provides better performance (although it will work only in this case).*

B. Full String class

string.h file

```
#ifndef STRING_H
#define STRING_H

#include <iostream.h>

class String
{
protected:
  // Internal form
  char *s;
  size_t len;

  // Constructor for use inside the class
  String(size_t);

  // Used in order to check that you can access
  // a character
  void check_index(size_t i);

public:

  // Constructors, destructor
  String(const char * =0);
  String(char);
  ~String();                              .../...
```

```cpp
.../...

  // Initializing
  String(const String&);

  // Assigning
  String& operator(const String&);

  // Information function
  size_t length() const
  { return len; }

  // Converting to const char *
  operator const char *() const
  ( return s; }

  // Indexing
  char& operator[] (size_t i);

  // Concatenating
  friend String operator+(String,String);
  String& operator+=(String);

  // Extracting sub-strings
  String operator() (size_t start,size_t end);

  // Exception for bad indexing
  class BadIndex;

};

// String input
istream& operator>>(istream& in,String& s);

#endif
```

exception.h file

```
#ifndef EXCEPTION_H
#define EXCEPTION_H

#include "string.h"

class Exception
{
protected:
  String name;
  Exception(char *s) : name(s) {}
public:
  Exception() : name("Exception")
  { }
  String type()
  { return name; }
};

#endif
```

string.c file

```
#include <string.h>
#include <strstream.h>

#include "exception.h"
#include "string.h"


class String::BadIndex : public Exception
{
  friend String;

protected:
  BadIndex(size_t index,size_t len);
  String mess;
public:
  String message()
  { return mess; }
};
                                      .../...
```

```
.../...
String::BadIndex::BadIndex(size_t i,size_t len)
  : Exception("string.BadIndex")
{
  char s[20];
  ostream buf(s,sizeof(s));
  buf<<i<<'\0';
  mess="Accessing character "+String(s)+
       " for a String of ";
  buf.seekp(0);
  buf<<len<<'\0';
  mess+=String(s)+" character(s)";
}

String::String(size_t n)
// Constructing a String of size n
{
  len=n;
  s=new char[n+1];
  s[len]='\0';
}

String::String(char c)
{
  len=1;
  s=new char[2];
  s[0]=c;
  s[1]='\0';
}

String::String(const char *ch)
{
  if(ch==0)
  {
    len=0;
    s=new char(0);
  }
  else
  {
    len=strlen(ch);
    s=new char[len+1];
    strcpy(s,ch);
  }
}
                                            .../...
```

```
.../...
String::~String()
{
  delete [] s;
}

String::String(const String& s0)
{
  len=s0.len;
  if(len==0)
    s=new char(0);
  else
  {
    s=new char[len+1];
    strcpy(s,s0.s);
  }
}

String& String::operator=(const String& s0)
{
  delete [] s;

  len=s0.len;
  if(len==0)
    s=new char(0);
  else
  {
    s=new char[len+1];
    strcpy(s,s0.s);
  }

  return *this;
}

void String::verify_index(size_t i)
{
  if(i>=len)
    throw BadIndex(i,len);
}

char & String::operator[] (size_t i)
{
  check_index(i);
  return s[i];
}
                                  .../...
```

```
.../...
String operator+(String s1,String s2)
{
  String res(s1.len+s2.len);
  size_t i;

  for(i=0;i<s1.len;++i)  res[i]=s1.s[i];
  for(i=0;i<s2.len;++i)  res[i+s1.len]=s2.s[i];

  return res;
}

String& String::operator+=(String s0)
{
  return *this = *this+s0;
}

String String::operator() (size_t start,
                           size_t end)
{
  check_index(start);
  check_index(end);

  String res(end-start+1);
  for(size_t i=start;i<=end;++i)
    res[i-start]=s[i];
  return res;
}

// Annex function for String input
// You do not need to use a static storage
// buffer, as this function dynamically allocates
// the required memory when you have fully
// entered the string

static char * input(size_t len,istream&
                    in,char separator = '\n')
{
  char c;
  char *res;

  in.get(c);

  if(c==separator)
  {
                                      .../...
```

C++ programming language

Appendix

```
.../...
    res=new char[len+1];
    res[len]='\0';
  }
  else
    res=input(len+1,in,separator);
    res[len]=c;
  }
  return res;
}

istream& operator>>istream& in,String& s)
{
  char *str=input(0,in);
  s=str;
  delete [] str;
  return in;
}
```

This example declares the `String` class as a friend of the `BadIndex` exception so that the `String` class can access the constructor of the `BadIndex` exception in the `check_index` function.

This example did not declare the `BadIndex` constructor as `public` in order to ensure that only the `String` class would be able to raise such an exception.

A

Abstract classes, *136, 141, 149*
Abstract data type
    tree structure, *11*
Access control, *117*
Acquiring resources, *199*
Ada programming language, *9*
Allocating memory, *29*
Andrew Koenig, *166*
Anonymous union, *21 - 22*
ANSI, *204*
ANSI X3J16 committee, *9*
Arguments
    by reference, *100*
    by value, *100*
    default values, *38 - 39*
    effective parameters, *41*
    formal parameter, *41, 44, 81, 105*
    passing, *41*
    passing arguments by address, *43*
    passing arguments by reference, *45*
    passing arguments by value, *42*
    passing by value, *89*
    real parameters, *42, 44*
Arithmetic expressions, *136*
Array of function pointers, *107*
Array of member function pointers, *107*
Assigning, *18*
Assigning derived classes, *127*
Assignment operators, *147*
AT&T Bell Laboratories, *9*

Base class, *116, 126, 149, 200*
Binary arithmetic operators, *74*
Bjarne Stroustrup, *9*

C

C preprocessor macros, *41*
C++ Builder, *125, 205*
C++ compilers for Windows environments, *205*
Canonical format, *82*
catch block, *194, 200*
cerr, *26*
cin, *26*
Class, *11, 26, 55*
    abstract classes, *141*
    access control, *57*
    assigning, *67, 89*
    assigning derived classes, *127*
    class member of a class, *101*
    compound assigments, *91*
    concrete classes, *141*
    constructing, *64*
    converting, *67, 96*
    converting from, *69*
    converting to, *67*
    definition syntax, *56*
    deriving, *115*
    destructor, *83*
    friend functions, *75*
    hierarchy, *115, 128*
    incrementing/decrementing, *78*
    initializing, *67, 87*
    initializing derived classes, *127*
    initializing references, *104*
    input/output, *80*
    members, *56*
    ostream, *81*
    pointers to members of a class, *107*
    private, *57*
    protected, *57*
    prototype, *89*
    public, *57*
    specification, *85*
    table of instances, *86*
Class composition, *122*
Class definition, *63*

Class derivation, *116*
Class hierarchy, *128, 130, 141*
Class inheritance, *116*
Class instance member of another class
    class member of a class, *101*
Class template, *202*
Classes and exceptions, *200*
CLU programming language, *9*
Comments
    C notation, *17*
    C++ notation, *17*
Concrete classes, *141*
const, *17, 61*
Constant pointer, *24*
Constant pointer to a constant, *25*
Constructing a derived class, *126*
Constructors, *64, 68, 84, 101, 147*
Converting from a class, *69*
Converting to a class, *67*
Converting with public derived classes, *121*
Copy constructor, *88*
Core dump, *205*
cout, *26*
cp, *170*
ctype.h, *158*

Data declaration, *18*
Data member, *63, 103*
Data types, *18*
    abstract , *11*
    base, *11*
    derived, *11*
Declaring, *18*
    constants, *23*
    functions, *36*
    with initialization, *18*
Default argument values, *38*
Default constructor, *126*
Defining data types, *10*
Defining functions, *36*
delete, *29*

delete operator, 31
Derivation
    private, 120
    protected, 119
    public, 119
    types of, 119
Derived class, 61, 126, 200
Derived class constructors, 118
Destructor, 147
Dynamic memory
    managing, 29
Dynamic typing, 12, 127, 131
    exceptions, 135
dynamic_cast function, 123

Effective parameters, 41
egcs compiler, 13, 20, 39
Encapsulation, 55, 117
Enumeration functions, 157
Enumeration types, 21
Environment, 13
Exception handler, 194, 204
exception.h, 205
Exceptions, 193
    propagating explicitly, 197
    system exception, 205
Explicit conversion, 68

float, 29
Formal parameters, 41, 44, 89
free, 29
Freeing memory space, 147
Friend, 81, 93, 122
Friend functions, 75, 95, 147
Friend keyword, 76
fstream, 168
Function, 10
    function description header, 45
    overloading, 50
    prototype, 45

return by reference, *93*
return by value, *89*
returning from, *47*
signature, *50*
with no return value, *20*
Function definition header, *36, 41*
Function description header, *45*
Function member, *86*
Function prototype, *10, 45*
Functions
    C++ input/output functions, *26*
    declaring, *36*
    defining, *36*
    friend, *75, 95*
    global functions, *36*
    inline, *40*
    member, *55 - 56, 59, 95*
    pointers to overloaded functions, *106*
    prototype, *36*
    pure virtual, *142*
    return type, *106*
    signature, *106*
    virtual, *130, 142*
Functions without arguments, *107*
Functions without return values, *107*

g++ command, *13*
Garbage collector, *31*
Global scope function, *34*
Going from C to C++, *9*

heap, *29, 50*

ifstream, *168*
Implicit conversion, *68, 72, 99, 179*
Indexing operator, *48*
Inheritance
    multiple inheritance, *12*
    single inheritance, *12*

Initialization constructor, *118*
Initializing, *18*
Initializing and assigning a Rational class, *67*
Initializing derived classes, *127*
Initializing references, *104*
inline expansion, *41*
Inline functions, *40*
inline keyword, *40*
Input/output, *94, 157*
Input/output stream library, *157*
Input/output with files, *167*
Input/output with memory, *172*
Instance, *11, 26, 55, 63*
Instantiated template, *179*
int, *29*
Interrupt level
 correspondence with system call, *107*
iomanip.h library, *166*
ios class, *157*
iostream library, *26, 80 - 81, 157*
isspace() function, *158*
istream class, *157, 168*
istrstream classes, *172*

Keywords, *17*
 ANSI C, *18*
 C++, *18*

Language elements, *17*
Linux, *13*
Local variable, *40*
lvalue, *48 - 49, 79, 93*

malloc, *29*
Manipulators, *166*
Member
 access control, *57*
 data, *55 - 56*
 functions, *55 - 56, 59*

private, 55
protected, 55
public, 55
Member data, 55
Member functions, 55, 61, 63, 76, 78, 89, 107, 147
    = ( ) ( ) -, 95
Members, 12
Method, 13
Microsoft Visual C++, 154
Module, 11
Modulus operator, 140, 146
Multiple derivation, 118, 150
Multiple inheritance, 153

N

new, 29, 66
new.h, 30
Non-member function, 78, 81

Object-oriented programming, 10
ofstream, 168
Operator
    +=, 92
    ==, 82
    >=, 82
    >>, 82
    <<, 34
    ~, 84
    <<(), 161
    >>(), 158
    ()(), 95
    ->(), 110
    %, 27
    ->, 110
    ::, 33
    < or >, 26 - 27
    arithmetic, 70
    association, 35
    associativity, 95
    binary arithmetic, 74
    commutative binary, 74

    index operator, *93*
    modulus, *146*
    multiplication, *70*
    overloading, *70, 94*
    priority, *35, 95*
    relational, *82*
    standard, *94*
    ternary, *146*
    unary minus, *70 - 71, 73*
Operator keyword, *69 - 70*
Operators C++, *26*
Ordinary conversions, *97, 121*
ostream class, *157, 168*
ostrstream classes, *172*
Overloading, *10, 65, 181*
    by member functions, *70*
    functions, *28, 50*
    non-member functions, *73*
    operators, *70, 94*
    pointers to overloaded functions, *106*
    resolving, *96*
    the - operator, *110*

Parameterized types, *182*
Parameters
    See Arguments
Parent classes, *122*
PASCAL, *10*
Passing arguments by reference, *45*
Passing arguments by value, *42*
Pointers to constants, *24*
Pointers
    constant pointer, *24*
    constant pointer to a constant, *25*
    pointer to a constant, *24*
    typed, *20*
    void, *20*
Pointers to members of a class, *107, 109*
Pointers to overloaded functions, *106*
Polymorphism, *12, 127*
Postfix incrementation, *79*

Prefix incrementation, *79*
printf function, *26, 80, 166*
Private derivation, *120*
Private members, *55*
Procedure, *10*
Propagating exceptions explicitly, *197*
Protected derivation, *119*
Protected members, *55*
Prototype, *36, 63, 71 - 72*
Public derivation, *119*
Public derived class, *116*
Public members, *55*
Pure virtual function, *142*

Real parameters, *42, 44, 89*
Releasing memory, *31*
Returning from a function, *47*
Root exception class, *206*
Runtime environment, *205*

scanf function, *26*
Scope of an object, *20*
Scope operator, *32, 108, 117*
set_new_handler(), *30*
Signature, *10, 50, 96, 106*
Simple inheritance, *153*
Single conversion, *96*
Single derivation, *118, 150*
Smalltalk, *150*
Standard input/output, *157*
Static data zone, *50*
Static member function, *109*
Static members, *109*
stderr, *26*
stdin, *26*
stdio.h, *163*
stdio, *26*
stdout, *26*
stream input/output, *26*

Streams, *157*
    formatting, *163*
strlen(), *84*
strstream classes, *172*
stsstream.h, *172*
struct, *21, 47, 55, 59*
Syntax analyzer, *138*
System exceptions, *205*

T

Template class, *182*
Template functions, *177*
ternary operator, *146*
this pointer, *61 - 62, 110*
throw keyword, *193*
Tree structure compiler, *136*
try block, *193*
Type
    constants, *23*
    declaring new type names, *23*
    enumeration, *21*
    explicitly converting, *32*
    void, *20*

U

Unary operator, *35*
Underlying C structure, *55, 60, 66 - 67, 84, 89, 118, 133, 147*
union, *21, 47, 55*
UNIX environment, *206*
UNIX programming, *9*
Unix systems, *157*
unsigned, *37*
User conversions, *97*
User data type, *10*

V

Variable
    global, *48*
Virtual base class
    constructing, *152*
Virtual destructors, *31*
Virtual function concept, *127*
Virtual functions, *130*, *142*, *147*
    internal implementation, *132*
Virtual functions table, *132*
Virtual keyword, *130*
Virtual member function, *13*
Virtual multiple derivation, *152*
Void type, *20*

▲ Quick Reference Guide ▲ Practical Guide ▲ Microsoft® Approved
▲ User Manual ▲ Training CD-ROM Publication

VISIT OUR WEB SITE http://www.editions-eni.com

Ask for
our free brochure

**For more information
on our new titles
please complete
this card and return**

Name: ....
....
Company: ....
Address: ....
....
Postcode: ....
Town: ....
Phone: ....
E-mail: ....

Please
affix
stamp
here

ENI Publishing LTD
500 Chiswick High Road
London W4 5RG